RECTIFYING INTERNATIONAL INJUSTICE

Rectifying International Injustice

Principles of Compensation and Restitution Between Nations

DANIEL BUTT

OXFORD
UNIVERSITY PRESS

Great Clarendon Street, Oxford, OX2 6DP,
United Kingdom

Oxford University Press is a department of the University of Oxford.
It furthers the University's objective of excellence in research, scholarship,
and education by publishing worldwide. Oxford is a registered trade mark of
Oxford University Press in the UK and in certain other countries

© Daniel Butt 2009

The moral rights of the authors have been asserted

First Edition published in 2009

All rights reserved. No part of this publication may be reproduced, stored in
a retrieval system, or transmitted, in any form or by any means, without the
prior permission in writing of Oxford University Press, or as expressly permitted
by law, by licence or under terms agreed with the appropriate reprographics
rights organization. Enquiries concerning reproduction outside the scope of the
above should be sent to the Rights Department, Oxford University Press, at the
address above

You must not circulate this work in any other form
and you must impose this same condition on any acquirer

Published in the United States of America by Oxford University Press
198 Madison Avenue, New York, NY 10016, United States of America

British Library Cataloguing in Publication Data

Data available

Library of Congress Control Number: 2008027800

ISBN 978–0–19–921824–0

For my parents

Acknowledgements

I have received a great deal of help and advice in the process of writing this book. I began working on international rectificatory justice while a graduate student in Oxford. My greatest intellectual debt is to David Miller, who not only supervised my masters and doctoral theses but taught me political theory as an undergraduate. It was David's work on nationality which first led me to begin thinking about these issues, and he has been a constant source of inspiration and support throughout. I am deeply grateful to him for all his efforts on my behalf, and would like to apologize for foisting the appellation 'international libertarian' upon him. Oxford is a wonderful place to do political theory, and over the years I have had conversations and arguments about the subject of this book with more people than I can possibly list here. I should like in particular, however, to thank the following for comments of various kinds on my work: Peter Barnes, Simon Caney, Clare Chambers, Jerry Cohen, Katherine Eddy, Cécile Fabre, Sarah Fine, Luc Foisneau, Denis Galligan, Natalie Gold, Robert Goodin, Axel Gosseries, Alan Hamilton, the late J.W. Harris, Dan Hawthorn, Poppy Hollman Ben Jackson, Rob Jubb, Dan McDermott, Lukas Meyer, Kieran Oberman, Avia Pasternak, Max Pensky, Mark Philp, Oliver Pooley, Jon Quong, Miriam Ronzoni, Ben Saunders, Christian Schemmel, Micah Schwartzman, Larry Siedentop, Julia Skorupska, Zofia Stemplowska, Mark Strathdene, Adam Swift, Patrick Tomlin, Bas van der Vossen, William Whyte, Steve Winter, Michael Wykes, and two anonymous reviewers for Oxford University Press. The examiners on my DPhil were Henry Shue and Hillel Steiner, both of whom provided extremely helpful comments, which have led me to rewrite the majority of the thesis for the purposes of this book. Chris Brooke kindly read the entire manuscript just prior to its submission, and commented upon it with great insight, and in tremendous detail. The book is much improved for his efforts, and I am beholden to him, although responsibility for the errors which remain is mine alone.

I should also like to thank audiences at the Conference of the Political Studies Association in Manchester; the 'Brave New World' Conference in Manchester; the Centre of International Studies in Cambridge; the International Symposium on Justice, Legitimacy and Public International Law, in Bern, Switzerland; the European Research Training Network on Applied Global Justice Workshop in Louvain, Belgium; and at Princeton University. I am particularly grateful to audiences at the Centre for the Study of Social

Justice lunchtime workshops, the Nuffield Political Theory Workshop, and the Oxford Graduate Political Theory Workshop, where I have presented multiple papers. This means that several individuals have seen me rehearse the same arguments over and over again, albeit in slightly different forms, on a number of different occasions. Clare Chambers, indeed, became convinced that my entire book consisted of a detailed response to Robert Fullinwider's driveway example, addressed in Chapter 4, so often did it come up in seminar discussion. I am obliged to all the participants in these forums for their help and patience. Versions of two sections of this book have appeared in print elsewhere. Part of Chapter 4 appeared as 'Nations, overlapping generations and historic injustice', *Canadian Journal of Philosophy* 37 (2007), 129–52. Part of Chapter 6 appeared as 'On benefiting from injustice', *American Philosophical Quarterly* 43 (2006), 357–67. I should like to thank the editors and publishers for permission to use this material here. I am very grateful to Dominic Byatt at Oxford University Press for his encouragement and patience throughout the writing of the book.

I have had three institutional identities whilst carrying out the work which has gone into this book: first, as graduate student at Wadham College, Oxford; second, as Research Fellow and Tutor in Politics at Keble College; and third, as Fellow and Tutor in Politics at Oriel College. In all three places I have found support, companionship, and intellectual stimulation, both from faculty and from students. I should particularly like to thank Mark Philip for his help over the last four years at Oriel. While at Wadham, I received funding for my doctorate from the UK Economic and Social Research Council (ESRC), for which I am very grateful. I have been fortunate to have been taught by some superb teachers, both before and during my time as a university student, and would like, in particular, to thank Nigel Bowles, Robert Currie, Paul Still, and the late James Hansford for their inspiration and encouragement over the years. My parents, Kenneth and Patricia Butt, have provided constant support throughout my fledgling academic career. I am deeply indebted to them, and dedicate the book to them both. Finally, Francesca Galligan has read a number of different incarnations of the manuscript and improved the contents of the book immensely. For this, I am deeply grateful. I am, however, unable to express the extent of my love and appreciation for her support throughout the entire period during which the book was written.

Contents

1. Introduction — 1
   1.1 Rectifying International Injustice – The Real World Context — 1
   1.2 Theory and Practice — 6
   1.3 Terminology — 22

2. Why Worry about Historic Injustice? — 31
   2.1 The Distinctiveness of International Rectificatory Justice — 31
   2.2 Does History Have Ethical Significance? — 34
   2.3 Departures from Initially Just Distributions — 37
   2.4 Departures from Initially Unjust Distributions — 41

3. International Libertarianism — 58
   3.1 International Libertarianism as an Account of Distributive Justice — 58
   3.2 The Principles of Just International Interaction — 65
      3.2.1 Core Principles of Just International Interaction — 66
      3.2.2 Further Principles of Just International Interaction — 67
   3.3 Judging Historical International Interaction — 72
      3.3.1 Historically Different Beliefs about Justice — 73
      3.3.2 The Recent Development of International Law — 75
      3.3.3 Justifiable or Excusable Departures from the Principles — 79

4. Compensation for Historic International Injustice — 97
   4.1 International Compensatory Justice — 97
   4.2 Identifying the Morally Relevant Counterfactual — 102
   4.3 Counterfactuals and Relational Justice — 115
   4.4 Benefiting from Injustice — 117
      4.4.1 Benefit and Duties of Assistance — 118
      4.4.2 Benefit and the Effects of Injustice — 122
      4.4.3 From Theory to Practice – Problems of Measuring Benefit — 130

5. Restitution and Inheritance — 140
   5.1 The Inheritance Model of Rectificatory Justice — 140
   5.2 The Justifiability of Inheritance — 141
      5.2.1 Property and Possession (1) — 145
      5.2.2 International Libertarianism and Historical Entitlement — 148
      5.2.3 Property and Possession (2) — 160
   5.3 Inheritance and Indeterminacy — 162

6. Nations, Overlapping Generations, and Historic Injustice — 174
  6.1 The Significance of National Identity — 174
  6.2 The Nature of Rectificatory Duties — 176
  6.3 Nations and Collective Responsibility — 178
  6.4 Nations and Overlapping Generations — 183
  6.5 Historic Justified Rights Infringements and Present Day Obligations — 188

  Conclusion — 195

Bibliography — 199
Index — 211

1

Introduction

1.1 RECTIFYING INTERNATIONAL INJUSTICE – THE REAL WORLD CONTEXT

The United Nations World Conference against Racism, Racial Discrimination, Xenophobia and Related Intolerance was held between 31 August and 8 September 2001 in Durban, South Africa. The Conference was widely portrayed in the West as having largely been a failure, with delegates unable to reach substantive agreement on two highly contentious issues that dominated the reporting of the proceedings of the Conference. The first was familiar, involving relations between Israel and Palestine. The second concerned a question that had only recently gained a significant amount of serious international coverage, that of whether Western countries should apologize and/or pay reparations for unjust actions performed in the colonial era, particularly (though not exclusively) in relation to their involvement in the slave trade. There was little consensus at the Conference, even among the African nations who sought to press claims upon their Western counterparts. Olusegun Obasanjo, President of Nigeria, argued in favour of an apology but against reparations, for while he maintained that, 'the legacies of several centuries of racial discrimination and dehumanisation through slavery, slave trade and colonisation have the deep and fundamental consequences of poverty... and marginalisation of Africans from the rest of the world,' he nonetheless said that, 'monetary compensation would hurt the dignity of Africans.'[1] Abdoulaye Wade, President of Senegal, ridiculed the reparations claims on the basis that he was the descendant of slave-owning African royals: 'If one can claim reparations for slavery, the slaves of my ancestors or their descendants can also claim money from me because slavery has been practised by all people in the world.'[2] But more representative of the bulk of the African delegates were the views expressed by Umberto Brown, International Secretary of the United States-based Black Radical Congress: 'The U.S. doesn't even want to take the first step and acknowledge slavery as a crime against humanity or acknowledge the continued suffering of Africans and African descendants. Instead, they say they "regret" that the slave trade happened. Forget regret. We want them to take responsibility.'[3]

Brown is unlikely to have been mollified by the outcome of the discussions, which, at the insistence of the European representatives, and following a walk-out by the United States, steered clear of any explicit reference to reparations, instead simply condemning and expressing regret for colonial practices. In one particularly striking instance, the United Kingdom successfully resisted pressure to label historic slavery as a crime against humanity, on the basis that it had not actually been illegal at the time. In the eyes of a number of observers, the Conference's treatment of the reparations issue had been at best a waste of time, at worst had diverted attention from other more pressing concerns ('The haggling between the Europeans and Africans over the slave trade and colonialism marginalised all debate on the huge problems of racism within Africa's borders today')[4] or had been positively harmful (The *Times* commented, in a remarkably hostile leader, that the 'enterprise has become a repellent throwback to the anti-American politics of resentment and hate that riddled the U.N. in the 1960s and 1970s').[5] The debate provoked a great deal of journalistic discussion worldwide, but the issues raised were largely put to one side following the terrorist attacks of 11 September 2001.

The aim of this book is to develop a set of principles that can be used to assess duties and obligations of compensation and restitution in an international context. The debate in Durban raised a wide range of questions – including the extent to which present day generations can be held responsible or accountable for the actions of their forebears, the nature of the enduring effects of historic wrongs, and the significance of the existence or absence of laws governing international interaction – that will be addressed in what follows. Such issues have only received significant attention in recent years. Many closely related issues have, of course, been raised in the past. The rights and wrongs of the colonial period have been extensively debated. Some African Americans in the United States have long claimed that they are owed compensation as a result of the enslavement of their ancestors, prompting a debate that has hovered on the edge of public consciousness since the radicalization of the civil rights movement in the 1960s. In the aftermath of the Second World War there were restitution claims that made explicitly moral arguments, based upon the injustice of, for example, Nazi Germany's actions, in a way which differed significantly from the reparations customarily imposed upon the losers of military conflicts by the victors. But it is only relatively recently that the issue of compensation for colonial practices has been raised in an international context. More typically, such arguments have been made within particular states, directed against the governments of those states by domestic minority groups. Thus, of the six chapters of his book *The*

Guilt of Nations that Elazar Barkan devotes to 'Colonialism and its aftermath', only one ('Restitution for slavery: opportunity or fantasy?') considers (in part) international cases, where it is claimed that governments, institutions, groups, or individuals of one state have obligations to, or valid claims against, such parties in other states.[6] There is far more philosophical literature available that considers compensation for historic wrongs from a domestic rather than an international perspective. This is not surprising, given that political philosophy has traditionally tended to consider questions of justice within a single, bounded state: John Rawls's *A Theory of Justice* sets the tone for this, as well as for so much else, in contemporary analytical theory.[7] As is increasingly commonly pointed out, however, interest in questions of international justice has grown in recent years, with inquiry that crosses over between the disciplines of political theory and international relations – two fields which have often paid scant regard to one another. Charles Beitz is generally credited with the revival of interest in questions of international justice within contemporary liberal political philosophy with his 1979 work *Political Theory and International Relations*, and by the time Rawls published his own contribution to the debate with his 1999 *The Law of Peoples* (a book based on his 1993 Oxford Amnesty Lecture of the same name) there was lively and far-reaching debate among political theorists on questions of international distributive justice.[8]

In *The Guilt of Nations*, Barkan couples a growing trend in domestic politics towards the consideration of compensatory and restitutive questions with a 'novel phenomenon': 'the demand that nations act morally and acknowledge their own historical injustices.'[9] He traces this initially to the end of the Second World War, and claims that there has been a quickening of this trend since the end of the Cold War, with its accompanying easing of international tension. It is perhaps not surprising that such questions tend to receive most attention when states believe that their security is not under threat, and so are of the opinion that they have more scope for ethical action. Given how rapidly the international security environment was transformed after 11 September 2001, mere days after the Durban summit ended, it may be the case that Durban, despite its failure, might represent the high-water mark of the reparations movement. This thought remains plausible, for example, when one considers the lack of political enthusiasm apparent when the issue was raised once more during the bicentenary of the abolition of the colonial slave trade in the United Kingdom in 2007. Although some other bodies, notably the Church of England, went some way towards endorsing the possibility that historic actions might give rise to contemporary obligations, the British government maintained the earlier position of expressing both sorrow and regret, while also seeking to differentiate the past from the present in terms of what is owed to others. The different terminology employed by the leaders of the relevant institutions is telling. Asked in a radio interview whether simply apologizing for historic actions was 'too easy' to be a morally appropriate response, Rowan Williams, the Archbishop of Canterbury, answered as follows:

> WILLIAMS: Yes, nobody I think has found an easy and morally clear way of figuring this. Are apologies too easy? Well they may well be, but they still have to be made I think, certainly an acknowledgement of the truth. It's not about lashing yourself with guilt over this, it's about saying 'well you know we belong to an institution which is in part shaped by this history, and ... we are here where we are and who we are partly because of terrible things that our forbears did – face it, get used to it, and you know make that history your history'. Then the question is, where are we now? And while it sounds simple to say, all right so we should ... pass on the reparation that was received in 1831 or whenever, exactly to whom? Exactly where does it go? And exactly how does it differ from the various ways in which we try to, to interact now with the effects of that in terms of aid and development and so forth?
>
> INTERVIEWER: But implicit in what you say is, is perhaps a need to make amends in some form?
>
> ARCHBISHOP: I think so, yes. If you are living off that kind of historic legacy, then you have a responsibility I think – you have a responsibility.[10]

By contrast, Prime Minister Tony Blair made the following statement:

> I believe the bicentenary offers us a chance not just to say how profoundly shameful the slave trade was – how we condemn its existence utterly and praise those who fought for its abolition – but also to express our deep sorrow that it could ever have happened and rejoice at the better times we live in today.[11]

Blair's words here reiterate the position put forward by the British delegation at Durban. 'Rejoicing in the better times we live in today' implies that wrongdoing is a matter of the historical record, rather than a contemporary concern. It suggests both that the slave trade itself no longer exists – a highly questionable assumption[12] – and that the historic slave trade does not give rise to present day obligations. Nonetheless, although African delegates were largely disappointed by the outcome of the 2001 sessions, a number of the agreed final resolutions point the way forward for the movement, if political will can be found amongst the states who signed up to the Declaration.[13] Article 98 of the Resolutions stresses the importance of teaching about the facts of history, 'with a view to achieving a comprehensive and objective cognizance of the tragedies of the past'. Article 99 acknowledges and regrets the 'massive human suffering' caused by, amongst other things, slavery and colonialism. Article 100 notes the initiative of some states to apologize and pay reparations 'for grave and massive violations committed.' Article 101 expressly endorses and appreciates the practice of apologizing for ancient wrongs. Perhaps most significantly, Article 102 notes: 'We are aware of the moral obligation on the part of all concerned States and call upon these States to take appropriate and effective measures to halt and reverse the lasting consequences of those practices.' What it means to acquire compensatory and restitutive obligations in an international context, how they are obtained, and how they may be discharged are precisely the questions which this book seeks to answer.

This book is an exercise in political theory. Most of the examples given are theoretical, and are not drawn from (though may correspond to) real world history. The aim of the book is to elucidate the moral principles that lie behind all consideration of the rectification of historic injustice. As such, the principles discussed are by no means relevant exclusively to the consideration of the aftermath of colonialism. Throughout the book, I use the term 'the rectificatory project' to describe the general aim of seeking to ensure that one's moral duties arising from historic injustice are fulfilled, whatever the nature of the historic injustice in question. The Durban Conference is, however, an appropriate place to begin for there are a number of reasons why the issue of relations between former colonial powers and their colonies is particularly significant to the principles under consideration. Colonialism raises a range of difficult philosophical issues. A wide variety of different forms of interaction may be considered under the headings of 'colonialism' and 'imperialism'. Although, as Ronald Horvath notes, 'it seems generally, if not universally, agreed that colonialism is a form of domination – the control by individuals or groups over the territory and/or behavior of other individuals or groups',[14] such a definition can be said to apply to a variety of actions, ranging from the violent conquest and suppression of a foreign people and the forcible appropriation of their resources and possessions, through various forms of direct or indirect political control, to the seemingly peaceful, and even consensual, exploitation of less powerful or wealthy non-nationals. Many would argue, of course, that various forms of colonialism persist in the modern world, but we can also speak meaningfully of a particular form of historical colonialism, based on forms of international interaction such as military invasion, subjugation, enslavement, and appropriation of resources, which most observers would (and do) readily condemn as both illegal and immoral if they were to occur in the present day. The actions in question often occurred at least several generations ago; were typically not illegal by the laws of the day, nor even necessarily considered to be morally wrong at the time; and frequently involved nations with very little prior interaction, which have often subsequently worked closely together, whether by mutual choice or not. All these characteristics of historical colonialism are significant when we come to assess what contemporary states owe one another as a result of past injustice in the present day. Although not all historic injustice which stands in need of rectification in the present day was colonial in nature, this book suggests that it is in their historic relations with their former colonies that many Western states find their most pressing rectificatory duties, which have been largely unrecognized and unfulfilled. In the following chapters, I argue that modern day individuals and groups face strong moral obligations to enquire into their national history, and to consider carefully the provenance of the resources and benefits to which they have access. I write this book as a British national, working within a British University. The evidence of Great Britain's colonial past is impossible to miss here in Oxford, most strikingly in the magnificent Codrington Library of All Souls College, built with profits from West Indian slave plantations. It is not hard to think of a myriad of ways in which I personally have benefited from forms of historical international interaction which are deeply controversial in the present day. The book does not represent an investigation of the kind I advocate into my own or anyone else's national past. Rather, it seeks to explicate the principles of rectificatory justice which such an investigation should employ, whoever is carrying out the investigation in question.

1.2 THEORY AND PRACTICE

The debate over the rectification of historic wrongdoing between nations is one which involves political actors, including elected representatives, interest groups, and the media, who seek to have an effect upon policy outcomes in the real world. This book aims to assist this debate. Its argument therefore aspires to a particular kind of practicality. It is becoming increasingly common to criticize a good deal of contemporary analytical political theory as being impractical, concerned as it is with what John Rawls described as 'ideal theory'.[15] In *A Theory of Justice*, for example, Rawls made it clear that, for the most part, he was considering justice within a well-ordered society, where 'everyone is presumed to act justly and to do his part in upholding just institutions'.[16] The real world evidently is not like this. Rawls accepted that questions of how we are to deal with non-compliance with justice are important in real world politics: 'Obviously the problems of partial compliance theory are the pressing and urgent matters. These are the things that we are faced with in everyday life' – and he referred explicitly to questions of compensatory justice in this context.[17] The issue of whether and how we should seek to rectify historic injustice is indeed a pressing political concern. We may believe that doing so will involve substantial transfers of resources between different states, or may involve other actions of great significance for particular individuals. Insofar as some of the beneficiaries of rectificatory action are likely to be some of the world's poorest people, it is not fanciful to suggest that whether or not we seek to rectify historic international injustice is a matter of life and death.

In dealing with the rectification of injustice, then, this is an exercise in non-ideal theory, in two separate senses. It does not seek to give an ideal-style account of how the world should be, and it need not necessarily be interpreted as giving an account of how the world should ideally proceed from its present non-ideal state. The first sense of non-ideal theory is the one most commonly found in contemporary writing. The purpose of much modern day analytical political theory is to give an account of what some element of an ideal society – and, by extension, an ideal world – would look like. For example, some writers seek to outline the principles of political and distributive justice which would obtain within a just society. Political theorists disagree over the extent to which such accounts should take account of empirical facts about the world: for example, by allowing for limitations of human psychology, or purported facts about human nature, to feature as component elements of theories of justice.[18] They may also disagree over whether the aim of ideal theory is to describe a kind of society which is at some level politically feasible, such as Rawls's claim that his theory is designed to describe a 'realistic utopia',[19] or to construct an admittedly infeasible but perfectly just alternative to our present society, in order to highlight our own shortcomings and, perhaps, suggest ideal standards to which we should aspire. Such disagreements may be framed in terms of 'practicality' and 'impracticality', in terms of whether a given ideal theory is, or should be, likely to be achievable in the real world. But there is a clear sense in which all those engaged in such enterprises are constructing theories of the ideal, and as such are bracketed together as theorists of 'ideal theory', in that, like Rawls, they describe just societies, where individuals fulfil their duties to each other. However, as George Sher notes, there is an alternative approach:

> ...in addition to treating existing societies as occasions for reflection about the ideal, or as sources of materials from which to fashion it, philosophers can also treat their lapses from the ideal as independent occasions for normative reflection – as distinct new sources of normative problems. When philosophers take this approach, they engage in what Rawls calls *non-ideal theory* or *partial compliance theory*, and what others call *the theory of the second best*.[20]

What does it mean to give a 'theory of the second best'? One way in which non-ideal theory can operate is by examining the appropriate response to departures from the ideal. This differentiates ideal theory from non-ideal theory in terms of its subject matter. Thinking about the rectification of injustice is clearly an exercise in non-ideal theory in this sense. So, for example, theories of punishment examine the requirements of justice in response to certain forms of wrongdoing. The subject matter is non-ideal in the sense that we would usually imagine that there would be no wrongdoing in an ideal society, but given that we live in a real world context where wrongdoing does exist, we nonetheless need to work out what justice requires of us. Similarly, a great deal of contemporary writing on international ethics is concerned with the non-compliance of other agents. Suppose that we believe that, in an ideal world, everyone would have enough to eat, as the rich would collectively fulfil a moral duty to transfer sufficient of their extra resources to those in desperate need – perhaps through, for example, voluntary contributions to some kind of global fund, or by paying a mandatory transnational income tax. In an ideal world, then, an individual's moral duty to the world's poor may well be satisfied by contributing her fair share to the global fund, or simply by paying her taxes. But what are her moral duties in a non-ideal world, where many of the world's rich do not do their fair share in helping those in need?[21] In both cases, non-ideal theory seeks to tell us what justice requires of us when we do not start from an ideal starting point. Non-ideal theory in this sense could be described as a 'theory of the second best', in that a situation where injustice is rectified is second best to a situation where no injustice occurs and so there is no need for rectification; but this is a rather different understanding of the idea of a 'theory of the second best' to that found in the work of some economists and political theorists, who argue that better outcomes can sometimes be achieved by aiming for some manageable target rather than for some infeasible or improbable ideal.[22]

This book looks at a question of non-ideal theory in its subject matter – it is concerned with how to respond to existing, real world departures from the ideal caused by international injustice. It is thus practical in the sense that it addresses a contemporary political debate. But it also seeks to attain a further kind of practicality, which I call 'double practicality', in that it aims to develop arguments which can realistically be employed by the protagonists in this real world debate. The key point here concerns the foundational premises which these protagonists accept. Chapter 2 argues that insofar as the rectification of injustice affects the distribution of resources, the content of one's theory of rectificatory justice will reflect one's theory of distributive justice. The less of a role that history plays in one's account of distributive justice, the less one will believe that the rectification of historic injustice requires a redistribution of resources in the present day. The book largely takes for granted a broad orientation on international distributive justice, which is labelled 'international libertarianism'. This reflects the idea that the principles which a range of political theorists believe govern international interaction are strikingly similar to the principles which libertarian writers, such as Robert Nozick, believe govern interaction between individuals at a domestic level.[23] As Chapter 3 argues, international libertarianism is supported by a significant number of political philosophers, many of whom advocate far more redistributive principles of distributive justice within the domestic sphere – including John Rawls himself. The international libertarian vision of a just world order is one governed by certain principles of justice which regulate interaction between states. These 'principles of just international interaction' are guided by two primary ideas: first, that certain forms of interaction between states, typified by unprovoked acts of aggression, are unjustifiable; second, that national self-determination should be respected unless the intervention of other states is required to prevent certain kinds of injustice. International libertarians hold that boundaries between different political communities have ethical significance. They are therefore generally resistant to claims that justice requires the redistribution of resources across state boundaries, other than when (at most) such redistribution is needed in order to raise those in other states up to some minimal level of well-being. As such, there are striking analogies with domestic libertarianism in terms of ideas such as respect for sovereignty, self-ownership, and the minimal state.

In terms of respect for sovereignty, the guiding principle of both accounts is that of non-intervention without proper cause. It is anticipated that, in the normal course of events, both individuals and political communities should be free to do as they please, providing that their actions do not infringe on the rights of others. Non-intervention, or non-interference as it is normally called in the domestic case, is the expected norm. Deviance from non-intervention requires special justification. In an international context, this becomes support for self-determination. The concept of self-ownership is a familiar one within a domestic libertarian context, and refers to the claim that an individual owns herself, where this is taken to refer to her body and to her talents. The concept of self-ownership also appears in an international context. Here, it refers to the right of a nation to the exclusive use of the natural resources within its territory. It may also be understood to refer to a relationship between the people of the nation and the territory on which they live; this may be taken as far as actually defining the nation in such a way as to make reference to the territory in question. Finally, both domestic and international libertarians express support for the minimal state, expressing scepticism as to the extent of legitimate state intervention. This is expressed within a domestic context in terms of opposition to taxing and spending for reasons other than providing basic communal services and ensuring individuals' security. The most important element of this is evidently the status given to private property. This concern is mirrored in terms of international libertarians' resistance to the open-ended international redistribution of resources, even if relatively demanding duties to assist non-nationals are endorsed. Rawls, for example, is explicit that the duties of assistance placed upon peoples require action only in order to achieve a particular objective; namely, bringing burdened societies into the Society of well-ordered Peoples.[24] As such, the duty of assistance 'is a principle of *transition*',[25] with a 'target and a cutoff point'.[26] Moves to afford further taxation powers to international bodies are therefore resisted.

International libertarianism is described in further detail in Chapter 3. It can be distinguished from two alternative approaches to questions of international justice, prescriptive realism, and cosmopolitanism, in that it seeks to delineate dedicated principles of international justice. Both realists and cosmopolitans deny that there is a distinct realm of international justice, for very different reasons. Prescriptive realism holds that states are justified in doing whatever is necessary to further their own self-interest. Realists therefore deny that international interaction either is or should be guided by considerations of justice. On the realist account, therefore, the suggestion that modern day states should seek to rectify the lasting effects of historic injustice makes little sense, since there is no such thing as historic international injustice. Cosmopolitanism denies that national boundaries have ethical significance. Thus, for cosmopolitans, the same principles of justice which apply domestically should apply internationally. So some cosmopolitans give highly redistributive accounts of international justice, advocating, for example, some version of global egalitarianism. Others, who argue for libertarian theories of entitlement domestically, argue for respecting property rights and oppose extensive redistribution both domestically and internationally. The significance of historic injustice is likely to be very different for these two types of cosmopolitans – as later chapters note, libertarians typically have very good reason to pay careful attention to the historical record – but what they have in common is that they deny that historic international justice requires dedicated scrutiny as apart from historic injustice in general, since they deny that there is anything which differentiates domestic from international distributive justice.

Prescriptive realism is discussed in Chapter 3. The position is often caricatured as holding that ethical principles simply do not apply to international relations, though it is perhaps more accurate to speak of the belief that the international sphere is a realm of necessity, where governments either have no choice, either practically or morally, but to pursue the self-interest of their own citizens. Reasons are given as to why the strong variant of this thesis – that states have no choice at all in how they deal with others, and have no leeway at all for moral action – should be rejected. Such a strong position is, in any case, now rarely asserted as an account of international justice (as opposed to a description of the *Realpolitik* of international relations) either by theorists or by real world political actors. Nowadays, almost all serious writers on the subject accept the existence of at least some minimal ethical constraints upon international actions. Furthermore, when expressions of exclusively self-regarding national interest realism are made in an overt manner in real world contexts, an obvious contemporary example being the initial form of the US Government's opposition to the Kyoto Protocol on Climate Change, they generally provoke a great deal of criticism, and are often subsequently rephrased in a less contentious manner. As such, even if we believe that, descriptively, self-interest guides the actions of political actors, the content of international political debate makes extensive reference to other-regarding moral principles.[27] If one accepts the existence of such principles, one needs at least an argument as to what should take place when the principles in question are contravened. This opens the door to the international rectificatory project. The questions at stake are, first, which historic actions count as acts of injustice, and, second, how we should respond in the present day to such acknowledged injustices. These are the issues which this book addresses.

The argument of this book, then, concerns the moral duties of contemporary political communities – it is not concerned with the question of whether fulfilling rectificatory duties is in the self-interest of these communities (aside, that is, from the sense of self-interest, which consists of their acting as moral agents). This is not to say, of course, that fulfilling the said obligations would *not* be in the interests of the communities involved. There are two plausible arguments from national self-interest that might motivate realists to adopt the rectificatory project. The first of these is straightforward: it might be the case that fulfilling rectificatory duties would be in a state's long-term interest in terms of its dealings with the state or states to whom its obligations were owed. This might particularly be the case if one believed either that one's national rectificatory duties were relatively slight, and amounted to little more than symbolic gestures such as making apologies, or if one thought that political pressure would mean that, over the long term, rectification of some kind would have to be made by many different states. There are other variations on this theme; for example, one might think that one's own nation's rectificatory obligations were relatively slight compared to one's rivals, and that fulfilling the said obligations would compel one's rivals to follow suit, thus gaining one's own nation a competitive advantage. In such a situation of assumed inevitability, one might gain a great deal of long-term goodwill by being the first mover. The second argument is perhaps more interesting, and stems from the national self-identity of the state with the rectificatory duties. It is now common for political philosophers to stress the benefits that communal membership and a sense of cultural identity can afford to individuals. Nationalists stress the role of one source of cultural identity in particular – the nation – and believe that one's national identity is, or can be, important to the quality of life of the individuals who make up the nation. Nations are characteristically understood by their members as being historically continuous entities; a nation is at least partly constituted by its members' beliefs relating to its past (regardless of whether these beliefs are accurate, or reflect a mythical history).[28] It is quite possible that in some situations this past may prevent a nation's members from embracing their national identity, for example, if they feel shame or guilt at the nation's historical actions.[29] One can imagine that this was the case in South Africa following apartheid, and the moves taken towards rectification and reconciliation there were at least partly oriented around the desire to allow South Africans to adopt a positive conception of South African nationality.[30] It seems not overly fanciful to think that knowledge of many Western countries' colonial past prevents a number of their citizens from embracing their national membership in a way they would like. A contemporary British example might be the poet Benjamin Zephaniah's recent refusal to accept an OBE – the initials stand for 'Order of the British Empire' – on the grounds that the award was associated with Britain's unjust colonial past. In an article for the *Guardian* newspaper, Zephaniah condemned the historic actions and lasting effects of the British Empire and the British establishment's refusal to embrace the rectificatory project:

> I get angry when I hear that word 'empire'; it reminds me of slavery, it reminds me of thousands of years of brutality, it reminds me of how my foremothers were raped and my forefathers brutalised. It is because of this concept of empire that my British education led me to believe that the history of black people started with slavery and that we were born slaves, and should therefore be grateful that we were given freedom by our caring white masters.... It is the institution of the monarchy that I loathe so very much, the monarchy that still refuses to apologise for sanctioning slavery... Why don't they just give me some of those great African works of art that were taken in the name of the empire and let me return them to their rightful place?[31]

In such cases, adoption of the rectificatory project might be seen to be in the nation's own self-interest, in that even if it costs money, it will allow for a higher degree of communal participation and unity.[32] It might even be possible to build an argument on explicitly realist premises which holds that, in such circumstances, Western governments have a moral duty to fulfil their rectificatory obligations: a duty they hold to their own nationals, rather than to foreign nationals.[33] My argument, however, will not address this question. The principles I examine are those which emerge as a result of unjust treatment of non-nationals. As such, they are duties owed primarily not to one's fellow citizens but to others.

The realist challenge, therefore, is largely put to one side. This leaves international libertarianism and cosmopolitanism as rival accounts of international justice.[34] Why adopt the international libertarian perspective when thinking about historic injustice? The straightforward reason is because of the popularity of international libertarianism. Chapter 3 lists some of the important political theorists who fall within the international libertarian camp, including such figures as John Rawls, Thomas Nagel, Michael Walzer, and David Miller along with many others. It would be quite wrong, of course, to suggest that international libertarianism is anything but deeply contentious at a theoretical level. A range of writers, including Charles Beitz, Thomas Pogge, Onora O'Neill, Darrel Moellendorf, and Simon Caney, again, along with many others, have challenged international libertarianism by putting forward opposing models of cosmopolitanism. Within the academy, therefore, opinion is deeply divided. When we look to real world beliefs about international justice, however, it is hard to resist the conclusion that there is much more backing for international libertarianism than for cosmopolitanism. As Cécile Fabre notes, 'Contrary to [cosmopolitanism], most people believe that borders *are* morally significant to establishing whether we owe anything to others, and that they are significant because national self-development matters.'[35] This vision also finds real world form in the provisions of international law, which explicitly uphold the principle of state sovereignty, subject to respect for the self-determination of other states and universally applicable human rights.[36] It is hard to maintain that there is a great deal of real world support for redistributive cosmopolitanism, which strongly suggests that to the extent that political theorists use controversial cosmopolitan premises, their work on rectificatory justice is likely to be of little use to those engaged in political argument in the real world.[37] Adopting the international libertarian perspective when considering the rectification of historic international injustice, therefore, allows for double practicality – it puts forward arguments which can realistically be used and endorsed by political actors engaged in real world policy disputes.

All this is straightforward for those who accept that international libertarianism is the right account of international distributive justice. With such a foundational argument in place, the argument concerning rectification would be non-ideal in the first sense outlined above – the ideal response to the non-ideal circumstances in which we find ourselves in the real world as a result of historic injustice. Those who accept international libertarianism tend to share the same foundational premises as those engaged in policy debates, and so their arguments on such questions are doubly practical. Although this book certainly looks at the foundational premises of international libertarianism, it does not go as far as endorsing them. My argument has a conditional character – *if* one accepts the international libertarian account of distributive justice, *then* one should consider the three morally relevant forms of potential connection with past wrongdoing which the book outlines. One can believe that such a project has both philosophical and political merit even if one is not an international libertarian. The real world policy debate over the rectification of international injustice is often confused, resting on conceptual mistakes and theoretical misunderstandings. Key ideas discussed in later chapters – including, for example, the role of counterfactual reasoning in calculating modern day benefit and harm (see Chapter 4), the justifiability of the inheritance of entitlements within an international libertarian framework (Chapter 5), and the significance of the claim that a failure to rectify injustice can itself constitute injustice (Chapter 6) – have been misunderstood by both political actors and academic theorists. This book seeks to redress this situation, and one might therefore hope that doing so would improve the quality of public debate, as well as clarifying the positions of those theorists who do accept international libertarian foundational premises, most of whom have paid little or no attention to the consequences of historic injustice for their accounts.[38] The aim is to enable such thinkers to reach a state of what Rawls calls 'narrow reflective equilibrium', whereby they aver a scheme of moral principles which is in keeping with their considered judgements about justice.[39] This is one reason for doing non-ideal theory in the second sense, whereby one does not argue for, or even necessarily accept, the foundational premises with which one is operating, and so is not committed to giving an account of how the world should ideally proceed from its present non-ideal state.

There is also another, perhaps more contentious reason for working within the international libertarian framework. This relates to the strategies pursued by those cosmopolitans who seek to effect a real world redistribution of resources. This book argues that the rectification of historic injustice is likely to involve a substantial redistribution of resources from rich to poor. Given the apparent lack of public support for global egalitarianism, for example, it may well be that the best political strategy for those who support extensive redistribution is not to seek to challenge the deeply held foundational principles of real world political actors, but to maintain that these very principles, if properly understood, call for a substantial redistribution of resources, even if this is not as complete a redistribution as egalitarians might wish for in an ideal world. Such an approach is similar to that which, on some accounts, has been adopted by Thomas Pogge. In recent work, Pogge has developed an institutional account of international justice which stresses the way in which the structure of international law and society actively harm the world's poor.[40] He claims that citizens of developed states are complicit in this injustice, since those who live in poverty in less developed states 'are being harmed through a badly slanted global order in whose continuous shaping and coercive imposition we are materially involved'.[41] As such, 'severe poverty is an ongoing harm we inflict upon the global poor'.[42] A key part of this argument is the claim that involvement in the perpetuation of the global economic order, through the everyday activities of those living in the developed world, infringes negative duties not to harm the world's poor. Pogge argues that 'ordinary moral thinking is committed to a hierarchy of moral reasons', which gives priority to negative duties not to wrong others, above even positive duties to protect one's next of kin from wrongdoing (and clearly above positive duties to protect unrelated foreigners from wrongdoing).[43] The account, therefore, is one which does not utilize controversial premises of, for example, egalitarianism derived from Kantian premises based on the moral equality of persons, but which bases duties to the world's poor on the nature of contemporary international interaction. Allen Buchanan has suggested that Pogge's argument has this form as it appears (to Pogge) to be the 'best argumentative strategy' to secure redistribution to those in need.[44] Buchanan surmises that rather than maintaining that we only have obligations to those who are or can be net contributors with us in a cooperative scheme, Pogge's point is rather that even if we do have some obligations to persons with whom we are not interacting, 'the fact of interaction grounds important, *and relatively uncontroversial* obligations of justice'.[45] Simon Caney speaks, in this context, of the appeal of 'Pogge's overall strategy of trying to build a case for global justice that is realistic and that seeks to work, so far as is possible, within the parameters of the modern world.'[46] The claim is that there are good strategic reasons to focus on the effects of international interaction, even if one in fact believes that we owe duties to all the world's poor regardless of the empirically contingent nature of contemporary international relations.[47]

A similar justification could be given for focusing on historic international injustice, defined in terms of violations of the principles of just international interaction. Pogge's definition of harm is contentious, resting upon the claims that, first, the existing world order causes harm to the world's poor, and second, that members of the developed world are implicated in this harm in such a way that they are failing to fulfil their negative duties to refrain from harming the world's poor.[48] He admits himself that many will find it hard to credit:

> That world poverty is an ongoing harm *we* inflict seems completely incredible to most citizens of the affluent countries. We call it tragic that the basic human rights of so many remain unfulfilled, and are willing to admit that we should

do more to help. But it is unthinkable to us that we are actively responsible for this catastrophe. If we were, then we, civilized and sophisticated denizens of the developed countries, would be guilty of the largest crime against humanity ever committed, the death toll of which exceeds, every week, that of the recent tsunami and, every three years, that of World War II, the concentration camps and gulags included. What could be more preposterous?[49]

The account of harm given in this book is much less controversial – it also rests upon negative duties to forebear from harming others, but draws upon paradigm cases of unjust international interaction, such as materially motivated aggression against other political communities, which are now almost universally accepted as being wrong.[50] This understanding of harm is straightforward, and defined in terms of active, usually deliberate, and typically violent wrongful damage to others' interests. An argument of duties to others grounded in this way is able to draw upon the powerful psychological force of arguments relating to rectificatory justice.[51] People do feel the force of rectificatory claims keenly. This is significant both at the level of determining what duties we hold in relation to others, and at the level of motivating us to fulfil these duties. To claim that individuals possess unfulfilled rectificatory duties to others is seriously to challenge their integrity as moral agents. It is therefore not surprising that the rectificatory project, while compelling to some, has also met with a good deal of spirited opposition in a real world context. Some people react with indignation and outrage to the suggestion that they possess rectificatory duties in the present which stem, in some cases, from the actions of their ancestors. The problematic implication here is that they are being held morally responsible for the actions of others – actions which were performed in many cases prior to their birth, and for which they simply cannot, on any account of moral agency, be held responsible. For understandable reasons, people react strongly when they believe that they are being blamed for something which is not their fault. The character of the (often conceptually confused) real world debate over apologies for historic wrongdoing has probably not helped matters in this regard. Insofar as it is commonly believed that the rectificatory project rests upon the absurd claim that present day individuals are in any sense morally responsible for the perpetration of historic injustice, the project has seemed outrageous to some, and ridiculous to others.

Nothing in this book rests upon such a claim. Instead, Chapters 4, 5, and 6 put forward three ways in which current generations within particular political communities may be linked, in a morally relevant way, to past wrongdoing, which may be broadly described in terms of benefit, entitlement, and responsibility:

1. Benefit: when one community is benefiting, and another is disadvantaged, as a result of the automatic effects of an act of historic injustice.
2. Entitlement: when one community has possession of property to which another community is morally entitled.
3. Responsibility: when one community is responsible for an ongoing injustice in relation to another community, understood in terms of an ongoing failure to fulfil rectificatory duties over time.

My claim is that, taken together, these morally relevant forms of connection mean that those living in the developed world possess significant rectificatory duties to many of those in less developed countries. The extent of these duties will depend, to a certain extent, on one's precise account of historic interaction – an account which this book does not seek to provide – but it does seem clear that if all three forms of potential connection are admitted, there will be significant overlap between the redistribution required by both cosmopolitan and international libertarian accounts. Properly understood, the motivating force of arguments based in rectificatory justice can be marshalled in support of international redistribution without holding present day individuals morally responsible for the actions of their ancestors.

There are therefore two complementary motives for cosmopolitans to argue for redistribution in relation to the rectification of historic international injustice. The first rests on the fact that such an argument is able to engage with the foundational premises of real world political actors, who typically reject cosmopolitanism. The second concerns the motivational force of ideas of rectificatory justice. It is one thing to hold that one's theory of justice or morality requires redistribution across national boundaries. International libertarians typically accept the existence of duties of assistance to those in desperate need. Yet, as many writers have observed, it is obvious that such duties of assistance are far from being fulfilled. The World Bank has estimated that, in 2001, over a billion people were below the minimal 'one dollar a day' international poverty line.[52] It is not simply a question of making the intellectual case in support of helping those in need. Opinion polls consistently show majorities in developed states as being – in theory – in favour of increasing aid to and encouraging development in the world's least developed countries.[53] Yet in real world political contexts, with multiple calls upon governmental funds, such views are only rarely translated into meaningful policy outcomes. Insofar as pursuing the international rectificatory project leads, in practice, to the fulfilment of duties of assistance, it can be seen as being complementary in nature to other approaches with similar goals, such as Pogge's emphasis on negative duties not to cause harm, and Peter Singer's account of positive duties to assist those in desperate need.

Such an approach is not without complications. There is undoubtedly an issue of intellectual honesty at stake – should political theorists who believe in egalitarian cosmopolitanism not try to convince others of the truth of their foundational premises, rather than merely pointing out that international libertarians ought to acknowledge the existence of rectificatory duties if they are to achieve a state of narrow reflective equilibrium? Some will worry that such a strategy fails to meet the need for principles of justice to be publicly justifiable.[54] It should be noted, however, that cosmopolitans need not disguise their own views, pretending to be international libertarians in public but secretly remaining cosmopolitans in private. (In this spirit, it is perhaps appropriate to acknowledge that my own ideal theory perspective on international distributive justice is both cosmopolitan and egalitarian, and so not international libertarian.)[55] Instead, the argument can be presented as one of seeking to reach a point of what Cass Sunstein calls 'incompletely theorized agreement' in the public sphere, whereby a given course of action can be agreed upon by individuals who hold different foundational premises.[56] Such a claim is somewhat complicated, of course, by the fact that there will inevitably be differences between the courses of action proposed by redistributive cosmopolitans, on the one hand, and by international libertarians pursuing the rectificatory project on the other. Claims relating to rectification do depend on the particular character of historic interaction. To claim that international libertarians should accept that the rectification of historic injustice requires substantial international redistribution is not, of course, to say that it requires the same degree of redistribution as that advocated by, say, egalitarian cosmopolitans, unless one's view is that historic injustice has been so prevalent as to call the legitimacy of contemporary holdings entirely into question.[57] So Nigel Dower, writing of the argument that nations should 'make recompense' for exploitation, argues:

> I think it is important not to base the moral argument for aid too firmly on it. To do so would be to incur the consequence of accepting that the very poor in a country which we were not exploiting would not be entitled to our concern.[58]

Onora O'Neill makes a related point in *Faces of Hunger*:

> ... if we cannot tell how far the predicaments of the present were produced by ancient wrongs, nor do much to tell which of those now alive have been so harmed, and which of them have benefited from those past violations, claims for compensation will be indeterminate and hard to allocate and so provide no certain remedy for the neediest.[59]

One need not accept all elements of these arguments. Chapter 3 notes that international libertarians can accept that it is unjust to exploit those in other countries. Chapter 4 addresses questions relating to the uncertainties of how to assess harm and benefit in connection with distant wrongs. But both Dower and O'Neill share a reasonable concern that there will be some very poor persons who will not be helped by a rectification of historic wrongdoing who would be aided if redistributive cosmopolitan principles of justice were realized. Should cosmopolitans be concerned about this?

It must be acknowledged that, ultimately, international libertarianism and redistributive cosmopolitanism are likely to have different practical implications. One approach allows for the justifiability of substantial and persistent inequalities between states, when these inequalities arise as a result of the legitimate self-determination of different political communities. The other typically calls for redistribution to limit or counter such inequalities. They do represent two very different takes on international distributive justice. But they need not be characterized as having widely divergent policy implications in the short term in relation to those in desperate need. International libertarianism, as has been noted, can accept the existence of duties of assistance to the very poor, and can even accept that features of the international economic and political order infringe the negative rights of the impoverished. So, making arguments in favour of aid to those in need which are based in the rectificatory project need not mean ignoring other possible grounds of duties to non-nationals. The facts of global poverty mean that there is a particular urgency to debates over global justice. For many of those involved in international politics, the question is one of which arguments are best able to marshal immediate support for those in desperate need. This book argues that such persons have good reason to think carefully about framing at least some of their arguments in relation to the rectification of historic international injustice, even if, in ideal theory terms, they reject international libertarianism and instead favour exclusively forward-looking principles of distributive justice.

This, then, is a second-form of non-ideal theory, which can readily be described as a 'theory of the second best'. Rather than seeking, ambitiously, to challenge the basic foundational premises of real world political actors, it seeks to bring about desirable change by engaging with existing beliefs about justice, and pointing out the unrealized progressive implications of these existing beliefs, properly understood. This is, in one sense, a conservative perspective on the efficacy of political theory.[60] One certainly need not maintain that all political theory need have this character. But in a world which is characterized both by widespread, life-ending injustice and by a theoretical chasm between the principles of justice advocated by many philosophers, on the one hand, and by most real world political actors, on the other, it surely has a place. Needs must when the devil drives.

One final point relating to the connection between theory and practice. This book is concerned with questions of rectificatory justice. In focusing on the 'rectificatory project', it argues that those living in the present days should fulfil any rectificatory duties which they possess to those who are still, in one of the three senses examined, suffering as a result of historic injustice. In asking who owes what to whom in a contemporary context, its primary focus is on the bearers of rectificatory duties. At a theoretical level, the focus on duties rather than rights is merely a matter of approach. In technical terms, the book employs a Hohfeldian model of claim rights in relation to rectificatory justice, whereby to say that an agent has a duty to rectify X is necessarily also to say that another agent has a right that X be rectified. Both duty holder and rights bearer must be identified if one is to claim that rectificatory justice requires action in the present. The emphasis on duty bearers, however, is potentially of practical significance in political terms. Some writers have expressed concern at the effects which a focus on backward-looking accounts of rights to rectification may have on the victims of injustice. Onora O'Neill, for example, finds the emphasis placed on the entitlements of the victim within rights-based accounts of compensatory justice problematic. Two potentially unfortunate consequences may arise. The first is that there may well be some individuals or groups who have suffered as a result of historic wrongdoing, but to whom no extant contemporary party possesses rectificatory duties. In such cases, there is a danger of positing a claim to compensation (and thus creating a potentially harmful sense of grievance) on the basis of injury suffered without specifying an agent with a correlative duty of rectification. Clearly, it is especially the case in the international arena that duties of compensation must be specifically fixed on particular agents with some morally relevant relation to the victim, since there is currently no obvious fallback institution, such as an international state, that has undertaken or could feasibly undertake to provide such compensation. The second, and related, potential consequence of a victim-centred approach is a common element of contemporary critiques of 'compensation culture'. O'Neill writes:

> When we ask what our rights are we no doubt assume that we and others are agents, but our first question is to ask what ought to be done for us, what we ought to receive from others. When we ask what our obligations are we begin by asking what we ought to do... [The rights-centred approach] invites a conception of oneself and others above all as victims, rather than as doers or citizens; it distracts allocation away from capacity for acting... Only the weak and powerless have reason to make the perspective of recipience and rights their primary concern.[61]

Political campaigns for the rectification of ancient wrongdoing are often criticized in this manner. It has been suggested that groups who continue to seek compensation for wrongs perpetrated against their ancestors or the restitution of property stolen in the distant past are harming themselves, regardless of the justice of their claims, by perpetuating a 'victim mentality', which adversely affects the future prospects of their own community. Such sentiments have frequently been expressed in relation to the debate in the United States over reparations to African Americans for slavery, from those within as well as those outside the black community. Thus, for example, John McWhorter, Associate Professor of Linguistics at Berkeley, criticizes Randall Robinson, author of *The Debt: What America Owes to Blacks* thus:[62]

> What kind of leading black thinker is one whose message for the black youth of America is...the measure of our strength as a group is how articulately we can call for charity? Its popularity notwithstanding, it is hard for me to accept that *The Debt* is really representative of my brethren's thinking on the subject of their place in America. Surely black people in all walks of life are increasingly realizing that pity has never gotten a race anywhere...[63]

This position, at least, is overstated, and evidently neglects the distinction between justice and charity. But nonetheless, it does seem possible that a viable argument of this kind could be made in certain contexts. Should we ignore the historical record, so as not to engender a 'victim mentality' in those who are due, as matter of justice, rectificatory action in the present day? The key question here concerns what we might call the location of the political initiative. What was seen in Durban was (largely) an approach to rectification based upon the rights claims of victims being resisted by the agents against whom the claims were being made. It *might* be the case that waging a long-term campaign of this kind is, in some circumstances, detrimental to the victim, in terms of their self-respect and their ability to develop, free from 'living in the past'. In such cases, it may well be sensible in practical terms to seek to move on from the past, and either put it to one side altogether, or pursue political initiatives based on the reconciliation of divided communities, rather than the attainment of justice. This, essentially, is a consequentialist argument, which claims that the costs of pursuing what one is owed as a matter of justice outweigh the benefits one would gain if one did in fact receive one's due. It does seem, however, that this is less likely to be the case if the political moves towards the rectification of injustice are initiated by the duty bearers, rather than by the rights holders. A stricter consequentialist test must be passed if the duty-centred approach, whereby agents willingly fulfil their rectificatory duties, is to be dismissed as counterproductive for the reason that it harmfully treats rights holders as victims. This is a rather different approach, and while it is not impossible that the costs of such an initiative might outweigh the benefits from the rights holders' perspective, it does seem less likely in practice. If we had good reasons to believe that the rectificatory project would, in fact, be harmful to the victims of historic injustice then of course it would seem sensible to hold that the pursuit of justice might be counterproductive. But this book puts such issues to one side – its focus is on what is owed by present day parties and to whom as a matter of justice. Clearly, the question of quite how these duties are to be best fulfilled is likely to be a difficult policy matter, which will principally need to be concerned with the best interests of the rights holders in question. But one must first give an account of what these duties are.

1.3 TERMINOLOGY

Finally, by way of introduction, it is necessary to address two terminological issues that often cause confusion within the context of the consideration of historic injustice.

1. Compensation and restitution

'Restitution' is a term which is used in different ways by different authors.[64] It can be taken to refer to the whole process of seeking to rectify historic injustice, and is often used in this way in both scholarly and popular discussion of righting past wrongs. Thus, for example, Richard Vernon uses the term to describe all elements of attempts to right historic wrongs, 'ranging from the literal return of the object that was taken (in whole or in part), through financial compensation based on estimates (somehow reached) of the value of the object, to apologies (or apology-like acts under various names) with or without accompanying compensation'.[65] By contrast, Onora O'Neill defines restitution much more narrowly, as only one possible part of rectificatory justice, and as conceptually distinct from compensation: restitution 'is a matter of restoring matters to those that obtained before wrong was done'; it corresponds specifically to the ruptured moral relationship between offender and victim, and unlike compensation, it 'cannot be vicarious'.[66] By way of laying out the legal context of the term, Peter Birks explains that, in common usage, the term has two meanings: 'There can be restitution of a thing or person to an earlier condition and restitution of a thing to a person.'[67] Confusion arises as the first sense of restitution here corresponds to the idea of compensation, whereby counterbalancing benefits are provided to make up for a particular loss. The second sense is conceptually distinct, and Birks identifies the idea lying at the heart of this second sense by suggesting that 'restitution is the response which consists in causing one person to give back something to another'.[68] These two senses of restitution are confusing, and have led to a degree of muddled thinking on the subject of the rectification of historic injustice, despite having been quite clearly separated in the past by writers such as Jeremy Waldron.[69] Therefore, I follow Birks in suggesting that we should keep the two terms quite separate. When I use the term 'restitution', I refer specifically to the return of misappropriated property. Compensation forms the subject of Chapter 4, and restitution is the subject of Chapter 5. I use the term 'rectification' to refer to restitution in the first, general sense, and, as noted, the term 'the rectificatory project' to describe the general aim of seeking to ensure that one's moral duties arising from historic injustice are fulfilled.

2. Nations and states
The second terminological issue relates to the differences between groups and entities such as nations, states, nation-states, and peoples. There is no agreed definition for any of these terms, and writers use them in different ways in different contexts.[70] The problem manifests itself even with the phrase 'international law', which, on some interpretations, refers to the law of states – not, in fact, of nations.[71] Insofar as nations are defined as particular kinds of self-identifying cultural groups, it is quite possible to have states that contain more than one nation, or nations split between two or more states.[72] In fact, philosophical debate over the rectification of injustice has often focused on precisely such cases, in relation, for example, to indigenous peoples. This book, however, is explicitly concerned with 'international' justice in the sense of justice between, not within, modern day self-governing communities. A question of historical rectification only falls within the remit of the book if the people of one modern day state have duties to persons who are members of other states. I refer to the latter class of persons as 'non-nationals'. In what follows, I use both the term 'state' and the term 'nation'. This is necessary, since modern day political agency is typically exercised through the state, and so political questions of duties to others arise primarily at a state level.[73] I generally use the term 'nation' when I am discussing the historical interaction of peoples. Here I refer (in David Miller's terms) to 'a community of people with the aspiration to be politically self-determining.'[74] Insofar as such communities were self-determining they were capable of acting unjustly to others, and regardless of their level of self-determination they could be treated unjustly and harmed themselves. The precise relation between historic nations and modern day states is often complicated: the most straightforward cases concern nation-states, where there is a close match between a historical cultural group and the population of a modern state, and this is generally the easiest example to bear in mind when conceptualizing problems of historical rectification. Inevitably, this is something of an abstraction, and might be thought to overlook the more complicated nature of many real world situations. However, the nature of my argument avoids a number of these problems. Chapters 4 and 5 work within a particular methodological assumption, whereby the populations of

current states are considered as innocent third parties in relation to historic injustice. The questions that are posed are (*a*) Have these modern day populations benefited, and non-nationals suffered, as a result of historic injustice? and (*b*) Are these populations in possession of property which might be said to belong to non-nationals? Such arguments make no assumptions about the relation of these modern day states to the nations originally responsible for the commission of injustice. The methodological constraint is removed in Chapter 6, which explicitly considers the extent of continuity between historic nations and their modern day counterparts.

NOTES

1. Chris McGreal, 'Secret talks to heal UN race split', *Observer* 2 September 2001.
2. Tim Butcher, 'Prejudice shows over slavery and reparations', *Daily Telegraph* 3 September 2001. The comment was, presumably, intended as a *reductio ad absurdum* of the reparations case, rather than an acknowledgement of the (not necessarily unreasonable) argument that various African royal families may possess significant rectificatory duties.
3. Rachel Neumann, 'Despite U.S. pullout, debate over reparations continues', *Village Voice* 5 September 2001.
4. Chris McGreal, 'UN race meeting ends in acrimony', *Guardian* 8 September 2001.
5. 'Debacle in Durban', *The Times* 29 August 2001.
6. Elazar Barkan, *The Guilt of Nations: Restitution and Negotiating Historic Injustices* (New York: Norton, 2000).The other five chapters consider indigenous groups (in general), Native Americans, Australian Aborigines, Maoris, and native Hawaiians. Much of the material on rectification for slavery applies to African American claims from the US Government.
7. John Rawls, *A Theory of Justice* (Oxford: Oxford University Press, 1972).
8. Charles Beitz, *Political Theory and International Relations* (Princeton: Princeton University Press, 1979); John Rawls, *The Law of Peoples* (Cambridge, MA: Harvard University Press, 1999).
9. Barkan, *The Guilt of Nations*, p. xvi.
10. Transcript taken from http://www.archbishopofcanterbury.org/525/ (accessed 13/02/2008).
11. Cited at http://news.bbc.co.uk/1/hi/uk_politics/6185176.stm/(accessed 13/02/2008).
12. On the contemporary slave trade, see Kevin Bales, *Understanding Global Slavery: A Reader* (Berkeley: University of California Press, 2005).
13. *Declaration of World Conference against Racism, Racial Discrimination, Xenophobia and Related Intolerance*, available at http://www.un.org/WCAR/durban.pdf/.

14. Ronald J. Horvath, 'A definition of colonialism', *Current Anthropology* 13 (1972), 45–57 at p. 47.
15. For example, see Colin Farrelly, 'Justice in ideal theory: a refutation' *Political Studies* 55 (2007), 844–64; but for powerful responses, see Zofia Stemplowska, 'What's ideal about ideal theory?' *Social Theory and Practice* 34 (2008), 319–40 and Adam Swift, 'The value of philosophy in nonideal circumstances' *Social Theory and Practice* 34 (2008), 363–87.
16. Rawls, *A Theory of Justice* (1972), p. 8.
17. Rawls, *A Theory of Justice* (1972), pp. 8–9.
18. G. A. Cohen, 'Facts and principles', *Philosophy and Public Affairs* 31 (2003), 211–45.
19. Rawls, *The Law of Peoples*, pp. 6–7.
20. George Sher, *Approximate Justice: Studies in Non-Ideal Theory* (Lanham: Rowman & Littlefield, 1997), p. 1. [Sher's emphasis]
21. This is discussed in Liam Murphy, *Moral Demands in Nonideal Theory* (Oxford: Oxford University Press, 2000).
22. See Robert E. Goodin, 'Political ideals and political practice', *British Journal of Political Science* 25 (1995), 37–56.
23. The term 'international libertarianism' is potentially confusing. As later discussion stresses repeatedly, it does not describe the perspective on international distributive justice of writers who are libertarians at a domestic level. In changing the foundational unit of libertarianism from individual to collective, the theory is completely transformed.
24. Rawls, *The Law of Peoples*, p. 111.
25. Rawls, *The Law of Peoples*, p. 118. [Rawls's emphasis]
26. Rawls, *The Law of Peoples*, p. 119.
27. My argument here follows that of Mervyn Frost on 'settled norms', which looks not so much at what political actors actually do but at the justification they feel necessary to give to their actions. See Frost, *Ethics in International Relations: A Constitutive Theory* (Cambridge: Cambridge University Press, 1996), pp. 105–6.
28. So Ernest Gellner famously writes that, 'Nationalism is not simply the awakening of nations to self-consciousness: it often invents nations where they do not exist', Gellner, *Thoughts and Change* (London: Weidenfeld & Nicolson, 1964), p. 168. For discussion, see Arash Abizadeh 'Historical truth, national myths, and liberal democracy: on the coherence of liberal nationalism', *The Journal of Political Philosophy* 12 (2004), 291–313.
29. See the discussion on national guilt and shame in Farid Abdel-Nour, 'National responsibility', *Political Theory* 31 (2003), 693–719.
30. The new South African constitution itself makes explicit reference to historic injustice, the preamble beginning: 'We, the people of South Africa, recognise the injustices of our past; honour those who suffered for justice and freedom in our land; respect those who have worked to build and develop our country; and believe that South Africa belongs to all who live in it, united in our diversity.' See Eduard Fagan, 'The constitutional entrenchment of memory', in Sarah Nuttall

and Carli Coetzee (eds.), *Negotiating the Past: The Making of Memory in South Africa* (Cape Town: Oxford University Press, 1998), 249–62.
31. See Benjamin Zephaniah, 'Me? I thought, OBE me? Up yours, I thought', *The Guardian* 27 November 2003.
32. In *On Nationality* (Oxford: Clarendon Press, 1995), David Miller points to a crisis in British identity, holds this to be a bad thing, and suggests a three point plan, involving: (*a*) an explicit debate about the character of national identity, (*b*) a constitutional settlement, including a written constitution, and (*c*) the introduction of civic education (pp. 78–82). My suggestion is that the adoption of the rectificatory project would also be a necessary step in reversing such a perceived decline in national identity.
33. The converse would also be true, in that on realist terms the government of a country whose sense of national identity would be lessened by paying compensation or effecting restitution would seemingly face a moral obligation *not* to seek to rectify past injustice.
34. As Cohen and Sabel have recently argued – and as Chapter 3 acknowledges – this is not to say that liberal political theorists need fall squarely into one camp or another, as it is quite possible to adopt one of a range of intermediate positions, holding that one has limited distributive duties to non-nationals. My claim is that such writers, along with more straightforward international libertarians, also need a distinctive account of international rectificatory justice. Joshua Cohen and Charles Sabel, '*Extra rempublicam nulla justitia*?', *Philosophy and Public Affairs* 34 (2006), 147–75 at p. 149.
35. Cécile Fabre, *Justice In a Changing World* (Cambridge: Polity, 2007), p. 103. David Miller argues in similar fashion in favour of his backward-looking national responsibility model, noting that whatever the theoretical appeal of present- or future-oriented accounts of international justice, this approach 'does not square with common opinion on the question of international distribution', Miller, 'Holding nations responsible', *Ethics* 114 (2004), 240–68 at p. 241n.
36. See Michael Walzer's account of the 'legalistic paradigm' in *Just and Unjust Wars* (New York: Basic Books, 1977).
37. For some, this may be sufficient reason to rule out redistributive cosmopolitanism at the level of justification, if one holds that one should take account of everyday beliefs when formulating principles of justice. David Miller has expressed support for a version of this position: 'I maintain that empirical evidence should play a significant role in justifying a normative theory of justice, or to put it another way, that such a theory is to be tested, in part, by its correspondence with our evidence concerning everyday beliefs about justice ... The aim is to achieve an equilibrium whereby the theory of justice appears no longer as an external imposition conjured up by a philosopher, but as a clearer and more systematic statement of the principles that people already hold' (David Miller, *Principles of Social Justice* (Cambridge, MA: Harvard University Press, 1999), p. 51). Miller does accept that this is a controversial view, since 'it may be

argued that to see justice in this way is to abandon its most critical function: our theory cannot judge an entire society, *including its beliefs*, to be radically unjust' (p. 279n [Miller's emphasis]). Evidently, it is just such a critical claim which is made by radical cosmopolitans who believe that everyday contemporary beliefs about justice are profoundly mistaken. See, for example, Peter Unger, *Living High and Letting Die: Our Illusion of Innocence* (New York: Oxford University Press, 1996). In any case, I do not follow Miller's approach here.

38. So Simon Caney claims that Rawls's failure to address this issue in *The Law of Peoples* creates a 'lacuna' in his account of international justice: 'It is hard to deny that the current distribution of wealth and power has been affected by previous injustice. This immediately raises the question of whether and to what extent compensation is owed to some because they have been treated unjustly in the past. Now my point here is *not* that Rawls must adopt principles of rectificatory justice. It is rather that, given the incontestable fact of previous exploitation, any satisfactory theory of international justice must address the question of whether there are duties of compensation (or reconciliation or even apology) ... What one cannot do, I think, is stay silent on the matter and this is what Rawls does' (Simon Caney, 'Survey article: cosmopolitanism and the Law of Peoples', *The Journal of Political Philosophy* 10 (2002), 95–123 at p. 119). David Miller, however, does address the issue, in particular in his *National Responsibility and Global Justice* (Oxford: Oxford University Press, 2007).

39. John Rawls, 'The independence of moral theory', *Proceedings and Addresses of the American Philosophical Association*, 48 (1974–5), 5–22 at pp. 7–8. It is quite possible, of course, that a proper understanding of the implications of their foundational premises may lead such theorists to revise these premises themselves, and so revise their understanding of – or reject – international libertarianism itself. What this book does not do is to challenge these foundational principles by subjecting them to thorough-going scrutiny, through an analysis of their strength compared to the foundational premises averred by others, such as cosmopolitans. This is why the approach is best described as one of seeking to achieve narrow rather than wide reflective equilibrium. See Rawls, 'The independence of moral theory ', p. 8; Norman Daniels, *Justice and Justification: Reflective Equilibrium in Theory and Practice* (Cambridge: Cambridge University Press, 1996), pp. 1–10. It should perhaps be underlined that Rawls's project is explicitly concerned with wide – not narrow – reflective equilibrium.

40. Thomas Pogge, *World Poverty and Human Rights* (Cambridge: Polity, 2002).

41. Pogge, p. 133.

42. Thomas Pogge, 'Symposium: *World Poverty and Human Rights*', *Ethics and International Affairs* 19 (2005), 1–7 at p. 1.

43. Pogge, p. 132.

44. Allen Buchanan, *Justice, Legitimacy and Self-Determination: Moral Foundations for International Law* (Oxford: Oxford University Press, 2004), p. 97.

45. Buchanan, p. 97 [my emphasis].
46. Simon Caney, 'Global poverty and human rights: the case for positive duties', in Thomas Pogge (ed.), *Freedom from Poverty as a Basic Right* (Oxford: Oxford University Press, 2007), 275–302 at p. 287, 44n.
47. In a recent interview, Pogge explicitly accepts that his emphasis on negative duties, at least, is strategic in nature: 'Yes, this emphasis is in part pragmatic. I do believe that most severe suffering in this world would be avoided if the rich countries merely fulfilled their duty not to harm. I also find, especially in the Anglophone countries, a great reluctance to take positive duties seriously. And this is most of my audience, an extremely powerful constituency in this world! I say to them: "I know what you expect from a lecture or essay about global poverty: an appeal to be more generous, to give more aid. But you will not get this from me. I am leaving positive duties aside and rest my case entirely on negative duties..." Many have criticized me for rejecting positive duties. Such criticisms are simply mistaken. By taking positive duties off the table in conversation with some particular audience, I am not denying such duties in any way. I am simply leaving them aside because I expect that no agreement can be reached. Of course I believe in positive duties. But I keep them out of much of my work to make it very clear that I need not appeal to them. I want to reach people Peter Singer cannot reach; and those people will tune out as soon as I talk about positive duties', Sandrine Berges, 'Interview with Professor Thomas Pogge', *Éthique et économique/Ethics and Economics*, 5 (2007). Peter Singer famously put forward an account of positive duties to those in desperate need in Singer, 'Famine, affluence and morality', *Philosophy and Public Affairs* 1 (1972), 229–43.
48. See Alan Patten, 'Should we stop thinking about poverty in terms of helping the poor?', *Ethics & International Affairs* 19 (2005), 19–27; Mathias Risse, 'How does the global order harm the poor?', *Philosophy and Public Affairs* 33 (2005), 349–76; Ser-Min Shei, 'World poverty and moral responsibility' in Andreas Follesdal and Thomas Pogge (eds.), *Real World Justice: Grounds, Principles, Human Rights, and Social Institutions* (Dordecht: Springer, 2005), 139–56.
49. Pogge, 'Symposium: *World Poverty and Human Rights*', pp. 1–2. See also Pogge, *World Poverty and Human Rights*, p. 145, which describes this phenomenon in terms of 'thoughtlessness'.
50. This is not to say that it is so widely accepted that such actions were wrong when performed in the different historical context of the past. This issue is addressed in Chapter 3.
51. John M. Darley and Thane S. Pittman, 'The psychology of compensatory and retributive justice' *Personality and Social Psychology Review* 7 (2003), 324–36.
52. Shaohua Chen and Martin Ravallion, 'How have the world's poorest fared since the early 1980s?', *The World Bank Research Observer* 19 (2004), 141–69 at p. 141. Some critics contend that this actually understates the extent of global poverty: see, for example, Thomas Pogge and Sanjay G. Reddy, 'Unknown: the

extent, distribution and trend of global income poverty' (2006) – available at http://ssrn.com/abstract=936772/.
53. See Henri-Bernard Solignac Lecomte, Ida McDonnell, and Liam Wegimont (eds), *Public Opinion and the Fight Against Poverty* (Paris: OECD, 2003).
54. For discussion with reference to Pogge, see Caney, 'Global poverty and human rights: the case for positive duties', pp. 300–1.
55. In terms of the terminology employed in Chapter 3, my position is one of non-relational egalitarianism.
56. See Cass R. Sunstein,'Incompletely theorized agreements', *Harvard Law Review* 108 (1995), pp. 1733–72.
57. This is, strikingly, a conclusion entertained at a domestic level by Robert Nozick in *Anarchy State, and Utopia* (New York: Basic Books, 1974), p. 231. Nozick's position is discussed in Chapter 2. It is equally striking that Nozick takes it for granted that rectification takes place within, rather than potentially between, societies.
58. Nigel Dower, 'World poverty', in P. Singer (ed.), *A Companion to Ethics* (Oxford: Blackwell, 1991), 273–83 at p. 275.
59. Onora O'Neill, *Faces of Hunger* (London: Allen & Unwin, 1986), p. 110.
60. For an articulation of this objection, see Goodin, 'Political ideals and political practice', p. 40.
61. Onora O'Neill, 'Rights to compensation,' *Social Philosophy and Policy* 5 (1987), 72–87 at p. 84.
62. Randall Robinson, *The Debt: What America Owes to Blacks* (New York: Plume, 2001).
63. John McWhorter, 'Against reparations', *The New Republic* 23 July 2001. See also McWhorter's *Losing the Race: Self-Sabotage in Black America* (New York: Perennial, 2001).
64. See the discussion in A. John Simmons, 'Historical rights and fair shares', *Law and Philosophy* 14 (1995), 149–84 at pp. 149–50n.
65. Richard Vernon, 'Against restitution', *Political Studies* 511 (2003), 542–57 at p. 543.
66. Onora O'Neill, 'Rights to compensation' *Social Philosophy and Policy* 5 (1987), 72–87 at p. 74.
67. Peter Birks, *An Introduction to the Law of Restitution* (Oxford: Clarendon Press, 1989), p. 10.
68. Birks, *An Introduction to the Law of Restitution*, p. 11. Birks in fact goes on to lay out a more precise definition of restitution in a legal context, so that: 'Restitution is the response which consists in causing one person to give up to another an enrichment received at his expense or its value in money' (p. 13). However, the conceptual distinction from compensation remains.
69. See Jeremy Waldron, 'Superseding historic injustice', *Ethics* 103 (1992), 4–28.
70. Rawls's preference for 'peoples' is somewhat idiosyncratic; for a discussion, see Simon Caney, 'Review article: international distributive justice', *Political Studies* 49 (2001), 974–97 at pp. 983–4.

71. Terry Nardin notes that so close have the notional links between nation and state become, 'that the English language now scarcely distinguishes them in many contexts. It allows us to speak of the "nation-state", "international relations" and the "United Nations," even though it is almost always states rather than nations which are being talked about', Nardin, *Law, Morality and the Relations of States* (Princeton: Princeton University Press, 1983), p. 43. See also Miller, *On Nationality*, pp. 18–19.
72. See David Miller, *Citizenship and National Identity* (Cambridge, MA: Polity, 2000), pp. 125–44.
73. This is in itself a simplification, as it overlooks perfectly valid arguments concerning the rectificatory obligations of, for example, multinational corporations. I leave such questions to one side, and focus exclusively on actions which can be taken by governments.
74. Miller, *On Nationality*, p. 19. Miller's full definition of nationality has five elements, and describes 'a community (1) constituted by shared belief and mutual commitment, (2) extended in history, (3) active in character, (4) connected to a particular territory, and (5) marked off from other communities by its distinct public culture', *On Nationality*, p. 27.

2

Why Worry about Historic Injustice?

2.1 THE DISTINCTIVENESS OF INTERNATIONAL RECTIFICATORY JUSTICE

The previous chapter observed that the specific question of rectifying *international* injustice has received little attention from political theorists. Why is this so? This chapter outlines a number of critical responses to the rectificatory project, and explains why largely they do not apply to international libertarian accounts of justice between states. It begins by examining the relationship between distributive and rectificatory justice. Within a domestic context, modern day liberal political theorists often advocate accounts of distributive justice which are essentially forward-looking. The actions of previous generations are seen as of only limited importance in determining who should have what in the present day. This means that writers have tended to advocate only limited degrees of redistribution to correct past wrongdoing – typically limited to actions committed in the relatively recent past, within, roughly speaking, a single generation. This is so both when they have thought about how to rectify departures from just initial starting points, and when they have confronted the more realistic problem of how to respond to injustice which occurs against a backdrop which would not be endorsed by ideal theory accounts of distributive justice. If one does have a forward-looking perspective on distributive justice – as many do at a domestic level – then it is quite right to think that the rectificatory project is of little consequence when it seeks to respond to distant wrongs, committed more than one generation in the past. Accordingly, a literature has developed, which, though largely sympathetic to political actors who advocate modern day redress in response to historic wrongdoing, denies that this is required as a matter of justice. What this approach overlooks, however, is the extent to which this nonchalance in the face of historic injustice cannot be sustained once one adopts backward-looking principles of international justice. This is precisely the approach of international libertarians, who characteristically advocate principles of just international interaction which do not require redistribution across political boundaries with the coming of each new generation. When one holds such a world view, the historical provenance of modern day advantages becomes crucially important. The extent to which the move from forward-looking to backward-looking accounts of international justice necessitates taking the rectificatory project seriously has not been fully appreciated.

It seems clear that a great deal of historic interaction between the world's different communities has been characterized by forms of behaviour that most people would readily condemn as unjust if they were to take place in the modern day. As Marshall Cohen writes, 'To an alarming degree the history of international relations is a history of selfishness and brutality. It is a story in which spying, deceit, bribery, disloyalty, ingratitude, betrayal, exploitation, plunder, repression, subjection and genocide are all too conspicuous.'[1] It is not hard to think of instances of when wars have been waged; people killed and enslaved; political regimes overthrown and property destroyed, damaged, or misappropriated for reasons which are now seen as clearly unacceptable; ranging from the naked pursuit of national self-interest to racist hatred of members of other communities. The extent to which it is appropriate to judge the actions of historical actors by contemporary moral standards is a controversial question, which will be addressed in the next chapter. But it does seem as if any attempt to think comprehensively about the rectification of historic injustice will have to consider a range of different kinds of human interaction – not only actions which took place within particular, bounded communities, but also instances when members of one community acted wrongfully and caused harm to members of another. When we consider the theoretical principles which tell us how to think about and respond to historical wrongdoing, we can ask whether the same principles should be used in both cases. Or is there anything distinctive about the rectification of historic *international* injustice specifically?

The answer to this question is a complicated one. Principles of rectificatory justice tell us how we should respond to injustice. They are thus clearly reliant on an account of what injustice is, or else we would not know when the need for rectification arises. But there are other ways in which the principles of justice which we endorse make a difference to how instances of injustice should be addressed. Rectificatory justice is not free-standing – it can only be properly articulated and examined with implicit or explicit reference to an understanding of justice in a broader sense. Of particular importance to the questions addressed by the rectificatory project is distributive justice. This is because it is concerned with cases where those morally responsible for the original acts of injustice in question are dead. When we ask how modern day duties and entitlements are affected by these historic actions, the primary issues which the project seeks to address are distributive in nature. We generally think that issues of punishment, of repentance, and of at least some senses of apology only arise within a context of moral culpability. Questions of rectificatory justice in response to historic wrongdoing are questions which concern the distribution of benefits and burdens in the present day. Claims that a given group is owed compensation as a result of the historic injustice of slavery, or that a valuable sculpture should be returned to the heirs of those from whom it was wrongfully misappropriated in the past, are claims about who should have what here and now. They are claims that operate in the real world, and that propose particular courses of action which affect the distribution of resources within, and between, societies. They are not the only issues at stake – we might think, for example, that historic wrongdoing raises questions of political justice, concerning the drawing of state boundaries, rights of self-government, and the terms of democratic inclusion and participation. As Chapter 1 indicated, furthermore, political demands for apologies can be made without any accompanying claims relating to compensation or restitution. But it is not unusual to maintain that distributive concerns lie behind many of these related issues – political actors, indeed, often maintain that campaigns to secure apologies are in fact intended as precursors to demands for substantive reparations, even if they are not presented as such.

Insofar as the rectificatory project does seem to call for a redistribution of resources in the present day, it makes recommendations as to who should have what. Questions of who should have what are typically characterized as matters of distributive justice. This has two implications. First, we need an account of how distributive and rectificatory justice correspond to each other before we can say what should be done in the present day in response to historic wrongdoing. Second, the question of whether the same principles can be used in relation to international cases as are used in domestic cases becomes apparent. Many people believe that different principles of justice apply in an international context from those that apply domestically, and in particular that what we owe, in distributive terms, to those of different nations is different from what we owe to our co-nationals. Even if one thinks that justice – in a broad sense – in the present day does not require serious consideration of the past treatment of one's fellow citizens within a modern day polity, it does not necessarily follow from this that one can also discount the historic treatment of members of other communities. If, in general, different principles of distributive justice apply within communities to those which apply between communities – which is, of course, a contentious claim – and if accounts of rectificatory justice cannot be derived in isolation from principles of distributive justice, then it may well be that rectifying *international* injustice specifically requires a distinctive theoretical approach.

In this chapter and the next, I look at the distinctive nature of claims relating to the rectification of international injustice. This chapter looks at the role of distributive justice in relation to accounts of rectificatory justice. This discussion allows us to see why a number of theorists have professed scepticism as to the desirability and urgency of rectifying historic injustice. The concerns which are thus raised, however, are shown to be drawn from particular understandings of distributive justice, which many see as being most plausible within the context of distributions within particular, bounded communities. I argue that the picture changes when we think about the role of rectificatory justice in connection with international libertarianism. The key distinction here is between forward-looking and backward-looking accounts of distributive justice. At a domestic level, most political theorists tend to advocate essentially forward-looking accounts, which pay only a limited amount of attention to the past, typically limited to the time span of a single generation. The rectificatory project is therefore seen as irrelevant insofar as it concerns actions performed further in the past. The exceptions to this are historical entitlement theories, which pay much closer attention to the claim that the actions of previous generations can make a difference to present day entitlements. Such accounts of distributive justice, therefore, are backward-looking, and so have to take the historical provenance of contemporary holdings much more seriously. Once we shift focus from the domestic level to the international, things change. Theorists who advocate forward-looking principles of distributive justice within political communities frequently favour backward-looking accounts of international justice. Their vision of a normative world order is not of one where resources are periodically redistributed between states, but is rather one of just interaction between sovereign entities, who are entitled to pass on advantages internally from generation to generation. It is in this context that the rectificatory project has real moral urgency.

2.2 DOES HISTORY HAVE ETHICAL SIGNIFICANCE?

Contemporary analytical political theory affords a central role to the idea of justice. In *A Theory of Justice*, John Rawls argued that justice is the first virtue of social institutions, as truth is the first virtue of systems of thought.[2] This reflects the peremptory force which is often attributed to justice claims. At least in relation to the public sphere, it is commonly thought that to agree that a given course of action is required by justice is to settle the question of what should be done. As Rawls writes, 'A theory however elegant and economical must be rejected or revised if it is untrue; likewise laws and institutions no matter how efficient and well-arranged must be reformed or abolished if they are unjust... Being first virtues of human activities, truth and justice are uncompromising.'[3] Quite how the different components of justice should be fitted together, however, both in theoretical terms, and when we come to apply our theories to the real world, is a difficult question. In particular, how should we conceive of the relationship between distributive justice, which concerns the just allocation of benefits and burdens, with rectificatory or corrective justice, which concerns the appropriate response to wrongful harm?[4] Both appear to be constitutive elements of justice, and yet it sometimes seems as if the apparent requirements of distributive and of rectificatory justice can pull in different directions. If we correct all the wrongful harm in the world, is there any reason to think we would be any closer to the ideals of distributive justice? Might we, in fact, perhaps even end up further away? To thinkers primarily concerned with questions of distributive justice, rectificatory justice, and, in particular, the rectification of ancient wrongs, can seem far from a pressing concern. It is common in the literature on this subject to find writers who believe that worrying about historic injustice is something of a red herring when we start thinking seriously about our moral rights and duties. The language characteristically used is instructive. Sympathy with real world political actors who seek redress is expressed,[5] and support is given for the role that the condemnation of historic wrongdoing can play in the way we conceive of ourselves and of our moral duties to others in the present day. The symbolic role of making apology and even of paying reparations is acknowledged, and it is accepted that the importance of such actions to the current day self-respect and political inclusion and recognition of particular, historically oppressed groups can be very significant, and so can, in some cases, give very strong reasons for action.[6] But it is explicitly denied that these are reasons of rectificatory justice in response to historic wrongdoing.[7] Justice is portrayed as essentially forward-looking: insofar as the practical effects of rectifying historic injustice serve to meet our contemporary obligations, it is not objectionable, but the reasons for this are not themselves historical.[8] So Jeremy Waldron writes that the rectificatory project can be trumped by 'an honest and committed resolve to justice for the future, a resolve to address present circumstances in a way that respects the claims and needs of everyone'. Such a resolve 'has priority over reparation which might carry us in a direction contrary to what which is indicated by a prospective theory of justice'. Although claims based on reparation and claims based on forward-looking principles will often coincide, 'it is worth stressing that it is the impulse to justice now that should lead the way in this process, not the reparation of something whose wrongness is understood primarily in relation to conditions that no longer obtain'.[9]

The key question here concerns the extent to which history may be said to have ethical significance. Are there good reasons for thinking that what happened in the past affects present day justice-based rights and obligations? This chapter examines this question. First, it looks at how accounts of distributive justice seek to rectify departures from just initial distributions. Second, it examines the extent to which history is deemed to have ethical significance when we come to think about unjust departures from real world distributions, which are not those which would be sanctioned by theorists' ideal theories. In both cases, the question is usually answered within a domestic context in such a way as to limit the relevance of historic injustice to a relatively short period of time – usually conceived of as a single generation. As will be seen, this attitude cannot be sustained by backward-looking international libertarians in an international context.

Is there, then, a tension between distributive and rectificatory justice? When considering this question, legal theorists typically start with a standard legalistic account of rectificatory justice, as reflected in the basic principles of tort law and the law of restitution. The principles of corrective justice embedded in tort law broadly hold that those responsible for wrongful losses are required to rectify the situation, insofar as doing so is possible, and to make up for the harm their actions have caused.[10] So Jules Coleman writes that, 'According to corrective justice, individuals have a duty to repair the wrongful losses for which they are responsible.'[11] The law of restitution is concerned with the class of actions where one person is required to give up to another an unjust enrichment received at her expense.[12] Both categories seek to address wrongdoing by requiring the transfer of resources between individuals: 'Corrective justice imposes the duty on the wrongdoer to compensate his victims for the costs his wrongdoing imposes on them. Restitutionary justice gives the victim the right to the wrongdoer's gains secured at her expense.'[13] I will call this the 'standard view' of rectificatory justice, since it reflects both existing legal practice and what might be thought of as an everyday, common sense approach to the effects of wrongdoing. Its full detail requires much more specification, and much of what follows in later chapters in dedicated to this task. Nonetheless, it can at least be interpreted in such a way as to incorporate the three forms of connection with historic injustice outlined in Chapter 1 and discussed in the remainder of the book, whereby one can possess rectificatory duties through responsibility for injustice, through benefiting from injustice, or through possessing property to which others hold entitlements. The important point for present purposes is that the standard view is explicitly historical: it looks to the past to give an account of what different individuals owe to one another in the present day, through seeking, in some way, to undo, reverse, or make up for the effects of injustice. The question then follows of if and how such a set of principles of rectificatory justice can be reconciled with theories of distributive justice. The point is that distributive justice is supposed to give us an account of who should have what, and yet rectificatory justice seemingly also requires, as a matter of justice, that we bring about particular distributions of property. Can these two sets of justice-based distributions conflict?

2.3 DEPARTURES FROM INITIALLY JUST DISTRIBUTIONS

Let us start by considering unjust departures from initially just distributions. Some writers have suggested that, on certain accounts of distributive justice, a conflict between rectificatory and distributive justice can indeed arise in such a context. Larry Alexander gives the example of a patterned distribution where each individual is to have equal shares, and which thus requires that A, B, C, and D each receive ten units of resources each. If A acts wrongfully in a way which destroys four units of D's goods, it seems as if the principle of equal shares requires that each of A, B, and C contribute one unit to D, whereas the principle of rectificatory justice outlined above would have it that A gives (at least) four units to D, resulting in a society whereby B, C, and D each have ten units but A only has six.[14] It looks as if either the principle of equal shares will have to be modified, by including, for example, some proviso whereby inequalities are not unjust if they come about as the result of holding wrongdoers responsible for the costs of rectifying harmful wrongdoing, or the standard model of rectificatory justice will have to be abandoned, and replaced by an alternative wholly derived from the 'equal shares' account of distributive justice, whereby the point of rectificatory justice is simply to correct inequalities, regardless of how they have arisen.

There does seem to be an irreconcilable difference between the standard account of rectificatory justice and the 'equal shares' distributive principle as outlined above. The theory of rectificatory justice suggested by the equal shares principle places no particular responsibility upon A as the wrongdoer, it merely assesses the capacity of agents to restore the conditions of material equality between persons. As such, it is an example of what Nozick describes as an end-state principle, which is unhistorical in that it is concerned solely with how things are to be distributed, regardless of how current resource holdings came about.[15] The 'equal shares' principle above is an example of what Nozick calls a 'current-time slice distribution', whereby to assess the justice of two given distributions 'one need look only at the matrix presenting the distributions'.[16] If there is a departure from the equal distribution, we do whatever is necessary to restore equality without considering how the departure from the just distribution came about. Nozick rightly points out that, 'Most persons do not accept current time-slice principles as constituting the whole story about distributive shares. They think it relevant in assessing the justice of a situation to consider not only the distribution it embodies, but also how that distribution came about.'[17] Current time-slice accounts of distributive justice necessarily contain their own accounts of rectificatory justice. In cases of deviation from the desired pattern, one should simply act to restore the structural distribution in question without worrying about how the deviation came about, meaning that the standard view of rectificatory justice seemingly drops out of the picture altogether. But it is not at all clear how significant this is in terms of identifying a general tension between distributive and rectificatory justice, since it is not obvious who actually endorses the kind of current time-slice principles that Nozick criticizes. The problem with the 'equal shares' approach to distributive justice is that it appears overly inflexible in maintaining that distributions in society must conform to such a rigidly defined distributive pattern, and this leads very quickly to outcomes which are wildly undesirable, both in consequentialist terms, and with regard to widely shared intuitions that accounts of who is to have what should pay at least some attention to how resource holdings came about in order to be fair. Thus, not only do distributive theorists generally accept basic criminal and penal institutions, which can affect levels of resource holdings in response to wrongdoing, they also typically allow movement away from abstract distributive patterns when such movement is the result of agents' freely made choices. The distributive principles which they outline are characteristically intended to regulate broad distributions over time. Thus, Stephen Perry has argued that, 'the most influential contemporary theories of distributive justice are dynamic rather than static'.[18] He argues, *contra* Nozick's depiction, that Rawls's account of distributive justice, for example, is (within certain limits) a matter of procedural rather than allocative justice, whereby distributions which happen to emerge are just if they are the result of institutions of the basic structure which tend over time to satisfy the difference principle.[19] Similarly, David Schmidtz contrasts Nozick's interpretation of the difference principle 'as a ground-level prescription for redistribution' with the 'canonical' interpretation of the difference principle 'as a way of evaluating basic structure',[20] and notes, 'To be sure, Rawls was a kind of egalitarian, but not a time-slice or even end-state egalitarian. The pattern Rawls meant to weave into the fabric of society was a pattern of equal status, applying not so much to a distribution as to an ongoing relationship.'[21] The radically egalitarian 'equal shares' account of distributive justice is deeply implausible, since it contains no role for the principle that choices for which individuals are responsible can affect the resource holdings to which they are entitled, even when they have deliberately chosen to inflict wrongful harm on other persons.[22] Other egalitarian accounts, such as the 'luck egalitarian' approaches of the likes of G.A. Cohen and Richard Arneson, instead accept that distributive shares can be affected by agents' freely chosen actions, and maintain that equality, properly understood, requires differential shares of resources for individuals not only in cases of deliberate malfeasance but also when inequalities are the consequences of bad luck to which individuals freely and consciously expose themselves.[23] An even stronger emphasis on individual choice and responsibility is found in libertarian accounts, such as Nozick's own historical entitlement model. These argue against the idea of imposing distributive patterns such as that of equal shares upon societies, on the grounds that to do so is to ignore and override the free choices made by individuals as to how they wish to use their own resources. Thus, Nozick argues that historical principles of justice 'hold that past circumstances or actions of people can create differential entitlements or differential deserts to things',[24] and puts forward the simplified maxim, 'From each as they choose, to each as they are chosen.'[25]

When distributive theorists accept that justice can require that individuals be held responsible for their choices, the apparent gap between the requirements of the standard approach to rectificatory justice and the demands of distributive justice seems much less apparent. Rectificatory justice emerges from the same concern with the fair terms of social interaction as does distributive justice, and, as such, both can be said to rest upon the same conception of the moral equality of persons. The key idea here is that, if we are to treat each other as moral equals, we will realize that fairness requires that we take responsibility for, and pay the costs of, some of our actions.[26] Different theorists disagree as to what extent our actions should give rise to differential shares, but pretty much everyone can sign up to the standard view of rectificatory justice, which corresponds to *wrongdoing*. So a concern with distributive justice certainly need not entail a disregard for rectificatory justice. When choice and responsibility play a role in a theory of who should have what, history becomes morally significant.

The implications of this for the distributive theorist are, however, potentially limited. The standard account of rectificatory justice given above makes explicit reference to 'the wrongdoer' – it is concerned, at least in the first instance, with the responsibility of the specific individual responsible for the wrongdoing. It is one thing to hold that actions which one performs within one's lifetime can generate differential entitlements and responsibilities to others, whether one is speaking only of the costs of wrongdoing, or more broadly in terms of generating entitlements to resources through one's efforts. It is another to hold that these actions can affect the life chances and entitlements of others – and theorists hold very different views on this matter. In particular, the question is left open as to what degree of redistribution is required at the start of each generation. A range of theorists accept principles of distribution with historical elements within individuals' own lifetimes, but reject the claim that inegalitarian advantages can justifiably be passed on from members of one generation to another. Precise reasons for this move vary, but a common theme is a concern for some version of equality of opportunity.[27] Even if we maintain that we should hold individuals responsible for some, or all, of the effects of their choices, then, it does not follow that their choices should affect the relative prospects of members of future generations. As Ripstein argues:

> An historical account of justice is not an account of a game with only one round, but of fair terms of interaction across generations. The idea that people should bear the costs of their activities is not the same as the idea that the sin (or bad judgment) of the parent (or grandparent) should shape the child's fortunes. Nor is an historical account of justice one in which those who lose in the first round must accept whatever terms others offer them.[28]

The result, in distributive terms, of adopting this kind of position is a broad antipathy to the justifiability of inheritance.[29] If distributive justice prohibits bequests and requires a significant or total redistribution of resources with each new generation, it seems as if the rectificatory project will have very limited scope, since the compatibility of rectificatory justice and distributive justice appears to be limited to a single generation. Such approaches are only backward-looking in relation to a single generation: other than in relation to individuals' own responsible choices, they are forward-looking. On this view, there is simply no distributive reason to worry about what happened in previous generations, since the actions of previous generations cannot affect modern day entitlements. This is the first reason why forward-looking theorists reject the rectificatory project, insofar as it involves assessment of actions performed by previous generations. In ideal theory contexts, forward-looking accounts of justice maintain that each new generation starts with a clean slate.

It is for this reason that the question of the rectification of older wrongs, whose original commission took place several generations ago, has received most scholarly attention from those who advocate backward-looking accounts of historical entitlement. Historical entitlement theorists such as Nozick explicitly reject the claim that justice requires redistribution with each new generation. Nozick argues that holdings are just, and so are not available for redistribution, insofar as they came about in keeping with three principles of distributive justice: the principle of just acquisition, by which individuals can come to possess property rights over objects; the principle of justice in transfer, by which entitlement to properly acquired property can be transferred from one individual to another; and the principle of rectification, by which illegitimate transfers of property are to be corrected.[30] Thus, respecting the autonomy of individuals means accepting their rights to transfer justly acquired property to whomever they want, including their children in subsequent generations. 'A person who acquires a holding in accordance with the principle of justice in transfer, from someone else entitled to the holding, is entitled to the holding.'[31] Of course, such an account is reliant upon an account of how individuals can come to acquire resources in such a way as to hold full property rights over them. But if such an account can be given, then the sense in which history can legitimately affect distributive justice is far more extensive than on the forward-looking model. As such, the historical entitlement account of justice in rectification can stretch across generations. There is no incompatibility between distributive justice and rectificatory justice here – which is precisely why one of Nozick's three principles of distributive justice *is* a principle of rectificatory justice.

2.4 DEPARTURES FROM INITIALLY UNJUST DISTRIBUTIONS

The foregoing account assesses the role of history in correcting departures from initially just distributions. The limited role which history plays in this account explains some of the reluctance political theorists who are not historical entitlement theorists at a domestic level have displayed in worrying about historic injustice. In looking at responsibility for wrongdoing in initially just contexts, it engages with one kind of non-ideal theory. It is not the only kind, however. The previous chapter noted that the term 'non-ideal theory' can be used to describe a range of different kinds of departures from the ideal. The foregoing discussion concerning the relation between distributive and rectificatory justice contains elements of both ideal and non-ideal theory. It imagines a just distribution, and then seeks to determine what rectificatory principles should govern unjust departures from this starting point. There is a sense in which any account of rectification pertains to the non-ideal, since the very idea of rectification implies that something has gone wrong, that there is some distortion or divergence which needs rectifying. One such possible divergence is that from an existing ideal. In some cases, it will be possible to restore the ideal; in others, this will not prove feasible, and justice will therefore require that the next best possible outcome be realized. Both situations are non-ideal in slightly different senses. In the former, a non-ideal outcome follows from the ideal, and the ideal is restored by means of rectification. In the second, the ideal outcome cannot itself be restored, but the outcome is nonetheless just, in that there is nothing else that can be done to render the outcome better from the perspective of justice. Consider a society constructed according to a given ideal principle of justice. Then suppose that one individual steals some of the property of another. Things have gone wrong in a number of ways. We have a distortion in the scheme of distribution, as one party is in possession of property which properly belongs to another. It may also be the case that the victim of the theft has been harmed other than by the loss of her property. Perhaps she feels her freedom and security are violated by the theft, perhaps the loss of the property disrupts plans which she has made. An account of rectificatory justice will have to deal with these consequences of the wrongful act. Returning the property to its rightful owner may not be sufficient – we may also need to require that the victim be paid further compensation, and/or that the wrongdoer be punished for her actions. In some cases, it may be that the effects of the act of injustice can be successfully rectified – perhaps the victim has not missed her misappropriated property, and so is content with its return and the genuine repentance and apology of the offender, or perhaps she can be fully compensated for any actual and opportunity costs suffered as a result of the property's absence.[32] In other cases, things may not be so straightforward – perhaps there is a sense in which the victim will never again feel secure in the possession of her property, regardless of how genuine the repentance, or how extensive the reparations, of the offender. Even though we may feel that the situation cannot ever fully be rectified, we may nonetheless maintain that there is an answer to the question of what justice requires of the offender. Suppose I slam down a piano lid upon the fingers of a gifted amateur pianist, irreparably damaging her fingers and preventing her from ever playing to the same standard again. Perhaps I am a rival musician and perform the action with malicious intent, perhaps I do it inadvertently in a fit of a culpably negligent exhilaration whilst applauding her performance. In either case, I owe her compensation. This claim is not dependent upon the claim that there is a certain amount of money which will fully make up for the loss, so that she is (in economic parlance) on the same indifference curve in terms of utility as before.[33] We may fully accept that making up such losses to some victims is impossible – the harm they have suffered may not be commensurate with money, or quite possibly with any act of rectification which the offender can perform, or which can be performed by any combination of agents.[34] Nonetheless, justice makes particular demands upon the offender, and sometimes on other agents, such as the community as a whole. The claim that 'nothing can compensate Y for X's actions' does not lead to the conclusion that 'X therefore owes Y nothing'; we generally think that X does still owe something, which may be a token or symbolic payment, or may indeed represent an ongoing effort to raise Y to as high an indifference curve as possible, in the full knowledge that she will never again be on as high a curve as she was before.[35] Once these rectificatory duties are met, the situation is clearly, in a sense, far from ideal, and is worse in a number of ways compared to the situation prior to the wrongdoing, but no agent possesses unfulfilled duties of justice in relation to another.

The situation is non-ideal in a further sense when we do not start from an initially just distribution, such as, on most accounts of distributive justice, in a real world situation. This is where the potential conflict between distributive and rectificatory justice becomes most apparent. Consider, for example, Arthur Ripstein's account of the compatibility of the two:

> [C]orrective justice is important because of a general picture of how fair terms of interaction justify their results. Provided that starting points are fair and tortious wrongs are righted, a set of holdings is legitimate if it is the result of uncoerced interaction.[36]

But what if we do not consider historic starting points to have been fair? Why then should we seek to rectify past wrongdoing? Consider the situation from the perspective of distributive justice within a given, bounded community. Many theorists do not seek to defend either existing or historic real world distributions within such communities. When asked how the distribution of benefits and burdens in such a society should, ideally, be ordered, some more or less extensive degree of redistribution is typically advocated. So, for example, a utilitarian might argue that property should be redistributed so as to maximize overall well-being, an egalitarian could advocate that resources should be redistributed according to some index of equality, and a prioritarian would typically maintain that justice requires redistribution so as to maximize the holdings of the worst-off members of society. Such theories may readily be categorized, following the argument of the preceding section, as forward-looking accounts of distributive justice, in that they do not accept that the actions of previous generations should make a difference to the entitlements of current persons, although they will typically accept that individuals' actions can affect their own entitlements. Whether the distributions favoured by forward-looking theorists will coincide with the apparent requirements of rectificatory justice seems entirely contingent, and unlikely in practice, given that, in real world contexts, we do not typically see historical distributions as being substantively just and fair, but as having arisen in ways which involved large measures of injustice and arbitrariness. As Robert Goodin has noted, 'Compensatory justice is profoundly conservative. Across its diverse range of applications, it usually serves to restore some *status quo ante*.'[37] Unless we have some good reason to prefer this *status quo ante* to the existing distribution, it seems that we will have no reason of distributive justice to advocate restoring the prior distribution. Even in cases where restoring the *status quo ante* does result in a just distribution, or, more likely, make a non-ideal distribution less unjust, it seems that the reasons for redistributing resources in keeping with the standard principles of rectificatory justice will not themselves be reasons of rectificatory justice, but of distributive justice.

Faced with this situation, a number of legal theorists have sought to deny the proposition that the point of rectificatory justice in the real world is to restore just distributions. Instead, such writers focus on the legitimacy of existing distributions, which may not be ideal, in that an alternative distribution could be more just, but which are tolerable, in that they do not cross some threshold of gross or manifest injustice. This, for example, is the account put forward by Jules Coleman. Coleman acknowledges that it is possible to think of distributions of property which are so unjust as to be illegitimate:

> In order for a scheme of rights to warrant protection under corrective justice... they must be sufficiently defensible in justice to warrant being sustained against individual infringements. Entitlements that fail to have this minimal property are not real rights in the sense that their infringements cannot give rise to a moral reason for acting... each of us can imagine political institutions that so unjustly distribute resources that no one could have a reason in justice for sustaining them by making repair.[38]

So there is a threshold of justice, a certain minimal level which real world holdings must reach if they are to be treated as legitimate. Such a threshold cannot be stated as part of a stand-alone principle of rectificatory justice, but must be assessed from the perspective of distributive justice.[39] But Coleman denies that existing real world holdings necessarily reach this threshold of injustice:

> No one I know believes that the underlying allocation of holdings in the United States, for example, exactly coincides with what distributive justice requires. On the other hand, it is not implausible to think that infringements of those holdings by the conduct of others normally gives rise to claims in justice to repair.[40]

He claims that although resource holdings in the United States are not those which a theorist of distributive justice would mandate, they are not so unjust that they can be justifiably overridden by individuals, acting in their private capacities. Even if we think that the US government could now, in the present day, justifiably reorder these resource holdings (which is a further claim from that which holds that society would now be more just had history happened in such a way that some resources now held by particular persons were in fact held by others), individuals are not entitled to take the law into their own hands and do this themselves. Legitimate holdings should generally be respected on account of their importance to persons: individuals take their levels of resource holdings into account when they frame life-projects, and may suffer serious harm if their legitimately conceived expectations are disrupted.

Liberals characteristically place great emphasis on the capacity of individuals to plan their lives, and to carry out these plans once made. Rawls, for example, argued that individuals have a highest-order interest in their capacity to frame, revise, and pursue their conception of the good. Significant concerns of individual autonomy give us good reasons to support principles and institutions of rectificatory justice which protect the capacity of persons to live autonomous lives by upholding their legitimate expectations, and reversing certain kinds of damage to them. So Robert Goodin identifies the importance of protecting such expectations as the normative basis for compensatory justice in a real world context, based on the following three principles:

1. People reasonably rely upon a settled state of affairs persisting (or, anyway, not being interrupted in the ways against which compensation protects them) when framing their life plans.
2. That people should be able to plan their lives is morally desirable.
3. Compensation, if sufficiently swift, full, and certain, would restore the conditions that people were relying upon when framing their plans, and so allow them to carry on with their plans with minimal disruption.[41]

Coleman's account of the justification of non-ideal property rights has the same character: 'Whatever their ultimate justice (or efficiency), schemes of holdings, and the norms regulating them, help to create stable expectations on which individuals can rely in coordinating their behavior with one another.' A system of property rights is an example of such a scheme. There is evidently a variety of possible schemes, and Coleman accepts that some will meet the demands of distributive justice better than others, but maintains that 'a range of these...will serve reasonably well in providing the framework within which individuals can formulate meaningful projects and plans, and make the necessary investments to execute them'.[42] Thus, the same concerns with human autonomy give us reasons both to seek to construct institutions which allow for the stable formation of legitimate expectations, and to uphold expectations once formed. There is no reason why such a claim need appear unduly problematic to the political theorist primarily concerned with forward-looking distributive justice. Indeed, it mirrors a general point sometimes made in an egalitarian context when considering the question of the extent to which it is reasonable for the rich to resist transitions from unequal to equal resource distributions, given that people factor the level of their resource holdings into their life projects.[43] The condition of legitimacy, understood in terms of sufficient defensibility with reference to a minimal threshold of justice, as opposed to full justifiability, is key. Suppose that my parents have managed to use their psychic powers to enslave the human race, have declared themselves Overlords of the Earthlings, and have promised me that I will one day inherit the entirety of the world's resources. This does not mean that these resources cannot be taken from me and redistributed when they die, regardless of how extensive my plans for the construction of stately pleasure domes. The consequence of respecting my expectations would be accepting a distribution so manifestly unjust that it could not possibly be thought to reach a minimal threshold of justifiability. But with the condition of legitimacy in place, the forward-looking theorist may well be willing to mitigate the demands of distributive justice in practice, and accept that an all-things-considered answer as to what should happen in non-ideal society should allow for the standard account of rectificatory justice, even if the eventual outcome is not actually optimal from the narrow viewpoint of distributive justice. Whether this means that there is indeed a conflict between rectificatory justice and distributive justice in non-ideal contexts, or whether a full account of distributive justice should take account of the significance of life projects and temper its requirements accordingly, becomes a largely semantic question – the outcome is again one whereby the forward-looking theorist of distributive justice seems able to support rectifying injustice.

As before, however, this amounts only to a limited recognition of the ethical significance of past interaction. A particular problem arises when we consider historic harmful wrongdoing – acts of injustice which occurred some considerable time ago. These typically involved direct harm both caused and suffered by agents who are no longer living. They may have involved the wrongful taking of property which was legitimately held, but not necessarily property over which owners had a strong entitlement in terms of distributive justice. Insofar as expectations were disrupted by a historic act of injustice, new plans of life have been formed by those affected, whether positively or negatively, and indeed seeking to rectify the historic wrongdoing may well disrupt these, more recent life projects. Goodin explicitly recognizes the force of this point in his account of the normative desirability of compensatory justice. His account requires that compensation be swift, and notes that 'we...seem to think that after a certain period of time, no compensation need be paid at all'.[44] He goes on to refer to the standard legal convention of a statute of limitations, which limits the amount of time within which claims for compensation can be made.[45] He notes that there are practical considerations why this should be so in some cases, the difficulty of collecting reliable evidence after a long period of time, for example, but goes on to claim that 'the most satisfactory reason for the practice seems to be that compensation is supposed to avoid interruptions to people's life plans; and such compensation would have no point long after the event, because by then that interruption would have already occurred'.[46] Jeremy Waldron makes similar arguments in relation to claims for the restitution of misappropriated property. For Waldron, legitimate expectations play a key role in assigning property rights over particular resources to individuals. But he also maintains that the right kind of expectations can only be engendered insofar as we have physical possession of the resources in question. If they are taken away from us, however unjustly, and we start to plan our lives anew without them, then our property entitlement lapses. Again, the passage of time undermines the point of rectificatory justice, and the original injustice has been, in Waldron's terms, superseded.[47]

In short, it looks as if a forward-looking theorist of distributive justice could accept the distributive elements of the standard view of rectificatory justice in relation to recent harmful wrongdoing as an element of non-ideal theory, but resist moves to seek to rectify historic injustice. If the consequences of historic injustice are not the result of choices made by agents living in the present day, and have not suddenly disrupted the life plans of contemporary persons, there seems no reason for theorists of distributive justice to seek to undo their effects *per se*, as opposed to pursuing the general goal of achieving distributive justice. For in the absence of these kinds of reasons, it looks as if the forward-looking elements of distributive justice reassert their priority in an all-things-considered account of what should be done. For example, Jeremy Waldron writes of the argument that we should seek to reverse the effects of historic injustice by reference to a counterfactual account of how things would be now had the injustice never occurred:

> The counterfactual approach aims to bring the present state of affairs as close as possible to the state of affairs that would have obtained if some specifically identified injustice had not occurred. But why stop there? ...Why not try to make things even better than they would have been if that particular unjust transaction, or any unjust transaction, had not taken place? Are we so sure that a smooth transition, untainted by particular injustice, from some early nineteenth-century status quo ante would leave us now where we actually want to be? Quite apart from particular frauds and exploitations, things were not marvelous in the nineteenth century. Many people lacked access to any significant resources, and many people had much more than what one might regard as a fair share. Why take all that as the baseline for our present reconstruction?[48]

The significance of historic distributions, then, for forward-looking theorists lies in the extent to which they contribute in the present day towards individuals' legitimate expectations, rather than in any structural feature they possessed. This suggests that, once expectations have been disappointed, and individuals' life plans have ceased being built around them, there is no reason to seek to restore the earlier distributions. This is the second reason why forward-looking theorists have characteristically paid little attention to the rectificatory project.

48   *Rectifying International Injustice*

What of backward-looking theorists? As previously noted, such theories seemingly have the theoretical capacity to take the rectification of historic injustice across generations seriously. The consequence of Nozick's political theory is that it is *possible* for a society characterized by extreme distributive inequality, or by the severe poverty of some but the affluence of others, to come about in keeping with the principles of justice. It follows that subsequent attempts by the state to redistribute property from one party to another will be illegitimate insofar as doing so ignores the justly acquired entitlements of property owners. Such a policy ignores the history by which the distribution came about, and treats resources as if they were 'manna from heaven':

> Whoever makes something, having bought or contracted for all other held resources used in the process...is entitled to it. The situation is *not* one of something's getting made, and there being an open question of who is to get it. Things come into the world already attached to people having entitlements over them.[49]

To return to the forward-looking argument of Jeremy Waldron, if it were the case that resource holdings in the nineteenth century had come about justly, but there had subsequently been unjust acts of misappropriation, we would indeed have compelling, justice-based reasons to seek to restore the previous distribution – the answer to Waldron's question, 'Why not try to make things even better than they would have been if any unjust transaction had not taken place?' would be 'Because such action would infringe the rights of property holders, and so be unjust.' Rights are, for Nozick, best seen as 'side-constraints' against the pursuit of particular goals, such as overall social utility – the fact that a given course of action would make things 'better' does not, for a historical entitlement theorist, entitle one to infringe property rights.[50] So it might be that what we are restoring is indeed a situation where 'many people lacked access to any significant resources, and many people had much more than what one might regard as a fair share', but if this was not unjust at the time – if historical poverty and inequality came about in keeping with the three principles of justice – then the historical entitlement theorist has no cause for concern derived from distributive justice.

The fact that Nozick's theory gives an account of how advantages could justifiably be transferred across generations, however, does not mean that this is what has happened in practice. We need not see Nozick as endorsing either the actual, real world distributions which we find in modern day societies such as the United States of America or the historical antecedents of these distributions. The point is that there is no reason to think that such existing distributions came about in keeping with the principles of justice in acquisition and transfer, since we recognize the pervasive injustice which has characterized how present day real world holdings have come about. If one considers the history of particular communities, it seems obvious that it is impossible to say which – if any – current day holdings have come about in keeping with the principles of justice in acquisition, transfer, and rectification. We simply do not have enough information about the history of individual resource holdings to work out who produced what, when, and under what circumstances. Therefore, on the basis of Nozick's own argument, real world resource holdings look open to challenge under the principle of rectification. Nozick himself realized this, although it is a point which has been ignored by many of those who claim to support his theory in a political context. At the end of his discussion of distributive justice in *Anarchy, State, and Utopia*, he accepts that it might be best to see some patterned principles of distributive justice as 'rough rules of thumb meant to approximate the general results of applying the principle of rectification of injustice'. So he suggests that, on the basis of particular empirical assumptions, one might end up endorsing, in response to historic wrongdoing, a version of the difference principle, on the basis that members of the least well off group in society have the highest probabilities of being the descendants of victims of the most serious instances of injustice. Regardless of whether we find such an approach plausible, he maintains that:

> ...an important question for society will be the following: given *its* particular history, what operable rule of thumb best approximates the results of a detailed application in that society of the principle of rectification? These issues are very complex and are best left to a full treatment of the principle of rectification. In the absence of such a treatment applied to a particular society, one *cannot* use the analysis and theory presented here to condemn any particular scheme of transfer payments, unless it is clear that no considerations of rectification of injustice could apply to justify it.[51]

He concludes that, 'Although to introduce socialism as the punishment for our sins would be to go too far', it is possible that the extent of past injustices is so great as to justify a more extensive, redistributive state in the short run. Within a given domestic society, then, it seems as if a historical entitlement theorist ought to be willing, from the perspective of distributive justice, to countenance a wholesale one-off redistribution of existing resource holdings as the best way of seeking to achieve justice in rectification. Libertarians who seek to defend individuals' rights over existing, real world property holdings cannot rely upon Nozick's account of how it would have been possible, in a different world, for holdings which resemble these holdings to have come about without infringing anyone's rights, because this is manifestly not how individuals' property rights have come about in the real world. Instead, it seems as if they will need a quite separate justification for these property rights, based upon, for example, some forward-looking consequentialist claim as to the value of affording individuals these kinds of property rights for the stable workings of markets, or on the harm which is caused when individuals' life projects are disrupted – regardless of how their holdings originally came about.[52] Such an account does not worry about who has what – the important thing is that some people have property rights, and that others have some opportunity (even if not an equal opportunity) to acquire their own entitlements. Quite how robust an account of property rights can be generated in this way is an open question; Loren Lomasky admits that these property rights are not as strong as Nozickian property rights, in that they must give way when others find themselves unavoidably in desperate need.[53] Paradoxically, the extent of historic injustice in a domestic context means that the rectificatory project is relatively uncomplicated for the historical entitlement theorist. The consequence of adopting the historical entitlement model in the non-ideal context of a society with a long history of complicated injustice is such a wholehearted acceptance of the rectificatory project that, in terms of the initial redistribution, the distinction between forward-looking and backward-looking models of distributive justice appears unclear. It seems as if we do not need to spend time worrying about who did what to whom and when – the distribution of existing property within a given society is altogether arbitrary, and so we find ourselves again in the context of a forward-looking discussion of how best to order society, balancing perhaps, our favoured distributive index or indices with the real world fact of legitimate expectations. But the extent to which this amounts to a conversion from a backward-looking to a forward-looking account of distributive justice is limited. First, as Nozick's invocation against socialism makes clear, the approaches are likely to differ on the question of what should happen following redistribution. It is open to the backward-looking theorist to argue that the redistribution of property should lead to agents possessing full rights over their resources. This would entitle them to engage in transfers in ways which would lead some to accumulate more resources than others, which could subsequently be bequeathed to subsequent generations.[54] Forward-looking theorists are likely to reject the inequalities which this would tend to create over time, and so insist on redistribution within each new generation. Second, it should be stressed that the historical entitlement theorist need not adopt this position if instead she is able to give an account of which holdings (should there be any) did in fact come about in keeping with the principle of justice in acquisition.[55] As Jonathan Wolff writes, 'Part of the libertarian position involves treating property rights as natural rights, and so as being as important as anything can be. On the libertarian view, the fact that an injustice is old, and, perhaps, difficult to prove, does not make it any less of an injustice.'[56] The argument for general redistribution is a contingent factor of the presumed all-pervasive nature of the effects of historic injustice within a given community. If society had developed in a different way, with, perhaps, less extensive interaction between persons than was typically the case in real world societies, or if it were the case that we had rather more information about the historical record, then a more limited form of rectification may be possible. This is significant when we come to assess international libertarianism, as will be argued in Chapter 5.

My argument in this chapter, then, is that the extent to which theorists assign importance to the rectificatory project depends upon the ethical significance of history within their accounts of distributive justice. This is why the content of our theory of distributive justice makes a difference to how we think rectificatory justice works. It follows that different accounts of distributive justice, which afford varying degrees of ethical significance to history, will give rise to different accounts of what an all-things-considered account of modern day justice requires. To suggest that egalitarian political theorists have no place for history in their accounts of justice is generally mistaken. The principle of the moral equality of persons, which is shared by the vast majority of contemporary theorists, requires that, in some circumstances, individuals be held responsible for their actions in ways which affect the level of benefits and burdens to which they are entitled in terms of distributive justice – especially, and fairly uncontroversially, when it comes to wrongdoing which harms other moral agents. But for those who broadly think that the distributive game begins again with each new generation, there is no point in looking to the historic actions of previous generations to work out what is owed to whom in the present day. History may matter, in the sense that it might be that the value and cost of contemporary benefits and burdens needs to be assessed in the light of the lasting effects of historic actions if distributions are to be fair, but this is a different matter from claiming that the actions of previous generations can actually create entitlements for present day individuals or groups.[57] History may matter in that people build the resource holdings to which they are accustomed into their life projects, and so even egalitarians might, in practice, condone rectification which restores unjust but legitimate property holdings so as to protect valuable expectations. But forward-looking theorists, in contrast to their backward-looking counterparts, have no reasons of justice to maintain that historic actions can, of themselves, determine entitlements to particular modern day distributions of benefits and burdens. So it is certainly open to the forward-looking theorist to dismiss the significance of the rectificatory project in an international context if – and only if – she maintains that international distributive justice has the same forward-looking character. This argument only holds insofar as one maintains both that justice requires redistribution with each generation *and* believes that this is so both domestically and internationally. If one rejects the claim that resources should be redistributed across the world with each new generation, as many do, then the door is reopened to the international rectificatory project, in terms of the sources of modern day *benefits*, of modern day *entitlements*, and of modern day collective *responsibility* in connection with historic wrongdoing. What one should not do, if one does hold different principles of domestic and international justice, is reject the domestic rectificatory project on the basis of the arguments presented above, and assume that the international rectificatory project has been dismissed in a similar fashion. It is a mistake to discuss international rectificatory justice in the same terms as domestic rectificatory justice if one holds significantly different principles of domestic and international distributive justice – as do many international libertarians. International libertarianism puts forward a backward-looking account of international distributive justice. Its focus on the principle of national sovereignty entails an opposition to attempts to redistribute resources across state boundaries, other than (at most) when doing so is necessary to fulfill minimal duties of assistance to those in need. The consequence is a resistance to global generational redistribution – international libertarians accept the backward-looking claim that the actions of individuals within one generation can legitimately affect the entitlements of their particular descendants. It is to an exposition of international libertarianism that we now turn.

NOTES

1. Marshall Cohen, 'Moral skepticism and international relations', *Philosophy and Public Affairs* 13 (1984), 299–346 at p. 299.
2. Rawls, *A Theory of Justice*, p. 4.
3. Rawls, *A Theory of Justice*, pp. 3–4.
4. 'Rectificatory' and 'corrective' justice are often treated as synonymous. In what follows, I prefer 'rectificatory' to 'corrective' justice, since, as will be seen, 'corrective justice' is sometimes taken by legal theorists to refer to compensation specifically, as opposed to restitution, which is bracketed off within 'restitutive justice'. I use 'rectificatory justice' to refer to both compensatory and restitutive obligations.
5. 'Repairing historic injustice ... is almost always undertaken by people of good will.' (Waldron, p. 27).
6. See Waldron, 'Superseding historic injustice' (pp. 6–7) and Vernon, 'Against restitution' (p. 545).
7. So Vernon argues, 'Not one word in this paper is intended to be critical of the return of land to aboriginal groups; of the monetary payments to the victims of racism or sexism or assault; or of apologies (if sincere) for the Inquisition, for the burning of Giordano Bruno or for the Boer War. What the article *is* against

is the idea that acts of this kind can be thought of as "restitutive"' (Vernon, 'Against restitution', p. 543).
8. O'Neill, 'Rights to compensation', pp. 86–7.
9. Waldron, 'Superseding historic injustice', p. 27. This point is made in the specific context of an argument relating to the supersession of Aboriginal claims. See also O'Neill, 'Rights to compensation,' p. 87.
10. The conception of 'responsibility' in this statement is deliberately broad, since tort law has to encompass a range of cases, such as liability for causing accidents, where culpability is open to question. As such, strict liability approaches hold that causal responsibility can be sufficient to give rise to compensatory duties, whereas others maintain that one must possess moral or outcome responsibility. The question of responsibility is discussed further in Chapter 6.
11. Jules L. Coleman, 'Corrective justice and property rights', in Rodney C. Roberts (ed.), *Injustice and Rectification* (New York: Peter Lang, 2005), 53–65 at p. 56. Coleman's language here reflects his 'mixed conception' of corrective justice, which replaces his earlier 'annulment' account. Whilst I think that the mixed approach is the most useful to adopt, I place no weight here on this claim – the important point is simply that corrective justice requires the redistribution of resources from one party to another in order to rectify wrongful losses. In some cases, the first party may be society as a whole, or innocent third parties, rather than the offenders themselves. For critical discussion of Coleman's shift, see Matthew Kramer, 'Of Aristotle and ice cream cones: reflections on Jules Coleman's theory of corrective justice' in B. Bix (ed.), *Analyzing Law: New Essays in Legal Theory* (Oxford: Oxford University Press, 1998), 163–80.
12. Birks, *An Introduction to the Law of Restitution*, p. 11. The question of what should count as an 'unjust enrichment' in legal theory and in moral theory is addressed in Chapter 4. The question of whether individuals face a positive duty to disgorge themselves of unjust enrichments can be left as an open question here, though my later argument makes it clear that in general I am sympathetic to the existence of a *moral* duty of this kind.
13. Jules L. Coleman, *Risks and Wrongs* (Cambridge: Cambridge University Press, 1992), p. 371. There is a semantic issue as to whether the law of restitution should be seen as part of, or should be distinguished from, corrective justice. *Contra* the line taken by Coleman above, Kit Barker argues that, for example, the restitution of a mistaken payment should be portrayed in terms of corrective justice, arguing that 'corrective justice embraces the broad objective of rectifying *individual injustices*, not simply the (narrower) concern to rectify *wrongdoing*' (Kit Barker, 'Unjust enrichment: containing the beast', *Oxford Legal Studies* 15 (1995), 457–75 at p. 470 [Barker's emphasis]). As noted, I use 'rectificatory justice' throughout in order to sidestep this issue.
14. Larry A. Alexander, 'Causation and corrective justice: does tort law make sense?', *Law and Philosophy* 6 (1987), 1–23 at p. 6.
15. Not all end-state principles are current time slice principles, for Nozick, since it is possible to have structural principles which 'operate upon a time sequence of

current time-slice profiles'. (*Anarchy, State, and Utopia*, p. 155.) So an egalitarian might resist the 'equal shares principle' by holding that resources should be distributed equally across individuals' whole lives. Such a principle would still be end-state, rather than historical, in Nozick's terms since there is no reference to the idea that entitlements can be created by individuals' past actions.

16. Nozick, *Anarchy, State, and Utopia*, p. 154.
17. Nozick, *Anarchy, State, and Utopia*, p. 155.
18. Stephen R. Perry, 'On the relationship between corrective and distributive justice' in J. Horder (ed.), *Oxford Essays in Jurisprudence*, (Oxford: Clarendon Press, 2000 – Fourth Series), 237–63 at p. 245.
19. Perry, 'On the relationship between corrective and distributive justice' pp. 245–6. See also Rawls, *A Theory of Justice*, pp. 86–8, and Samuel Freeman, *Rawls* (Abingdon: Routledge, 2007), pp. 125–7.
20. David Schmidtz, *Elements of Justice* (Cambridge: Cambridge University Press, 2006), pp. 56–7.
21. Schmidtz, *Elements of Justice*, p. 201.
22. This is not to maintain that responsibility must be the central element of plausible theories of distributive justice – merely that it needs to play some role. For general scepticism as to the significance of responsibility in this area, see Matt Matravers, *Responsibility and Justice* (Cambridge: Polity, 2007).
23. See G.A. Cohen, 'On the currency of egalitarian justice', *Ethics* (1989), 906–44, and Richard Arneson, 'Equality and equal opportunity for welfare', *Philosophical Studies* 54 (1988), 79–95.
24. Nozick, *Anarchy, State, and Utopia*, p. 155.
25. Nozick, *Anarchy, State, and Utopia*, p. 160. The full, less snappy version of the maxim runs: 'From each according to what he chooses to do, to each according to what he makes for himself (perhaps with the contracted aid of others) and what others choose to do for him and choose to give him and choose to give to him of what they've previously been given (under this maxim) and haven't yet expended or transferred.'
26. See Arthur Ripstein, *Equality, Responsibility and the Law* (Cambridge: Cambridge University Press, 1999).
27. See Rawls's account of 'fair equality of opportunity', *A Theory of Justice*, pp. 83–90. For a left libertarian perspective, see Peter Vallentyne, 'Brute luck, option luck, and equality of initial opportunities,' *Ethics* 112 (2002), 529–57.
28. Ripstein, *Equality, Responsibility and the Law*, p. 44.
29. See, for example, D. W. Haslett, 'Is inheritance justified?', *Philosophy and Public Affairs* 15 (1986), 122–55; Janna Thompson, Taking Responsibility for the Past: Reparation and Historical Injustice (Cambridge: Polity, 2002), pp. 107–12. The objection here is to inheritance insofar as it creates significant inequalities: liberal theorists are generally willing to allow limited bequests, especially in relation to the likes of family heirlooms, insofar as equality of opportunity is not affected. For accounts which afford individuals limited quotas of inherited assets, see Liam Murphy and Thomas Nagel, *The Myth of Ownership: Taxes*

and Justice (Oxford: Oxford University Press, 2002) and Stuart White, *The Civic Minimum: On the Rights and Obligations of Economic Citizenship* (Oxford: Oxford University Press, 2003). Rawls does allow inheritance, but only insofar as 'the resulting inequalities are to the advantage of the least fortunate and compatible with liberty and fair equality of opportunity'. *A Theory of Justice*, p. 279. For further discussion, see Michael B. Levy, 'Liberal equality and inherited wealth', *Political Theory* 11 (1983), 545–64 and Guido Erreygers and Toon Vandevelde (eds.), *Is Inheritance Legitimate?* (Heidelberg: Springer-Verlag Berlin, 1997).

30. Nozick, *Anarchy, State, and Utopia*, pp. 150–3.
31. Nozick, *Anarchy, State, and Utopia*, p. 151.
32. Whether this should be characterized as a return to the ideal can be left as an open question. Although the ideal distribution of resources has been restored, and although the victim is (stipulatively) unharmed in the long run by the injustice, we may feel that the act of acknowledging wrongdoing and repenting leaves the wrongdoer permanently altered. Claudia Card has written insightfully on this subject, adapting Bernard Williams' idea of 'moral remainder' to describe the ongoing feelings of the moral agent who has admitted wrongdoing and has sought to rectify her actions. See Claudia Falconer Card, 'Rectification and remainders', in Edward Craig (ed.), *Routledge Encyclopaedia of Philosophy*, (London: Routledge, 1998), available at http://www.rep.routledge.com/article/L082/; Claudia Card, *The Atrocity Paradigm: A Theory of Evil* (Oxford: Oxford University Press, 2002), pp. 167–70; Bernard Williams, 'Ethical consistency', *Proceedings of the Aristotelian Society*, supplementary volume 39 (1965), 103–24 at p. 117.
33. This overly simplistic formulation reflects Robert Nozick's account of full compensation, (*Anarchy, State, and Utopia*, p. 57), which is discussed further in Chapter 4.
34. On the role of compensation in restoring 'moral equality' between victim and offender, see Gerald Gaus, 'Does compensation restore equality?', in John W. Chapman (ed.), *Nomos XXXIII: Compensatory Justice* (New York: New York University Press, 1991), 45–81.
35. There are, of course, cases where any effort by the offender to make either full or symbolic reparation will be rejected by the victim, and where an insistence on doing so will in fact make the victim worse off. It seems clear that in such cases the offender does indeed face a duty to do nothing, with the result that the restoration of equilibrium between victim and offender is indeed impossible.
36. Ripstein, *Equality, Responsibility and the Law*, p. 270.
37. Goodin, 'Compensation and redistribution', p. 143.
38. Coleman, *Risks and Wrongs*, pp. 352–3.
39. Coleman, 'Corrective justice and property rights', p. 65. See also Perry: 'Distributive justice often contributes to the legitimacy of an entitlement that corrective justice protects, and in that sense there is a normative connection between the two.' 'On the relationship between corrective and distributive justice', p. 237.

40. Coleman, *Risks and Wrongs*, p. 353.
41. Goodin, 'Compensation and redistribution' in John W. Chapman (ed.), *Nomos XXXIII: Compensatory Justice*, 143–77 at p. 152.
42. Coleman, 'Corrective justice and property rights', p. 64. See also Waldron, 'Superseding historic injustice', pp. 18–19. This issue is discussed further in Chapter 5.
43. See, for example, Thomas Nagel, *Equality and Partiality* (New York: Oxford University Press, 1991), pp. 169–74.
44. Goodin, 'Compensation and redistribution', p. 172n.
45. Of course, it is one thing to say that a claim must be made within a particular time frame (in other words that the victim of injustice must appeal for compensation within a specified period of time following the act in question) and another to say that claims which are made become invalid after a particular period of time. We may (though we need not) support the former claim without supporting the latter.
46. Goodin, 'Compensation and redistribution', p. 172n.
47. Waldron, 'Superseding historic injustice', pp. 18–19. Waldron's position here is discussed in Chapter 5.
48. Waldron, 'Superseding historic injustice', pp. 13–14.
49. Nozick, *Anarchy, State, and Utopia*, p. 160.
50. Nozick, *Anarchy, State, and Utopia*, p. 33.
51. Nozick, *Anarchy, State, and Utopia*, p. 231 [Nozick's emphasis].
52. In the former case, David Schmidtz argues that, 'Dwelling too much on the past is wrong for the same reason that ignoring the past altogether is wrong: Excess in *either* direction reduces stability in transactions, thus making it harder to go forward in peace' (*Elements of Justice*, p. 212). Loren Lomasky opposes the rectificatory project with reference to the life projects of those currently in possession of property: 'No radical upheaval of property rights now can in any degree make redress for rights violations that happened centuries ago. Just the opposite is the case: a confiscation of property preparatory to bringing about the Brave New World would sin against the rights of contemporary individuals to be secure in the possession of the property they are actually using in the ongoing pursuits of their projects' (*Persons, Rights, and the Moral Community* (New York: Oxford University Press, 1987), p. 145). In each case, if very strong property rights are to be defended, we need extremely good reasons as to why we should attach so much importance to stability in transactions or to individuals' life projects, given that there are other goals that a political community may seek to pursue by means of the redistribution of property. Say we accept the possibility of a forward-looking, non-redistributive libertarianism; would it be possible to construct a parallel account of *international* libertarianism? I am even more dubious as to the plausibility of such a project than in the domestic case, especially as it would have to sidestep the substantive arguments relating to the generation of national entitlements presented in Chapter 5. I will merely note here that even if such a non-historical account was able to avoid

the restitution based arguments of Chapter 5, it would still be susceptible to the arguments from benefit in Chapter 4, and responsibility in Chapter 6. So even forward-looking international libertarians have good reason to take the rectificatory project seriously.
53. Lomasky, *Persons, Rights, and the Moral Community*, p. 126.
54. It is not clear that backward-looking theorists *need* to accept this – they could argue that individuals should only be afforded limited rights over the redistributed property, and thus be prevented from using it in certain ways, including, for example, giving it away to others in general, or bequeathing it to their descendants in particular, while still maintaining that different distributive principles apply to property which is initially justly acquired.
55. Lomasky argues that although past injustices are causal contributants to current holdings, 'Those holdings may not be upset unless to do so would be to reclaim rights wrongfully usurped and to make restoration to the rightful possessors', *Persons, Rights, and the Moral Community*, pp. 145–6.
56. Jonathan Wolff, *Robert Nozick: Property, Justice and the Minimal State* (Cambridge: Polity, 1991), p. 116.
57. So, the fact that a sculpture was created by the ancestors of a given group, with a shared communal identity, might mean that this sculpture has a particular value to them, which other sculptures do not. A fair scheme for the distribution of ancient sculptures should take this intense preference into account, but it does not settle the issue by creating an entitlement to the sculpture for the group. If another group has an equally intense preference as a result of a shared aesthetic appreciation of the sculpture, this should also be taken into account.

3

International Libertarianism

3.1 INTERNATIONAL LIBERTARIANISM AS AN ACCOUNT OF DISTRIBUTIVE JUSTICE

The previous chapters observed that many political theorists adopt one set of principles of distributive justice when it comes to benefits and burdens within their own communities, but a different set when it comes to looking at relations between political communities. This chapter lays out the account of distributive justice – international libertarianism – which is used in the rest of the book to assess present day duties and obligations arising from historic injustice. It consists of three sections. The first outlines international libertarianism as a backward-looking account of international distributive justice, in contrast with forward-looking redistributive cosmopolitanism. The second gives details of the principles of just international interaction, which international libertarians argue should regulate relations between different political communities. While the contrast in the first section is with cosmopolitanism, here international libertarianism is differentiated from prescriptive realism. International libertarians reject the claim that the international sphere is governed by conditions of anarchy and necessity – instead, they accept at least some minimal moral constraints on international action. I list both core principles, which characteristically are endorsed by international libertarians, and which distinguish them as a group from prescriptive realists, and further principles, which international libertarians may, but need not, accept. Finally, the third section considers the probity of using these principles, which international libertarians believe constrain the conduct of international relations in the present day, to judge historic international interaction.

Chapter 2 argued that the international rectificatory project appears to be of limited significance for redistributive cosmopolitans, insofar as they advocate forward-looking accounts of distributive justice, which maintain that resources should be redistributed anew each generation, without regard to political boundaries. The situation is different, however, for those who hold backward-looking accounts of international distributive justice which afford sovereignty over their own resources across generations to political communities. It is now time to say more about international libertarianism, and distinguish it from cosmopolitanism as a theory of international distributive justice. A range of different writers have put forward positions, which mean that they are, in my terms, international libertarians, and they have been characterized in a number of different ways. The best-known assignation is probably that of Charles Beitz, in his distinction between 'cosmopolitan liberals' and 'social liberals' who writes that 'social liberalism holds that the problem of international justice is fundamentally one of fairness to societies (or peoples), whereas cosmopolitan liberalism holds that it is fairness to persons'.[1] Most notable among the social liberals, of course, is Rawls himself, who, in *The Law of Peoples*, resisted the attempts of cosmopolitans such as Beitz and Pogge to apply versions of the difference principle to the world as a whole.[2] His broad position has been explicitly defended by some writers, such as Samuel Freeman and Mathias Risse.[3] Others have put forward accounts with similar policy prescriptions, but which are somewhat different in terms of their justifications for these positions: examples here include Thomas Nagel, Michael Blake, and Andrea Sangiovanni.[4] One should also include advocates of what has been called ethical or liberal nationalism, including David Miller and Yael Tamir, on my account, as well as Michael Walzer[5] together with those who adopt the 'Society of States' approach, such as Terry Nardin and Mervyn Frost.[6] These writers inevitably differ in the precise nature of their accounts, but they are united in opposition to both redistributive cosmopolitanism and prescriptive realism. What, then, is the basis of their account of international distributive justice?

International libertarians hold that distributive duties are owed primarily to fellow members of our own political communities. The extent to which those who are not members of one's own community have been characterized as significantly different, in some regard, from oneself has varied from time to time and from place to place, but the idea that what we owe to fellow members of our group is in some way distinct from what we owe to individuals who are not group members is one which many have found to have ethical significance, for a range of different reasons. Insofar as an argument is cosmopolitan, it resists this idea. The cosmopolitan perspective is derived from some kind of a denial of difference. Charles Jones defines the cosmopolitan standpoint as 'impartial, universal, individualist, and egalitarian',[7] and Brian Barry writes, 'At the heart of moral cosmopolitanism is the idea that human beings are in some fundamental sense equal.'[8] From this perspective, what individuals have in common is more significant than what separates them. Arguments between cosmopolitans and non-cosmopolitans, then, turn on the question of difference. When a non-cosmopolitan argues that some difference between particular individuals justifies treating them in divergent ways, a cosmopolitan can make one of two responses. She can either deny that the difference described by the non-cosmopolitan exists, or she can accept the existence of the difference, but deny its moral relevance.

In some respects, we are all cosmopolitans now. In contrast to earlier times, no one of any ethical integrity would deny the moral personhood of human beings of other nationalities, although differences persist over the extent to which we should extend personhood to certain contested categories, such as those with serious mental disabilities, very young children, foetuses, and different types of animals. The claim that members of one nation are in some way inherently inferior to members of another and so need not be treated with the respect due to human beings is now typically treated with the contempt this deserves, and this marks an acceptance of one sense of the ideal of equality, and indeed constitutes a degree of progress in our moral relations with one another.[9] The degree to which this marks a substantial acceptance of egalitarianism, however, is very limited. It is quite possible to be cosmopolitan in some regards – and thus hold that individuals are of equal moral worth and so should in some sense be treated equally – whilst still accepting that there can be good reasons to treat different people differently in particular circumstances. In particular, there is deep disagreement over the extent to which an acceptance of the moral equality of persons gives rise to principles of distributive justice which are (*a*) universally applicable and (*b*) egalitarian in nature. So, for example, libertarians can maintain that their standpoint on distributive justice is cosmopolitan in Jones's terms, which is to say that they are impartial, universal, individualist, and indeed to some degree egalitarian insofar as they accept the moral equality of persons, without accepting the egalitarian *distributive* claim that resources within a given community should be allocated according to some index of equality.[10] Such thinkers are cosmopolitans, but not redistributive cosmopolitans.[11]

In terms of international distributive justice, the debate between those who are commonly described as 'cosmopolitans' and those who are not concerns the ethical significance of boundaries between different political communities. Cosmopolitans hold that these boundaries do not have ethical significance, and that it is a mistake to think that the distributive duties one holds in relation to one's fellow nationals are different in nature from those held with regard to non-nationals. As above, this position can be held for one of two reasons. For some, political boundaries between different groups of people simply cannot make a difference to the duties we owe to others. Such writers adopt what Andrea Sangiovanni has called a non-relational conception of distributive justice: 'Those who argue that principles of distributive justice have a *nonrelational* basis reject the idea that the content, scope, or justification of those principles depend on the practice-mediated relations in which individuals stand.'[12] So non-relational theorists do not scrutinize the empirically contingent relationship between different individuals. They argue that individuals stand in a position of moral equality in relation to one another, and, crucially, that this moral equality means that principles of distributive justice should disregard boundaries between different political communities. David Richards, for example, argues that international relations should be governed by 'moral reciprocity'; not a relational conception of reciprocity, which looks to what one gains and loses from one's interaction with others, but a non-relational concern for others based on the Kantian idea of treating persons as equals: 'the moral idea of reciprocity, which invokes this idea of equality, is not that of reciprocal actual advantage, but the ethical idea of treating persons in the way one would oneself reasonably like to be treated.'[13] The outcome is an endorsement of a global version of Rawls's original position which disregards individuals' national identity, since 'one's membership in one nation as opposed to another and the natural inequality between nations may be as morally fortuitous as any other natural fact.'[14] For non-relational cosmopolitans, there is – necessarily – no distinction between domestic and international distributive justice.[15]

The distributive implications of non-relational cosmopolitanism are certainly controversial. Suppose that the world is divided into two completely separate continents, each with an equal set of raw materials. Two entirely distinct communities emerge, one on each continent. For various reasons, the first develops more rapidly than the second, across a number of different generations. Each community is self-sufficient, and no individual suffers hardship or is unable to pursue a minimally decent life, but individuals in the first community do have greater access to advantages than those in the second. Now imagine that technology improves to the extent that the two continents become aware of each other's existence, and of their respective resource holdings. There is no interaction between the two, but it would be possible for the people of one continent costlessly to transfer resources to the people of the other. Do questions of distributive justice even arise in this context? There is a deep divide between different theorists on this issue. For some it is obvious that they do, given that the question of where one is born seems to be arbitrary from a moral point of view. To others, it is equally obvious that they do not. From this perspective, questions of distributive justice only arise when individuals interact with one another in particular kinds of ways. So, for example, despite his having invented the device of the original position, Rawls's account of distributive justice in *A Theory of Justice* is explicitly relational – it addresses the fair terms of cooperation within a given society, understood as a cooperative venture for mutual advantage.[16]

On this account, those on one continent may well have duties to those on another, but these are best understood in terms of natural duties to aid others in distress when one can do so without excessive cost to oneself, and negative duties not to cause certain types of harm. For Rawls, these are non-relational 'natural duties', which 'hold between persons irrespective of their institutional relationships; they obtain between all as equal moral persons'.[17] They are not, however, duties of distributive justice. So, for example, Jonathan Wolff argues as follows:

> In the film 'The Man Who Fell to Earth' David Bowie plays a creature in human form from an alien planet which is desperately short of water. It is hard to sustain the thought that we have a duty of justice to part with some of our water to help them. Of course we might think we have some moral duties to help, but justice is not the whole of morality.[18]

Wolff suggests, therefore, that 'the applicability of norms of justice presupposes some sort of cooperative relations or interaction: not necessarily mutually advantageous economic exchange, but some level of shared fate and entangled lives'.[19] The question, then, for those who adopt relational theories of justice, is what kind of association or interaction is necessary in order for relations of distributive justice to obtain between persons. If one is to be a relational cosmopolitan, one therefore needs to make both a normative claim and an empirical claim. The normative claim concerns the kind of interaction which one believes is necessary to bring distributive justice into play. The empirical claim maintains that the relevant form of interaction exists, as a matter of empirical fact, in the modern day world between all persons. Evidently, the more extensive the degree of interaction specified in the normative claim, the more scope is afforded to the opponents of cosmopolitanism to deny that the empirical claim holds. So, for example, Darrel Moellendorf's account of cosmopolitanism is relatively minimalist in terms of the normative claim: he argues that 'association' is sufficient to bring about duties of justice. 'Association' here means more than mere interaction, but only in terms of degree. It arises when people interact in certain ways through politics or commerce: 'if...established social practices or institutions regularly affect the highest order moral interests of a person, that person is in association with all of the others who act within the constraints of those practices or institutions.'[20] Moreover, once we are in association with others, we share the same distributive duties to all of our associates, the degree of association is not morally relevant in terms of distributive justice: 'There is no good reason to think that a tighter association should entail that the interests of one's close associates should be given priority over the interests of other associates.'[21] If this is one's position, it is reasonably unproblematic to maintain that, given the nature of international commerce and increasing levels of interdependence between states, the peoples of the world are in association with one another.

The conjunction of the normative claim and the empirical claim thus lead to redistributive cosmopolitanism. Other cosmopolitans make different normative claims, and thus face different empirical challenges. Some have argued, for example, that Rawls errs in failing to extend his principles of justice to the world as a whole, since interdependence means that all the peoples of the world can plausibly be said to be members of the same scheme of social cooperation, and are thus entitled to a fair share of the fruits of this cooperation via the difference principle. Charles Beitz, for example, argued in *Political Theory and International Relations* that 'the membership of the original position should be global rather than national because national societies are not, in fact, self-sufficient; the system of global trade and investment, organised within a structure of international institutions and conventions, constitutes a scheme of social cooperation in Rawls's sense'.[22] This argument, then, accepts (for the sake of argument) Rawls's own relational normative claim as to the circumstances of justice, but seeks to show that he has drawn the wrong overall conclusion due to the failure of his empirical claim. Other writers have sought to oppose Beitz on this, again disputing his interpretation of the empirical evidence.[23]

International libertarians oppose both the non-relational and the relational accounts of cosmopolitanism. Against non-relational cosmopolitans, they insist that different principles of distributive justice can obtain between different individuals depending on the nature and/or degree of their association and interaction. Against relational cosmopolitans, they deny that the kind of interaction and association which one finds in the real world is of the kind which would mean that the same distributive principles would obtain between all persons. They thus affirm the moral salience of a particular kind of difference between persons. Inevitably, writers disagree as to what precisely this morally salient difference might be. All, however, dispute Moellendorf's claim that mere association is sufficient for the circumstances of justice to arise. Instead, there is something about the nature of particular political communities – be they conceived in terms of states, nations, or peoples – which differentiates members from non-members in a morally significant fashion. This might just be a result of the extent of interaction, if one believes that the degree of interdependence within a political community is much greater than that which obtains between nationals and non-nationals. Michael Walzer, for example, suggests that questions of distributive justice only emerge if 'we can tell a story of engagement and responsibility'.[24] In response to the claim that global interdependence means that this condition is met, he maintains that current levels of interaction are insufficient for distributive duties to others to arise:

> A number of writers have argued in recent years that evolving patterns of global proximity, knowledge, and interaction make us all responsible for one another. The tendency is indeed clear, and this is the story that needs telling if the requirements of justice are to be expanded. But I am inclined to think that, for now at least, ordinary moral principles regarding humane treatment and mutual aid do more work than any specific account of distributive justice.[25]

David Miller's position is similar, in that it rests upon the absence of a particular kind of community at a global level. His domestic account of distributive justice is explicitly egalitarian, but he denies the claim that the whole world should be seen as a single community in such a way as to give rise to egalitarian distributive duties:

> A community of the kind that supports egalitarian principles of justice must...have at least the following three features. Members must have a shared identity, an awareness that there is something distinctive about them that holds them together in a single unit; there must be common understandings or common purposes that give the community its ethos; and there must be an institutional structure that acts on behalf of the community, in particular overseeing the allocation of resources among the members. Now although in the contemporary world there are clearly forms of interaction and cooperation occurring at the global level...these are not sufficient to constitute a global community. They do not by themselves create either a shared sense of identity or a common ethos. And above all there is no common institutional structure that would justify us in describing unequal outcomes as forms of unequal treatment.[26]

Other writers pick up particular aspects of this approach. For liberal nationalists such as Yael Tamir, it is the mutual partial concern which members of particular communities have for one another which is key.[27] Others stress the fact that members of self-governing communities are subject to the same coercive laws. Thomas Nagel's complicated account, for example, argues that what he calls socio-economic justice 'depends on positive rights that we do not have against all other persons or groups, rights that arise only because we are joined together with certain others in a political society under strong centralized control'.[28] Thus it is not sufficient for the circumstances of justice to obtain that individuals be common members of a cooperative enterprise for mutual advantage. Instead it is the 'complex fact' that we are both responsible for and subject to the coercive laws of the state which is significant: society takes, and imposes, decisions in our names, and as such we are entitled to reject arbitrary inequalities between societal members.[29] Michael Blake also focuses on coercion, arguing more straightforwardly that 'a concern with relative economic shares... is a plausible interpretation of liberal principles only when those principles are applied to individuals who share liability to the coercive network of state governance'.[30] Sangiovanni claims that we owe particular duties to those within our own state as a result of the idea of fair reciprocity: 'those who have submitted themselves to a system of laws and social rules in ways necessary to sustain our life as citizens, producers and biological beings are owed a fair return for what those who have benefited from their submission have received.'[31] The detail of the different theories is unimportant for our current purposes. The key element which they all have in common is opposition to redistributive cosmopolitanism. Although the principles of distributive justice which they endorse in relation to domestic societies are often highly redistributive, they do not require a generational redistribution of resources across national boundaries. It follows from this that the history of international interaction – and thus historic international injustice – is morally significant for international libertarians. What still remains to be seen is what kinds of international interaction such writers consider to be unjust.

3.2 THE PRINCIPLES OF JUST INTERNATIONAL INTERACTION

International libertarians, then, maintain that certain kinds of boundaries between political communities have ethical significance in terms of distributive justice. What we owe to our fellow nationals is different from what we owe to non-nationals. The international libertarian vision of the world is one of sovereign political communities exercising self-determination and controlling their own futures. This is not to say, however, that we are justified in extending moral concern exclusively to our fellow nationals. We owe certain negative duties to those in other states, and we may indeed have positive moral duties to them. International libertarianism can be characterized as an intermediate position on international ethics, lying between cosmopolitanism, which denies that political boundaries have any ethical significance, and prescriptive realism, which in extreme form denies that there are any moral constraints on the pursuit of national self-interest. International libertarians reject the claim that the contemporary international arena is characterized by necessity and anarchy, a Hobbesian state of nature in which self-interested actions can be justified with reference to pre-emptive self-defence. Instead, they accept the existence of certain forms of moral constraint upon their treatment of non-nationals. In this section, I identify a limited set of principles of just international interaction which are accepted by a wide range of both political philosophers and by real world practitioners.[32] These can be divided into core principles, which all international libertarians accept regulate international conduct, and further principles, concerning which international libertarians can disagree. If one accepts a range of further principles, it is possible to develop the principles into a more demanding account of international justice that places considerable duties and constraints upon international actors, and whose implementation would involve a substantial reform of real world political practices. It is crucial, however, to appreciate that even this more demanding account is very different from redistributive cosmopolitanism. Insofar as redistribution is called for, it is intended to maintain fair interaction and to prevent those in other states from falling below minimal levels of well-being. International libertarianism is, at most, concerned with fairness in commerce and trade, and sufficiency in other states. Redistribution is always targeted – it falls short of the generational reallocation of resources called for by egalitarian cosmopolitans. This is sufficient for the international rectificatory project to be significant in connection with past injustice.

I first lay out the core principles, before introducing the further elements of the more demanding account.

3.2.1 Core Principles of Just International Interaction

The key to the core principles is a commitment to the basic principles of international law and a respect for national sovereignty and self-determination. This can be expressed in a number of different ways, but there are two basic principles at the heart of just international interaction:

1. States should refrain from forceful intervention in the affairs of other states, other than (*a*) when acting in response to aggression, or (*b*) to prevent certain kinds of human rights violations.
2. States should comply with voluntarily made treaties and agreements.

The detail of each is, of course, complicated and disputed, and a wide array of difficult cases arise where the guidance of the principles is limited. For example, principle (1) is phrased in such a way as to allow states to use force both in order to defend themselves and others against aggression and potentially also to intervene in other states in order to prevent particular levels of human rights violations. In practice, the content of each of these exemptions from a universal prohibition against the use of force is extremely controversial. What constitutes a sufficient danger to one's security to justify the use of force in self-defence, and what degree of force is legitimate, are difficult questions, particularly in relation to pre-emptive action against perceived threats. Under the principles of just international interaction, forceful intervention from the motive of economic interest, for example, is impermissible. The extent to which humanitarian intervention can be justified in terms of the interests of the people of the state in whose affairs one is intervening is also very far from settled, as is clear from the extent to which a large number of contemporary states insist that their human rights records are a matter for domestic and not international concern. If it is generally accepted that intervention of some kind is legitimate in extreme cases such as genocide, marginal cases are far more controversial. Furthermore, there is disagreement as to whether (1b) should be interpreted as *permitting* or *requiring* intervention to prevent human rights violations. The interpretation of principle (2) is also controversial; for example, some suggest that the obligation to honour international agreements does not extend to compelling states to uphold the full content of international human rights agreements, insofar as these agreements contain positive rights to welfare as well as negative rights of security. Thus, certain Western states have traditionally argued that some human rights are 'aspirational' in nature, rather than imposing definite duties in the present day. While it may be the case that there are a significant number of cases where it is not clear whether the principles are being violated or not, it is also the case that the principles do allow us to identify clear instances of unjust international interaction. With this in mind, the paradigmatic case of unjust international action is self-interested aggression.

3.2.2 Further Principles of Just International Interaction

The core principles are sufficient to ground a set of duties to non-nationals, and to allow us to identify certain instances of unjust international interaction. As such, they are all that is necessary to commence consideration of the rectificatory project, given the further contention that a great deal of historic international interaction contravened these principles. It is quite possible to believe that there are further principles which also apply, however, meaning that one believes that one has a more extensive set of duties to non-nationals, without having to adopt a substantively cosmopolitan position. All the principles are open to more or less demanding interpretations. These should certainly not be taken as a definitive set of further principles; rather the aim of what follows is merely to give an indication of how more demanding principles can be added to the core principles. The further principles in question are as follows:

1. States should not harm non-nationals.
2. States have duties of reciprocity to non-nationals.
3. States should not exploit non-nationals.
4. States have duties of assistance to non-nationals.

Each will be briefly considered in turn.

1. States should not harm non-nationals.
The core prohibition on self-interested forceful intervention can be expanded into a more general prohibition on causing harm to non-nationals. Thus, for example, Janna Thompson draws upon Michael Walzer's legalistic paradigm of international relations to describe a 'Just Interaction Theory':

> According to this conception, the respect for the equal entitlement to self-determination forbids states and their citizens from disrupting, harming, destroying or negligently allowing to be harmed or destroyed, the rights and well-being of individuals of another state or their political institutions against their will (except in self-defence or to prevent gross acts of inhumanity).[33]

Evidently, this goes beyond the paradigmatic cases of aggression against other states, by referring more generally to actions which disrupt or harm the well-being of non-nationals, whether by design or negligent omission. Part of what this might mean falls under the heading of duties of assistance, and will be discussed in (4) below. But there are a range of cases where there is a clear causal link between the actions of one state and the harmful impact of these actions on others. Some of these are uncontroversially unacceptable. Thus David Miller's account of illegitimate intervention goes beyond the prohibition of force, speaking of 'the duty to abstain from materially harming another state, either by acts of military aggression or by physical damage in the form, say, of pollution that is exported across national boundaries'.[34] The prohibition of harm beyond this point is controversial, however, on account of the difficulties faced in distinguishing between different actions which damage the interests of non-nationals. The key point here is that it cannot be right to say that any actions which harm non-nationals' well-being are unacceptable, as such an extensive principle would seemingly rule out virtually all competitive interaction. The problem is akin to that which accompanied Mill's attempts to outline the 'harm principle' in *On Liberty*.[35] One potentially plausible restriction is to prohibit 'exploitative' harm specifically, and this is addressed in (3) below. The prohibition of harm beyond this point is hard to assess, but could potentially be defined in terms of economic well-being.[36] As Chapter 1 noted, the work of Thomas Pogge demonstrates that it is possible, with a sufficiently expansive understanding of what constitutes harm, to conclude that multiple aspects of the current international economic order and the structure of international law are positively harmful to the world's poor, and so leave the affluent states of the world open to charges of acting unjustly in contexts seemingly far removed from the paradigm cases of armed intervention. For our purposes, it is sufficient to note that a number of the putative harms included on such an account stem from the interdependent nature of the modern international system. The vast majority of putative cases of historic harm can be addressed under the core prohibition against self-interested forceful intervention, or the further principles relating to exploitation and duties of assistance.

2. States have duties of reciprocity to non-nationals.
The key idea of reciprocity is that one should gain a fair return from one's contribution to a scheme of cooperation. For some, this is the central idea lying behind relational accounts of distributive justice. Allan Gibbard, for example, suggests that Rawls's account of justice as fairness in *A Theory of Justice* is best seen as a theory of fair reciprocity:

> Rawls proposes that justice is fairness in exchange, but on a grand scale: it is fairness in the terms governing a society-wide system of reciprocity. The system consists in each person's supporting a basic social structure and drawing benefits from it. The citizen of a well-ordered society is motivated to return benefits fairly, and this general motivation becomes a motivation to conform to the rules of a social structure he considers fair.[37]

So reciprocity, for international libertarians, can provide justice-based reasons for redistribution within political communities. As noted above, Sangiovanni bases his defence of domestic egalitarianism, but opposition to global egalitarianism, explicitly on fair reciprocity.[38] International libertarians need not insist, however, that there are no reciprocal obligations to those in other states. One can agree that a degree of mutually advantageous international cooperation exists without accepting that it gives rise to the same kind of obligations which one has to one's fellow nationals. So Miller, for example, argues that, regardless of the existence of formal agreements to provide aid, or indeed of natural duties to provide aid, there exist, 'obligations of reciprocity, arising from practices of mutual aid whereby states come to one another's assistance in moments of need.'[39] As an example, he cites the 'emerging convention' of the international provision of emergency relief following natural disasters. Again, this is of relatively little significance to the consideration of historic actions, insofar as it is an emerging convention, so the obligations in question may be said to be a relatively recent development. It may be that international libertarians are willing to accept that other forms of international cooperation in the present day give rise to reciprocal obligations to non-nationals; the crucial point is that these are limited, and do not amount to the same kind of obligations which are owed to fellow nationals.

3. States should not exploit non-nationals.
A great deal of contemporary discussion of international interaction concerns the phenomenon of international exploitation, which for our purposes can be broadly defined as the situation in which a state takes unfair advantage of non-nationals.[40] This emerges as a result of the manifest inequalities of power and resources which obtain between contemporary states. Thus, Miller suggests that states possess a duty 'not to exploit states that are one-sidedly vulnerable to [their] actions'.[41] In some cases, the exploitation may be categorizable as forceful intervention, which is prohibited under the core principles, as when one state threatens another with military sanctions if they do not act in a particular way. Thus, for example, de-Shalit claims that Jordan was exploited by Iraq in the Gulf War of 1991, when Iraq used its military superiority to force Jordan to allow goods to be transported through Jordan: 'The threat was implicit but clear: that if it did not, Iraq would bomb it using missiles against which Jordan had no means of defence.'[42] Other cases, where the threatened sanctions are not military but are economic in nature, are less straightforward.

There is an extensive philosophical literature on exploitation, and to a large extent how one understands the term will determine whether one believes that, for example, the benefits that developed states gain in international trade from their advantaged bargaining position are exploitative.[43] Thus, while Steiner holds that the core characteristic of exploitation is that, 'it involves a mutually self-interested, consensual exchange in which what one party transfers is – but need not have been – of greater value than what is received in return',[44] he insists that, 'on a liberal theory of exploitation, x's failure to sell for more than it did is exploitative only if that underselling is occasioned by a rights violation'.[45] On this model, it would seem that cases of exploitation would be covered by the core principles of just international interaction. By contrast, Miller insists that, 'rights violations are neither a necessary nor a sufficient condition for exploitation to occur', and develops an account which makes reference to both departures from benchmark equilibrium prices, and to bargaining advantages which one party uses to induce the other to engage in the relatively less beneficial exchange.[46] This account refers to the relative positions of the parties. Goodin instead refers to their absolute levels of well-being, holding that exploitation consists of wrongful behaviour that violates a particular moral norm: namely, that of 'protecting the vulnerable'. He concludes, 'we all have a strong moral responsibility to protect the interests of those who are particularly vulnerable to (i.e. those whose interests are strongly affected by) our own actions and choices, regardless of the particular source of their vulnerability.'[47]

For our purposes, it should be noted that one need not depart from Steiner's liberal account of exploitation to find unequal international transactions morally problematic if the inequality stems from, or is affected by, historic injustice. Even if unequal transactions *per se* are untroubling, this may not be the case if the inequalities stem from ancient wrongdoing. Subsequent disadvantageous, albeit consensual, transactions could thus be said to constitute unjust harm. This is discussed within the context of morally relevant counterfactuals in Chapter 4. Furthermore, if one is persuaded by Goodin's account of general obligations to the vulnerable, then the nature of historic interaction between nations may make certain current practices particularly troubling. If we were to believe that our historic actions meant that we had particular duties to protect certain non-nationals, then not only to have failed to fulfil our rectificatory duties but furthermore to be exploiting the non-nationals in question in the current day would seem monstrous from a moral point of view. Thus, Goodin speaks of a 'flagrant violation' of the duty to protect the vulnerable when persons 'positively play for advantage against those they are duty-bound not only not to press advantage against but actually to protect'.[48] We will return to the issue of international exploitation in Chapter 4.

4. States have duties of assistance to non-nationals.
The core principles allow for the possibility of justifiable intervention in the affairs of another state for humanitarian reasons, to prevent certain degrees of human rights violations. However, many writers go further than this and argue that in certain circumstances other states have a duty to intervene, either against the apparent wishes of the government of the state in question to protect human rights, or at the request (or with the cooperation) of this government to alleviate suffering or assist with development. Thus, for example, Rawls argues that, 'Peoples have a duty to assist other peoples living under unfavorable conditions that prevent their having a just or decent political and social regime.'[49] This form of duty may, for our purposes, be fixed at a low level (no positive duties to non-nationals whatsoever, or bare subsistence – providing famine relief, for example) or at a high level (incorporating extensive positive duties in relation to subsistence, housing, education, health-care, and socio-economic development). It may therefore involve one-off transfers of resources to address immediate need, ongoing assistance to encourage development, or the imposition of sanctions or even military intervention to seek to reform or remove particular political regimes. In any case, difficult questions must be answered concerning the distribution of the burdens of

assistance between different states, particularly in circumstances where other agents fail to fulfil their duties.

It may be thought that an acceptance of these duties of assistance lessens the analogy between domestic libertarians and international libertarians. Domestic libertarianism, after all, is customarily associated with the claim that those in poverty do not have a justice-based right to assistance. Two points may be made in response to this. First, it is not necessarily the case that an acceptance of a duty of assistance commits one to the strong claim that those in need have a right that they be assisted. Nozick, after all, is quite happy to accept that the wealthy have duties to be charitable to the poor, and should act in such a manner – his claim is rather that the poor do not have an enforceable right that they be assisted. Duties of assistance are not generally expressed in terms of enforceable rights in an international context, for the obvious reason that there is no body analogous to the state at a domestic level which is capable of acting as an agent of enforcement. (This is not to say that international libertarians need to maintain that these duties do not correlate with enforceable rights – just that they need not do so necessarily. It is often not clear what different writers think about this.) Furthermore, domestic libertarians need not even resist the conclusion that the poor have a right to assistance *in extremis* – this is a point which is openly accepted by Loren Lomasky, for example.[50] Second, and more importantly, the key point here is that what is being proposed still falls short of the redistributive cosmopolitan position. Even at their most generous, these duties refer to absolute rather than relative levels of welfare. They seek to ensure that non-nationals reach a given level of welfare, but do not require redistribution to conform to a pattern beyond this point. Rawls explicitly contrasts his position with that of redistributive cosmopolitans on this point. Duties of assistance only apply insofar as other societies are unable to realize just institutions: 'Once that end is reached, the Law of Peoples prescribes no further target such as, for example, to raise the standard of living beyond what is necessary to sustain those institutions.'[51] As such, even demanding conceptions of duties of assistance have cut-off points. Insofar as the redistribution such principles mandate is limited, there is potentially significant scope for the requirements of the rectificatory project.

3.3 JUDGING HISTORICAL INTERNATIONAL INTERACTION

The principles of just international interaction, then, are equivocal on the question of positive international obligations but require that states refrain from forceful self-interested intervention in the affairs of others, other than when acting in self-defence or to prevent certain violations of human rights. It seems that if we apply even these minimal principles to what is known of human history, the inescapable conclusion is that the dominant characteristic of international relations has been extensive injustice. The potential implications for the rectificatory project are obvious. If we are to judge the past by contemporary moral standards, it looks as if the injustice which may require rectification is staggering in its scope. Is it right to apply these standards to past events? There are two broad ways that an argument against doing so might proceed. The first way maintains that historic international relations were not governed by what we now hold to be the principles of just international interaction, because they were governed by a different set of principles. The second way accepts that historic international relations were, in the first instance, governed by the principles of just international interaction, but maintains that departures from them may have been permissible for morally compelling reasons in particular circumstances. The question, then, concerns the status of the principles of just international interaction. Does their contemporary acceptance represent moral progress, the result of the development of our understanding of our moral obligations to others? Or do they derive their force from particular, contingent features of the contemporary international arena? Or were there particular features present in the past which justified contraventions? In each case, the argument in question must make reference to some morally significant difference between the current day and the past, and maintain that this difference means that we should apply different standards to the two periods. What might such a morally significant difference be? In this section, I dismiss two possible candidates derived from the first approach. I argue that neither the claim that previous generations affirmed different principles of just international interaction nor the observation that international law represents a relatively recent development gives us a good reason to think that it is wrong to judge historical interaction by widely shared contemporary standards. An alternative candidate derived from the second approach, which holds that the different nature of the historical international arena may have permitted some departures from the principles of just international interaction, is then considered.

3.3.1 Historically Different Beliefs About Justice

It has already been noted that the widespread acceptance of the principles of just international interaction is a relatively recent phenomenon. Is it significant that historical persons advocated principles of justice in relation to international relations which are different from those affirmed today? This claim is not in itself troubling, unless one (implausibly) adheres to a version of moral relativism, which maintains that morality is wholly constituted by the moral beliefs of agents, and so varies from time to time depending on the extant set of moral beliefs.[52] The purpose of the rectificatory project is to determine what constitutes the morally appropriate response to acts of injustice. This process necessarily involves what may be called judgement or criticism. Actions and institutions are assessed in terms of their accordance, or otherwise, with principles of justice. It is important to be clear as to what this means. Contemporary historians tend to be dubious as to the propriety of using current moral standards to judge the past. There are a number of strands to this disquiet, but one of them relates to a project assumed by a number of historians in the past: namely, that of allocating moral praise or blame to historical figures. The worry seems to be that a misjudgement is made if the moral worth of individuals is judged on the basis of ethical concepts and standards with which they were not familiar. There is a sense in which allocating culpability, in particular, for failure to live up to contemporary standards may seem unfair (even though there may be circumstances in which we are prepared to afford especial praise to those who seemed able to transcend the conventional morality of their day). But we need not necessarily go this far in our judgement of the past. As G.A. Cohen argues:

> We can distinguish between how unjust past practices (e.g. slavery) were and how unjust those who protected and benefited from those unjust practices were. Most of us (rightly) do not condemn Lincoln for his (conditional) willingness to tolerate slavery as strongly as we would a statesman who did the same in 1999, but the slavery institution itself was as unjust in Lincoln's time as it would be today.[53]

Cohen goes on to note that sound judgements about the justice and injustice of people are more contextual than those pertaining to the rules within which they operate, and must take account of, amongst other criteria, the nature of contemporary institutions and levels of intellectual and moral development. So it is that, 'The morally best slave-holder might deserve admiration. The morally best form of slavery would not.'[54] He does not develop his position further, and so he is not committed to the strong claim sometimes made by historians that we should only judge the people of the past by the moral standards of the day.

The point can perhaps be seen most clearly if we consider the possibility that certain historical moral beliefs rested upon factual premises which we now know to be false. Suppose, for example, that a nation based its attitude to foreigners on a belief that only fellow nationals were, as a matter of scientific fact, human beings. We now know this not to be the case. So we might suppose that, were they to have access to our body of scientific knowledge, they would be forced to revise their views, and adopt different principles for regulating their conduct with foreigners. It follows that they would concur with our modern day judgement that their moral beliefs were, as a matter of fact, wrong (which is not, of course, necessarily to say that they were wrong to hold them). If we think that they were not at fault in believing such things, then we might well conclude that they deserve no moral disapprobation at all, even though the actions they performed were unjust. Of course, we may well suppose that the relationship outlined above between scientific knowledge and moral reasoning does not conform with real world practices. It may be, for example, that scientific beliefs in the past were formed as a result of, and in order to give support to, existing cultural beliefs (Allen Buchanan refers to this phenomenon as 'culturally induced factual ignorance'),[55] and the assessment of moral blame in such circumstances may well be a different matter. We might want to say that individuals, and communities, bear moral responsibilities to scrutinize the foundations of their moral beliefs to the best of their ability so as to ensure their rationality, and that a failure to do so leaves them open to judgements of moral culpability. But regardless, the judgement in relation to the injustice of the actions in question remains. The issue of the intentions of the perpetrators of injustice, of the nature of their inner judgements, is not irrelevant; if they are known to the victim, they may significantly affect the nature and degree of the harm suffered, and so may be of consequence when we assess what would constitute compensation. But the aim of the rectificatory project is not the judgement of the moral worth of historic individuals, it is consideration of the lasting effects of injustice.[56]

3.3.2 The Recent Development of International Law

The second candidate for morally significant difference between present and past is the relatively recent development of international law. The key point here is that international law, as it has developed in the twentieth century, now incorporates the principles of just international interaction. This fact is frequently cited by contemporary authors who argue for the normative force of the principles. Consider, for example, Michael Walzer's description of the 'legalist paradigm'. In *Just and Unjust Wars*, he bases his account of what constitutes unjust aggression between states on 'the conventions of law and order'.[57] So it is that the prohibition against aggression, and the right of self-defence in response to such aggression, reflects the current state of international law on the subject. As Article 2(4) of the Charter of the United

Nations stipulates, 'All members shall refrain in their international relations from the threat or use of force against the territorial integrity or political independence of any State'. Nardin writes:

> [Walzer's] view is that one can distinguish lawful and unlawful uses of force between states, that is, distinguish just from unjust wars... An unjust war does not merely interrupt peace (understood as a condition of calm marked by the absence of fighting), it violates the lawful order that guarantees states their independence and territory.[58]

So just and unjust wars are distinguished by reference to contemporary international law. But this leaves open the question of the relation between the principles of just international interaction and international law, for the development of these elements of international law is a relatively recent phenomenon. In earlier times, it was believed that quite different legal provisions covered international relations. In medieval times, the primary focus of international law consisted of treaties.[59] Obligations to non-nationals emerged solely as a result of promissory obligations which were voluntarily made to others. In making a treaty with another state one forms a special relationship with the other party, and as such acquires promissory obligations to others. As with any such promissory obligation, the duties and entitlements in question are not absolute, and can be trumped by other moral obligations in certain circumstances. But nonetheless, the breaking of treaties without such a compelling good reason constitutes an act of injustice. Janna Thompson uses instances of treaty violations as 'obvious test cases' for accounts of obligations stemming from historical injustices. She describes instances of violations of treaties with indigenous peoples in New Zealand and the United States, and argues:

> Governments, most people agree, should keep their promises. Promises, to be sure, are obligations, all things being equal. The law and common sense allow that there can be good excuses for not keeping an agreement: it may have been made under duress or in ignorance; it may be vitiated by unforeseen circumstances or moral considerations. However, it is difficult to suppose that the British Crown, or the New Zealand and American governments that inherited its powers and responsibilities, had a legitimate excuse for what they did.[60]

It seems that we should treat such non-excusable examples of treaty violations as cases of injustice, if we accept Thompson's premise that 'governments... should keep their promises'. It is also true that, in the present day, we generally believe that it is wrong to fail to comply with the more extensive provisions of contemporary international law, and certainly with the elements of international law which uphold the principles of just international interaction. As with domestic accounts of political obligation, there are different accounts of why we might think that states have an obligation to obey international law. The most widely cited candidate is consent theory – the idea that states should keep to the provisions of international law as they have agreed to do so, reflecting the fact that international law has largely developed through the use of treaties. But it is also possible to build an account based on fair play, which stresses the benefit states receive from other states' compliance with the law, or on states' obligations to uphold fair and/or just institutions. In any case, it seems that it would be possible to argue that principles of just international interaction have moral force precisely because they are enshrined in international law. This suggests an alternative account of historic international injustice, whereby we scrutinize the actions of historic actors in order to ascertain whether they were illegal under the terms of the international law of the time, instead of retrospectively applying contemporary norms stemming from subsequent law making. The claim, then, is that the principles of just international interaction are inappropriate to the assessment of times which predate the development of contemporary international law. The development of international law represents a morally relevant difference between the past and the present, whether we think that this is because of the voluntary acceptance of promissory obligations, or the changed context of international relations.

This conclusion should be rejected. We can accept many of the preceding arguments – that treaty violations are paradigmatic examples of historic injustice, that the principles of international interaction have only recently been incorporated into international law, that breaking international law in the current day is wrong, and even that modern day states have promissory obligations not to contravene the principles of just international interaction which they did not have in the past – without accepting the further conclusion that it is the incorporation of the principles into international law which gives them their binding moral force. Suppose, it is well known that I like cutting people's heads off. If I promise you that I will spare you, and not cut your head off, it is true that I break my promissory obligation to you if I do subsequently decapitate you. But this does not make the breaking of the promise constitutive of the wrong done to you. There is clearly a further sense in which you have been wronged, just as there is a sense in which nations who were, for example, attacked or invaded prior to the development of international law, were wronged. You are, in a sense, wronged twice: once for the broken promise, certainly, but also once for the decapitation.[61]

The key point here is that just as we believe that I have a moral duty not to decapitate you, so we believe that political communities have moral duties not to commit acts of aggression against each other. The way most political philosophers express this is to say that contraventions of the principles of just international interaction infringe the rights of those adversely affected.

We are not speaking here (in the first instance, at least) of legal rights, but moral rights. The most straightforward way to think about the rights involved stems from an acknowledgement of the interest of the rights holders, which the principles seek to serve. Joseph Raz holds that an individual, X, has a right 'if and only if X can have rights, and, other things being equal, an aspect of X's well-being (his interest) is a sufficient reason for holding some other person(s) to be under a duty'.[62] Thus, the principles maintain that individuals have a sufficiently important interest in life, liberty, security, and self-determination to hold foreign nationals and governments under a duty to forebear from hostile self-interested intervention.

What is the source of these rights? If we are to maintain that the principles of just international interaction obtain regardless of their express legal provision, that is, independently of their creation as a result of promissory obligations, then it seems that we must show that they correspond to what are normally called *human rights*, described by Feinberg as 'that subclass of moral rights that are said, in virtue of their fundamentally important, indeed essential, connection with human well-being, to belong equally and unconditionally to all human beings, simply in virtue of their being human'.[63] If we accept the existence of such rights, then we would normally accept that they exist independently of their legal recognition. Feinberg describes such rights as the right to life as being held against 'the world at large'; they, 'being based on reasons derived from moral principles, are binding on the consciences of other persons', and, as such, 'can exist prior to or independently of their recognition by the state':

> Hence, they are, in the appropriate sense, *moral rights*. When they are recognised by the state they acquire support from reasons of an additional kind derived from legal rules and thus become legal claim-rights against one's fellow citizens.[64]

But they are moral claim-rights against other human beings in any case. As such, all that the incorporation of the principles of just international interaction into international law has done is to give legal weight to pre-existing moral duties. And these moral duties are justified by the interest of the rights holders they serve. Justifying these rights from first principles is a difficult task, and so most theorists are content to rely to some extent on our intuitive beliefs about morality. Walzer, for example, writes:

> Individual rights (to life and liberty) underlie the most important judgments that we make about war. How these rights are themselves founded I cannot try to explain here. It is enough to say that they are somehow entailed by our sense of what it means to be a human being. If they are not natural, then we have invented them, but natural or invented, they are a palpable feature of our moral world.[65]

Insofar as we think historic actions contravened the rights of historic individuals, we need make no appeal to the provisions of positive law to label them unjust. Indeed, some writers are willing to go further, and argue that human rights violations can be described not just as injustices but as crimes, even in the absence of legal prohibition. Alan Gewirth draws on his extensive theorizing as to the source of human rights to argue that 'to wage aggressive war in the motivational sense of aiming to subjugate other persons or groups is a crime':[66]

> What makes [such actions] crimes is that they are offenses against or violations of basic human rights. The criteria for the existence and contents of such rights and for their violations can be ascertained by objective rational methods of ethical analysis. They are quite independent of the enactments of positive statute laws.[67]

For some, there is something inherently anachronistic about assigning human rights to historical peoples, prior to the codification of international law.[68] But this is a semantic point. Nothing is lost for the purposes of the rectificatory project if reference is made to moral or natural rights. The key point is that we describe violations of these rights – however defined – as acts of injustice.

3.3.3 Justifiable or Excusable Departures from the Principles

We have considered, and rejected, the view that the principles of just international interaction only have normative force as a result of their incorporation into international law. But the observation that the international arena has been transformed by, amongst other things, the development of international law suggests a third approach to the consideration of past contravention of the principles. It might be suggested that although the development of international law does not, of itself, transform the nature of nations' obligations to each other, it is indicative, and part of, a changed international context which has allowed different modes of interaction. This approach is suggested as a result of engagement with the neo-realist school of international relations. It has been argued that an acceptance of the principles of just international interaction entailed a rejection of the extreme prescriptive realist position, which maintains that states are justified in pursuing any course of action which is in their national interest. A belief that the principles currently obtain, however, is not incompatible with a belief that the prescriptive realist position was justifiable in the past. Therefore, it is necessary to consider the realist position in greater detail.

Kenneth Waltz's neo-realist account of the nature of international society is often cited as paradigmatic of the realist approach to international morality.

Waltz argues that the anarchical nature of the structure of international society dictates the policy choices states make in their dealings with each other. Thus, he 'postulates anarchy as part of a generative structure, constraining and encouraging states to behave in important ways, regardless of their leaders' motives, avowed goals, or domestic state–society relations.'[69] This is, in the first instance, a descriptive realist claim, in that it seeks to explain the actual workings of real world international relations, but it has significant normative conclusions. If a state's actions are dictated by the nature of international society, then it seems problematic to maintain that they should act otherwise. It might be that actions which violate the principles of just international interaction are forced upon states, and thus are performed out of necessity. The position is described by Osgood and Tucker:

> If the struggle for security, independence, and survival itself is a necessity that men may deny but one from which they cannot escape, so must be the *ultima ratio* of this struggle ... in employing force to preserve the nation's independence and survival, the statesman only does what he cannot help but do. To insist, however, that these actions raise moral dilemmas and form the proper object of moral judgment is to misapprehend their nature and significance.[70]

One interpretation of such arguments is to suggest that choice is literally missing at the level of international diplomacy.[71] In fact, this conception of necessity is far too strong. Many contemporary writers have observed that modern day states seem to exercise a good deal more discretion in their choice of policies than this would suggest.[72] As Michael Walzer argues, 'Judgments of necessity in this sense are always retrospective in character – the work of historians, not historical actors.'[73] In fact, such claims are rarely made by thoughtful contemporary realists. As David Mapel explains, when realism is understood as a philosophical response to the likes of pacifists and just war theorists, it represents the claim that, 'morality should not *always* govern state conduct.'[74] In suggesting that necessity may 'compel' a state to act in a particular fashion, it is not being argued that the state is literally incapable of acting in another fashion. Rather, it is an argument about actions which states feel 'compelled' to take, in that doing so is necessary in order to serve some particular level of national interest. This is normally expressed in terms of self-preservation, or of the defence of the common life of the community, which is conceptually linked to the basic interests of the polity's members. One might say that a political community acts from the motive of necessity when the actions it performs are necessary in order to protect the vital interests of its members. Again, we can describe these interests in terms of life, liberty, security, and self-determination. As such, Osgood and Tucker describe the meaning of necessity being invoked here as a moral, rather than a natural, imperative.⁷⁵ Mapel expresses the central argument of prescriptive realism in relation to *ius ad bellum* as the claim, 'that strict observance of legal and moral prohibitions against aggression must sometimes compromise the state's security or survival'.⁷⁶ Crucially, then, for realists, this moral necessity can justify infringements of the principles of just international interaction, including the central prohibition against aggression. This is in contrast to the international libertarian claim that no state is justified in using force against another to further their own ends unless acting in genuine self-defence. Other than when responding to immediate threats to their sovereignty or security, no modern day state may claim self-preservation as justification for its actions. This is why international libertarians are not prescriptive realists.

The challenge to the rectificatory project posed by prescriptive realism, however, lies in the suggestion that these moral prohibitions may not have obtained in the past. For example, it might be argued that the modern world, for some polities, at least, is more secure than was the case previously. This claim would draw attention to the emergence of institutions of international society in the twentieth century, such as the United Nations, and of the transformation of international law itself. No causal argument need be made here about the independent force on states' actions of legal institutions; it might be that, once in place, they constrain political actors, or it might be that they merely reflect political changes that have already taken place. Of course, the degree of security enjoyed by the states of the developed world can easily be overstated, by overlooking the dangers posed by threats such as nuclear proliferation and international terrorism, for example. But what is clear is that the threats and challenges facing such states in the present day are, at least, qualitatively different from how they were. The states of the developed world characteristically no longer face threats to their sovereignty arising from the threat of invasion. International libertarian advocates of the principles of just international interaction claim that the contemporary world cannot be accurately characterized as a violent Hobbesian state of nature; a war of all against all. One reason for this is the growing connections between, and the interdependence of, many states. Stanley Hoffmann outlines the nature of this new international system, characterized by an unprecedented increase in the density of international relations:

> We now live in the first truly global international system and it is characterized by two highly important phenomena. The first is the nuclear revolution. The invention of nuclear weapons has created formidable new dimensions of insecurity and, as one statesman after another has proclaimed, highlighted the bankruptcy of the traditional approach to security as a zero-sum game. The second phenomenon is economic interdependence in an increasingly integrated

world economy. This has meant both that domestic politics, and particularly domestic public policies in economic and social matters, are at the mercy of outside forces and that domestic needs and demands can often be met only by international cooperation.[77]

Both developments compel states to work together, so that the dominant mode of international relations becomes one of cooperation rather than conflict. A loss for one state is by no means necessarily a gain for its rivals. The detail of the analysis is not important here; all that need be noted is the claim that modern day states may have more leeway for action without threat to their security than their predecessors.

The suggestion, then, is that it is not the case that the tenets of international law give necessary and sufficient reasons for keeping to the principles of just international interaction. As argued previously, these principles have independent normative force even in the absence of international law. But it might be the case that the combination of the existence of positive international law in the present day which reflects and reinforces these principles and of a political backdrop characterized, for example, by globalization and interdependence, means that modern day states have no good reasons *not* to keep the principles. By contrast, we might think that some, and potentially many, historic international actions were characterized by necessity. They took place within a context of intense conflict between states, and this context meant that actions which would not be justifiable in the present day were necessary in order to guarantee national self-preservation. So a rejection of the view that modern international relations are best characterized as taking place within an anarchic state of nature is compatible with a belief that such a situation did obtain in the past. If we do believe this to be true, there are three broad approaches we can adopt in terms of historical judgement of actions we would now condemn as unjust. The first two are as follows:

1. We can sustain our judgement, and hold the actions to be unjust.
2. We can reverse our judgement, and hold the actions to be just.

This suggests a new model of historical scrutiny, where actions are not only examined to see if they represent violations of the principles of just international interaction but where the context of the actions is also examined. Obvious cases of class (1) would be attacks on other nations motivated by racism or greed. Given that we have rejected the strong realist line that anything a state does is motivated by necessity, there is no reason we cannot unproblematically label right-infringing actions, which we do not deem to be necessary to ensure national self-preservation, as unjust. Are there examples of class (2) cases? It might appear that examples might be historic actions which can be justified in terms of self-defence, but which would not be counted as such in the present day due to the absence of an immediate threat, such as an attack on another state justified by reference to the idea of pre-emptive self-defence.[78] The important point to note here is that actions taken in self-defence in response to aggression should not be seen as violating the rights of other parties. Gewirth argues that national self-defence is legitimate 'for the purpose of repelling unjustified aggression', and goes on to note:

> The killings in such a defensive war have a moral status similar to other means of self-defense. A partial analogue is found in the domestic criminal law. When a judge sentences a criminal to prison, he infringes the criminal's right to freedom, but he does not violate that right insofar as the sentence is justified; on the contrary, the punishment he imposes is itself an expression and defense of the human right to basic well-being. In a parallel way, to kill or injure someone in self-defense does not violate the attacker's human right to life or physical integrity. So human rights, consisting in rights to freedom and well-being, are protected rather than violated when war is resorted to in order to repel aggression that aims to violate those rights.[79]

The problem with the extension of class (2) to pre-emptive self-defence is that this justification of the use of force operates at a high level in that it proclaims the outcome to be just. Indeed, Gewirth's argument here is that the outcome of justified self-defence is *more* just than the pacifist alternative, as fighting back protects, rather than violates, human rights in a broad sense. An important corollary of this for our purposes is that such actions do not give rise to compensatory duties in relation to those whose rights are infringed. Rodin writes:

> ...when somebody justifiably kills an aggressor in self-defense we say that the aggressor has been harmed but not that he has been wronged. The aggressor (or his estate) is not in a position to demand compensation or an apology for the act.[80]

So a legitimate claim that a given action was performed in self-defence shuts the door completely on the rectificatory project. As a number of writers have noted, such attributions of moral righteousness are difficult (at least) in the field of pre-emptive self-defence since they rely upon the political judgement of those making the decision as to the probability of the threat they face. The problem is that if one expands the conception of aggressive provocative action, one moves away from the idea of pre-emptive war, designed to respond to a certain or near certain threat from those wishing one harm, towards preventive war, designed to ward off a potential future threat. Mapel argues that 'war can also be an indispensable means of defending the state against grave but nonforceful threats',[81] but it is very hard to see how the consequences of an aggressive, violent response to a nonforceful threat can be defended as just. It seems, then, that when we come to look at historic aggression, we will find cases which fall readily into class (1), and may find cases which we categorize as class (2), but will also find cases where classification seems more complicated. It is useful here to look at the categorizations employed by historians. For example, the military historian Michael Howard mentions Vattel's division of wars into 'the necessary, the customary, the rational and the capricious'.[82] He identifies a range of motives for war, some of which allow relatively straightforward categorization:

> There have certainly been occasions when states have gone to war in a mood of ideological fervour like the French in 1792; or of swaggering aggression like the Americans against Spain in 1898 or the British against the Boers a year later; or to make money, as did the British in the war of Jenkins' Ear in 1739; or in a generous desire to help peoples of similar creed or race, as perhaps the Russians did in 1877 and the British dominions did in 1914 and 1939.

Tellingly, however, he continues:

> But in general men have fought during the last two hundred years neither because they are aggressive nor because they are acquisitive animals, but because they are reasoning ones: because they discern, or believe they can discern, dangers before they become immediate, the possibility of threats before they are made.[83]

A good many historic actions, it would seem, are neither straightforwardly unjust nor just. Such actions are taken not genuinely in self-defence, but out of a concern for national self-preservation, which can mean more than simply protecting the lives of their citizens. As Osgood and Tucker note, the domestic analogy with individual self-preservation does not always hold: 'what is the "self" that is to be preserved in the case of the nation?'[84] In a situation of international conflict, states have typically sought first to maintain and secondly to maximize their level of power and of material holdings, and, at times, those of their allies. The suggestion is that concern for their own long-term future, for friends and families, and for the well-being of the polity as a whole, may have caused historic individuals and peoples to contravene the principles of just international interaction in a way which, it might be claimed, could be justified in terms of national self-preservation, as opposed to self-defence in the proper sense of the concept. As such, they may have acted on mere suspicions that others might, in the future, cause them harm, and as such have harmed quite innocent persons.[85] Or they may have knowingly harmed innocent persons who posed no immediate, or even conceivable, threat to themselves, in order to protect themselves, or to minimize even the possibility of their welfare being threatened.[86]

How should we consider such cases? We can, of course, bite the bullet and allot them unequivocally to category (1) or (2), and pronounce the outcomes to be either wrongful or righteous. Idealists such as Rodin naturally tend towards the former option, realists to the latter. Clearly, if the former option is taken, no challenge is posed to the rectificatory project. The latter option cuts across the great body of established philosophical opinion as to duties of respect for persons and is, I would suggest, broadly incompatible with any kind of theoretical commitment to human rights. As such, it is highly unlikely to be adopted by those committed to the principles of just international interaction in the present day. One response in the literature is to invoke a new category, relating to 'excusable' actions. For example, Mapel suggests that when many realists purport to defend seemingly immoral actions, they are in fact seeking to excuse them; to exculpate those responsible for the choices which lead to them. He seeks to explain the pressure placed upon states, when threatened, to look to their own survival regardless of the costs to innocent third parties, arguing that a combination of elements, such as psychological pressure and the immense value one puts on one's own survival, might explain, 'why the state should at least sometimes be excused for violating principles of morality when collective security is threatened.'[87] So he notes that:

> ...although individuals should not assign this sort of value to their own survival or to the survival of the state, we may be reluctant to blame them, or blame them fully. In choosing to act unjustly, we might say, they only do what anyone but a saint would do.[88]

It should be clear from the discussion of Section 3.3.1 that such a solution is of little use to the rectificatory project, insofar as we are largely indifferent to the moral worth or otherwise of those responsible for historic actions. The focus of our enquiry is on the lasting effects of unjust actions. As such, the moral character of those responsible for the actions is of little significance.

There is, however, a further option. We might, following Judith Jarvis Thomson (and latterly Joel Feinberg and Loren Lomasky), describe the actions in question as *justified rights infringements*, so that:

3. We can qualify our judgement, and hold the actions to be justifiable, in the sense of being permissible, without endorsing the outcomes of the actions as just.

Feinberg develops his model of justified rights infringements with reference to a subsequently widely cited example, that of the imperiled backpacker.[89] He writes:

> Suppose that you are on a backpacking trip in the high mountain country when an unanticipated blizzard strikes the area with such ferocity that your life is imperiled. Fortunately, you stumble onto an unoccupied cabin, locked and boarded up for the winter, clearly somebody else's private property. You smash in a window, enter, and huddle in a corner for three days until the storm abates. During this period you help yourself to your unknown benefactor's food supply and burn his wooden furniture in the fireplace to keep warm. Surely you are justified in doing all these things, and yet you have infringed the clear rights of another person.[90]

The important point of Feinberg's account from the perspective of rectificatory justice concerns the obligations of the backpacker following his actions. Feinberg believes 'we would not think it inappropriate' to express our gratitude and regrets to the homeowner afterwards, but this, even, is not the end of the matter, for 'almost everyone would agree that you owe *compensation* to the homeowner for the depletion of his larder, the breaking of his window, and the destruction of his furniture'.[91] Thus, his claim is that even though certain rights infringements might be justifiable, they nonetheless impose compensatory duties on the infringer. His conclusions in this area are not limited to the field of property rights. It can even be justifiable to infringe on another agent's right to life. The examples he has in mind are not the most obvious cases of self-defence, where it might be supposed that one has a right to defend oneself against a malevolent aggressor without infringing on her right to life, or acquiring duties of compensation to her or to her heirs. However, citing Judith Jarvis Thomson's arguments, he points out that, 'there are some rare cases... of justified killing of innocents whose rights to life *are* thereby infringed – 'If you are an innocent threat to my life (you threaten it through no fault of your own), and I can save my life only by killing you, and therefore do kill you, I think I do owe compensation, for I take your life to save mine."[92] Loren Lomasky concurs with this conclusion. He notes that the 'benchmark for permissible rights infringements will be set higher for harms to persons than harm to property', but contends that 'even infringements of the right to life – which, necessarily, are uncompensatable to the victim – can be rationally justified under conditions of extreme urgency'.[93] Janna Thompson specifically invokes Feinberg's backpacker example in citing just such a description of some colonial practices:

> The invasion by Europeans of the lands of indigenous people in the Americas, Australia, New Zealand and Africa has often been excused by the following argument. 'Once indigenous nations came within the ambit of European exploration and exploitation, a European invasion was inevitable. Those individuals and nations hungry for gold, land or power were not going to leave indigenous people alone. The only question was which European nations would seize the

opportunities. If England had not assumed control over Australia, New Zealand and as much of North America as it could grab, some other nation would have done so – to the detriment of vital British interests.' The argument claims that the agents in this case – nations, individuals and companies – were acting under the force of circumstances – they had little choice but to do what they did, and thus were not culpable for the crime of aggression, any more than the backpacker was culpable for invading the cabin.[94]

The imperatives confronting the colonialists were similarly stressed by Frederick Lugard in 1926:

> The partition of Africa was...due primarily to the economic necessity of increasing the supplies of raw materials and food to meet the needs of the industrialised nations of Europe. If my reader will...contrast the condition of squalor and misery in which the bulk of the people of these islands lived in 1816 with the conditions...in 1891, he will realise how insistent had become the prevailing demand alike for the food-supplies and for the raw materials which were the product of the tropics...Europe was impelled to the development of Africa primarily by the necessities of her people, and not by the greed of the capitalist.[95]

The suggestion, then, is that there could be a class of historical actions which infringed the rights of historical persons and/or groups but which did not constitute acts of injustice *per se*. Such a judgement accepts that the actions in question infringed the rights of others, but justifies the actions in terms of the rights of self-preservation of those committing the actions. Such judgements are most appropriate when we consider individuals and groups who stand as innocent third parties in relation to the rights infringers. This would not describe actions legitimately taken in pre-emptive self-defence, but it could potentially be extended to instances of preventive self-defence, and to instances where the rights of groups who did not even pose a potential threat were justifiably infringed. If any instances of colonialism are to be defended in terms of national self-preservation, the justification is likely to take such a form. Such an account would obviously need a great deal of detail, and would need to consider precisely what actions might be legitimately undertaken against innocent third parties in the name of self-preservation. Actions which involve the use of lethal force against innocents are likely to be extremely difficult, although not necessarily impossible, to justify.[96] The problem for the putative defender of colonialism here concerns the wantonly bloody character of much of colonial history. If one is to excuse historic actions as justifiable, then it must be the case that they are proportionate to the threat faced, and do not involve the unnecessary use of force. Even if one thought that colonialism, understood as a broad policy, was potentially justifiable, this would not justify each and every colonial enterprise, and it would certainly not justify the manner in which Western countries often pursued their national interest with little or no regard for the welfare of those they subjugated.

Let us accept, for the sake of argument, that a plausibly persuasive account of how *some* historical actions were justified rights infringements could nonetheless be given. For the sake of this book, all that needs to be accepted is that historical justified rights infringements could have taken place. The important conclusion for the rectificatory project is that, unlike cases where actions against aggressors are justified by reference to self-defence, justified rights infringements do not close the door on rectificatory justice, in that those responsible for the actions face duties to pay appropriate compensation. If this is not done, they act wrongly and unjustly. Even if we accept that the action is justified, the outcome of the action will itself be unjust unless rectified. It seems clear that if we are to seek to justify a significant number of historic actions as justified rights infringements, then in most cases this rectification has not taken place. This failure to rectify in itself constitutes an injustice, which needs to be considered along with any other historic injustice. This is not necessarily the end of the matter, however, as it might be argued that a historic failure to fulfil rectificatory duties was *itself* justified in terms of national self-preservation. Should such instances count as acts of injustice? We will return to the matter in Chapter 6.

NOTES

1. Charles Beitz, 'Social and cosmopolitan liberalism', *International Affairs* 75 (1999), 515–29 at p. 515.
2. Rawls, *The Law of Peoples*, pp. 112–20.
3. Samuel Freeman, *Justice and the Social Contract: Essays on Rawlsian Political Philosophy* (New York: Oxford University Press, 2007); Mathias Risse, 'What we owe to the global poor', *The Journal of Ethics* 9 (2005), 81–117.
4. Thomas Nagel, 'The problem of global justice', *Philosophy and Public Affairs* 33 (2005) 113–47; Michael Blake, 'Distributive justice, state coercion, and autonomy', *Philosophy and Public Affairs* 30 (2002) 257–96; Andrea Sangiovanni, 'Global justice, reciprocity and the state', *Philosophy and Public Affairs* 35 (2007), 3–39.
5. Miller, *On Nationality*; Yael Tamir, *Liberal Nationalism* (Princeton: Princeton University Press, 1993); Walzer, *Just and Unjust Wars*.
6. Nardin, *Law, Morality and the Relations of States*; Frost, *Ethics in International Relations* (Cambridge: Cambridge University Press, 1996).
7. Charles Jones, *Global Justice: Defending Cosmopolitanism* (Oxford: Oxford University Press, 1999), p. 15.

8. Brian Barry, 'International society from a cosmopolitan perspective', in David Mapel and Terry Nardin (eds.), *International Society: Diverse Ethical Perspectives* (Princeton: Princeton University Press, 1998), 144–63 at p. 146.
9. For discussion, see Bernard Williams, 'The idea of equality', in *Problems of the Self: Philosophical Papers' 1956–1972* (Cambridge: Cambridge University Press, 1973), 230–49.
10. For example, see Tom Palmer, 'A Cosmopolitan Theory of Justice' (Oxford D.Phil. thesis, 2000). Left libertarians are characteristically cosmopolitan, but supportive of generational redistribution. Hillel Steiner has written extensively on this subject: Hillel Steiner, *An Essay on Rights* (Oxford: Blackwell, 1994); 'Territorial justice', in Simon Caney, David George, and Peter Jones (eds.), *National Rights, International Obligations* (Boulder, Colorado: Westview, 1996), 139–48; 'Hard borders, compensation and classical liberalism' in David Miller and Soheil H. Hashmi (eds.), *Boundaries and Justice: Diverse Ethical Perspectives* (Princeton: Princeton University Press, 2001), 79–88.
11. Others use the terminology of 'strong cosmopolitanism' and 'weak cosmopolitanism', or 'radical' and 'mild', to make a similar point. See the exchange between Miller and Caney following publication of Caney's 'Review article: international distributive justice': David Miller, Caney's 'International distributive justice: a response', *Political Studies* 50 (2002), 974–7; Simon Caney, 'A reply to Miller', *Political Studies* 50 (2002), 1013–18.
12. Sangiovanni, 'Global justice, reciprocity and the state', p. 6.
13. David A.J. Richards, 'International distributive justice' in J.R. Pennock and J.W. Chapman (eds.), *Nomos XXIV: Ethics, Economics, and the Law* (New York: New York University Press, 1982), 275–99 at p. 278.
14. Richards, 'International distributive justice', p. 290.
15. For other nonrelational accounts, see, *inter alia,* Charles Beitz, 'Cosmopolitan ideals and national sentiment', *Journal of Philosophy* 80 (1983), 591–600; Simon Caney, *Justice Beyond Borders: A Global Political Theory* (Oxford: Oxford University Press, 2005), Onora O'Neill, *Bounds of Justice* (Cambridge: Cambridge University Press, 2000); Kok-Chor Tan, *Justice Without Borders: Cosmopolitanism, Nationalism and Patriotism* (Cambridge: Cambridge University Press, 2004).
16. See Rawls's account of the 'circumstances of justice', *A Theory of Justice*, pp. 126–30.
17. Rawls, *A Theory of Justice*, p. 115.
18. Jonathan Wolff, 'Rational, fair, and reasonable', in P.J. Kelly, *Impartiality, Neutrality and Justice: Re-reading Brian Barry's Justice as Impartiality* (Edinburgh: Edinburgh University Press, 1998), 35–43 at p. 41.
19. Wolff, 'Rational, fair, and reasonable', p. 41.
20. Darrel Moellendorf, *Cosmopolitan Justice* (Boulder, Colorado: Westview, 2002), p. 32.
21. Moellendorf, *Cosmopolitan Justice*, pp. 45–6.

22. Charles Beitz, 'Cosmopolitan ideals and national sentiment', p. 595. Beitz is here summarizing his earlier critique of Rawls; in this article, he goes on explicitly to lay out his own, non-relational account of cosmopolitanism.
23. See Brian Barry 'Humanity and justice in global perspective', in Goodin and Pettit (eds.), *Contemporary Political Philosophy: An Anthology* (Oxford: Blackwell, 1993), 525–40 at pp. 531–2 and Christopher Brown, *Sovereignty, Rights and Justice: International Political Theory Today* (Cambridge: Polity, 2002), p. 173; but for a defence of Beitz, see also Simon Caney, *Justice Beyond Borders*, pp. 109–10. I return to this argument in Chapter 4.
24. Walzer, 'Response', p. 293.
25. Walzer, 'Response', p. 293. For Walzer internationally, as for Nozick domestically, 'justice is not the whole of morality' (p. 293).
26. David Miller, 'Justice and global inequality', in A. Hurrell and N. Woods (eds.), *Inequality, Globalization, and World Politics* (Oxford: Oxford University Press, 1999), 187–210 at p. 190.
27. Yael Tamir, *Liberal Nationalism*, pp. 95–116.
28. Nagel, p. 127.
29. Nagel, pp. 128–9.
30. Blake, p. 258.
31. Sangiovanni, 'Global justice, reciprocity, and the state', pp. 26–7.
32. For characteristic accounts of these principles, see Rawls, *The Law of Peoples*, p. 37; Michael Walzer, *Just and Unjust Wars* (New York: Basic Books, 1977), 61–3; Miller, *On Nationality*, pp. 104–5; Frost, *Ethics in International Relations*, pp. 106–10; Nardin, *Law, Morality and the Relations of States*, pp. 269–70.
33. Janna Thompson, *Justice and World Order* (London: Routledge, 1992), 78.
34. Miller, *On Nationality*, p. 104.
35. For discussion, see John Gray, *Mill On Liberty: A Defence* (London: Routledge, 1996), 48–69.
36. Ironically, one potential consequence of widening the prohibition on harm might be to widen the category of actions which constitute aggression, and so justify states in using force in self-defence. Thus, David Mapel describes prescriptive realists as holding that, 'in some situations, it may be indispensable for the state to act "aggressively" and therefore "unjustly" in order to avoid a nonforceful danger that will prove no less fatal than military conquest.' (David R. Mapel, 'Realism and the ethics of war and peace', in Terry Nardin (ed.), *The Ethics of War and Peace: Religious and Secular Perspectives* (Princeton: Princeton University Press, 1996), 54–77 at p. 59). It should be noted, of course, that it does not necessarily follow that widening the criterion of unjustifiable harm also widens the right to self-defence: the claim that A should not do X to B does not necessarily imply that B is justified in using force against A in the event of X.
37. Allan Gibbard, 'Constructing justice', *Philosophy and Public Affairs* 20 (1991), 264–79 at p. 266. Rawls endorses this characterization in *Political Liberalism* (New York: Columbia University Press, 1993), 17n.
38. Sangiovanni, 'Global justice, reciprocity, and the state', p. 26.

39. Miller, *On Nationality*, p. 105.
40. More precisely, de-Shalit delineates four versions of international and transnational exploitation: 'There are four types of exploitation in the international arena: exploitation between states, exploitation within state A, the beneficiaries of which are mainly people in state B; exploitation of individuals from one country by another state in which they work; exploitation of individuals from one country by individuals in another state, in which they work', Avner de-Shalit, 'Transnational and international exploitation', *Political Studies* 46 (1998), 693–708 at p. 693.
41. Miller, *On Nationality*, p. 104.
42. De-Shalit, 'Transnational and international exploitation', p. 695.
43. See, for example, Wertheimer's list of sixteen contemporary definitions of exploitation, in Alan Wertheimer, 'Exploitation', in Edward N. Zalta (ed.), *The Stanford Encyclopedia of Philosophy (Winter 2001 Edition)* available at http://plato.stanford.edu/archives/win2001/entries/exploitation/.
44. Hillel Steiner, 'Exploitation: a liberal theory amended, defended and extended', in A. Reeve (ed.), *Modern Theories of Exploitation* (London: Sage, 1987), 132–48 at p. 132.
45. Steiner, 'Exploitation: a liberal theory amended, defended and extended', p. 141. For criticism of the application of the liberal theory of exploitation to the international arena, see de Shalit, 'Transnational and international exploitation', pp. 698–702.
46. David Miller, 'Exploitation in the market', in Reeve (ed.), *Modern Theories of Exploitation*, 149–65 at p. 153.
47. Robert Goodin, 'Exploiting a situation and exploiting a person', in Reeve (ed.), *Modern Theories of Exploitation*, 166–200 at p. 187. Goodin's account goes further and argues for a positive duty of assistance to take measures to assist those who are particularly vulnerable to one's actions.
48. Goodin, 'Exploiting a situation and exploiting a person', p. 188.
49. Rawls, *The Law of Peoples*, p. 37. For discussion, see *The Law of Peoples*, pp. 105–20. See also Miller, *On Nationality*, p. 105, and 'National self-determination and global justice', in Miller, *Citizenship and National Identity* (Oxford: Polity, 2000), 81–96.
50. 'Is it the case that those in exigent straits may demand welfare goods *as a matter of right*? The answer, I think, is yes. If a person is otherwise unable to secure that which is necessary for his ability to live as a project pursuer, then he has a rightful claim to provision by others who have a surplus beyond what they require to live as project pursuers', Lomasky, *Persons, Rights, and the Moral Community*, p. 126. Paul Russell argues that Nozick should also accept this claim: see Russell, 'Nozick, need and charity', *Journal of Applied Philosophy* 4 (1987), 205–16.
51. Rawls, *The Law of Peoples*, p. 119.
52. I do not have space here to put forward the many reasons why I find this and related positions implausible. I give an account of moral relativism and its relation to the rectificatory project in Daniel Butt, 'Principles of Compensation

and Restitution in International Justice' (Oxford D.Phil. thesis, 2005). Here I restrict myself to the following two points: (*a*) Even if one is committed to *cultural* ethical relativism, and so holds that morality is different for different cultural communities, it does not follow that one need endorse *historical* ethical relativism, and hold that morality is different in different historical periods. The focus on rectificatory duties here is significant – in assessing the duties of one's own community one is appealing to that community's own developed moral principles. It is far from clear what constitutes 'different historical periods' for the historical ethical relativist, given that contemporary societies have gradually developed from their historical forebears, and often share many of the same moral principles (on this, see Allen Buchanan, 'Judging the past: the case of the human radiation experiments', in Ronald Munson (ed.), *Intervention and Reflection: Basic Issues in Medical Ethics* (Belmont, California: Wadsworth, 2000), 525–30 at p. 527). (*b*) It is quite possible to be broadly cultural relativist, especially in relation to, for example, socially determined meanings of justice and morality within particular cultures, and accept the existence of universally applicable prohibitions on certain kinds of human interaction. See, for example, Michael Walzer's account of 'reiterative universalism' in *Thick and Thin: Moral Argument at Home and Abroad* (Notre Dame: Notre Dame University Press, 1994). Accepting even minimal moral constraints on the conduct of international relations is sufficient for the rectificatory project to have force.

53. G.A. Cohen, *If You're an Egalitarian, How Come You're So Rich?* (Cambridge, MA: Harvard University Press, 2000), pp. 211–12n.
54. Cohen, *If You're an Egalitarian, How Come You're So Rich?*, p. 212n.
55. Allen Buchanan, 'Judging the past: the case of the human radiation experiments', p. 528.
56. Bernard Williams also seeks to mark out judgements about justice specifically as being different from moral judgements about the past in general. He first points out that, '... an assessment in terms of justice can, more obviously than others, be conducted without involving the unhelpful question of whether anyone was to blame' (p. 165), before suggesting that, 'it may be that considerations of justice are a central element of ethical thought that transcends the relativism of distance' (p. 166) Bernard Williams, *Ethics and the Limits of Philosophy* (London: Fontana, 1985). On this, see also his *Shame and Necessity* (Berkeley: University of California Press, 1993).
57. Walzer, *Just and Unjust Wars*, p. 61.
58. Terry Nardin, 'Philosophy of war and peace', in Edward Craig (ed.), *Routledge Encyclopedia of Philosophy* (London: Routledge, 1998), available at http://www.rep.routledge.com/article/S066/.
59. Georg Schwarzenberger describes the premises of medieval international law as follows: (*a*) In the absence of an agreed state of truce or peace, war was the basic state of international relations even between independent Christian communities. (*b*) Unless exceptions were made by means of individual safe

conduct or treaty, rulers saw themselves entitled to treat foreigners at their absolute discretion. (c) The high seas were no-man's-land, where anyone might do as he pleased. Cited in Mark B. Salter, *Rights of Passage* (Dordecht: Lynne Rienner, 2003), p. 16.
60. Janna Thompson, *Taking Responsibility for the Past*, p. 4.
61. Some theorists of punishment suggest that certain crimes involve, in a sense, two wrongful acts: one committed against the immediate victim and one against society as a whole. If so, we could (perhaps fancifully) suggest that the decapitation constitutes four wrongful acts: harming both victim and society by both decapitating and promise breaking.
62. Joseph Raz, *The Morality of Freedom* (Oxford: Clarendon Press, 1986), p. 166.
63. Joel Feinberg, 'Voluntary euthanasia and the inalienable right to life', *Philosophy and Public Affairs* 7 (1978), 93–123 at p. 97.
64. Feinberg, 'Voluntary euthanasia and the inalienable right to life', p. 96.
65. Walzer, *Just and Unjust Wars*, p. 54. This claim is later developed through his idea of 'reiterative universalism' in terms of empirically common prohibitions: 'These prohibitions constitute a kind of minimal and universal moral code. Because they are minimal and universal (I should say almost universal, to protect myself against the odd anthropological example), they can be represented as philosophical discoveries or inventions...We might best think of them not as discovered or invented but rather as emergent prohibitions, the work of many years, of trial and error, of failed, partial and insecure understandings...', Walzer, 'Interpretation and social criticism', in Sterling M. McMurrin (ed.), *The Tanner Lectures on Human Values* (Salt Lake City, Utah: University of Utah Press, 1988), 1–80 at pp. 22–3.
66. Alan Gewirth, 'War crimes and human rights', in Aleksander Jokić (ed.), *War Crimes and Collective Wrongdoing* (Oxford: Blackwell, 2001), 48–56 at p. 50.
67. Gewirth, 'War crimes and human rights', p. 51. For such an objective ethical analysis, Gewirth refers readers to his works *Reason and Morality* (Chicago: University of Chicago Press, 1978), chapters 1–3 and 'The epistemology of human rights', *Social Philosophy and Policy* 1 (1984), 1–24.
68. James Nickel, 'Human rights' in Edward N. Zalta (ed.), *The Stanford Encyclopedia of Philosophy (Summer 2003 Edition)* available at http://plato.stanford.edu/archives/sum2003/entries/rights-human/.
69. Martin Griffiths, *Realism, Idealism and International Politics: A Reinterpretation* (London: Routledge, 1992), p. 78.
70. Robert Osgood and Robert Tucker, *Force, Order and Justice* (Baltimore: The Johns Hopkins University Press, 1967), p. 253.
71. See Arnold Wolfers, *Discord and Collaboration* (Baltimore: Johns Hopkins University Press, 1962).
72. See, for example, Andrew Linklater, *The Transformation of Political Community: Ethical Foundations of the Post-Westphalian Era* (Cambridge: Polity, 1998).

73. Walzer, *Just and Unjust Wars*, p. 8. Gregory Raymond goes so far as to suggest that the popularity of the discourse of necessity in diplomatic circles is a consequence of the difficulties which political leaders face in making decisions: 'A growing body of psychological research suggests that rather than being rational calculators who dispassionately weigh the costs and benefits of alternative courses of action, national leaders are emotional decision makers who are beset with doubts, struggle with painful trade-offs, and have a limited capacity to process the intelligence reports that they receive about the capabilities and intentions of their rivals.' (Gregory A. Raymond, 'Necessity in foreign policy', *Political Science Quarterly* 13 (1998–9), 673–88 at p. 685). Faced with the stress of taking important decisions under such circumstances, it is not surprising that those with the responsibility for decision-making attribute the policy not to their own choices but to situational factors.
74. David R. Mapel, 'Realism and the ethics of war and peace', p. 54. It should be noted that the less nuanced versions of realism are nonetheless extremely commonly expressed.
75. Osgood and Tucker, *Force, Order and Justice*, p. 267.
76. Mapel, 'Realism and the ethics of war and peace', p. 55.
77. Stanley Hoffmann, 'The political ethics of international relations', in Joel H. Rosenthal (ed.), *Ethics and International Affairs: A Reader* (Washington D.C.: Georgetown University Press, 1999), 28–49 at p. 35.
78. In contemporary international law, claims of preemptive national self-defence are most often judged in relation to the *Caroline* doctrine of 1838, which requires that a state demonstrate '...necessity of self-defence, instant, overwhelming, leaving no choice of means, and no moment for deliberation.' For discussion, see David Rodin, *War and Self-Defense* (Oxford: Oxford University Press, 2002).
79. Gewirth, 'War crimes and human rights', p. 50.
80. Rodin, *War and Self-Defense*, p. 30.
81. Mapel, 'Realism, war and peace', p. 59.
82. Michael Howard, *The Causes of Wars* (London: Maurice Temple Smith, 1987), p. 12.
83. Howard, *The Causes of Wars*, p. 15.
84. Osgood and Tucker, *Force, Order and Justice*, p. 271. The legitimacy of the domestic analogy in this context is questioned at length by David Rodin in *War and Self-Defense*.
85. The classic example of a preventive war of this kind is the Third Punic War, between Rome and Carthage (149–146 B.C.). For discussion, see Charles W. Kegley Jr. and Gregory A. Raymond, 'Preventive war and permissive moral order', *International Studies Perspectives* 4 (2003), 385–94.
86. Two possible examples emerge from the two World Wars. Walzer considers, and rejects, the possibility that the German attack on Belgium of 1914 was motivated by necessity (*Just and Unjust Wars*, pp. 240–2). He cites the speech of

Chancellor von Bethman Hollweg to the Reichstag on August 4, and Bethmann Hollweg's justification of Germany's actions is particularly interesting for our present purposes: 'Gentlemen, we are now in a state of necessity, and necessity knows no law. Our troops have already entered Belgian territory. Gentlemen, that is a breach of international law... The wrong – I speak openly – the wrong we thereby commit we will try to make good as soon as our military aims have been attained' (p. 240). Regardless of our view of the rights or wrong of Germany's actions, it is interesting that the Chancellor's justification – acknowledging and apologizing for the wrong, pleading necessity and promising to pay compensation – correlates closely to the account of justified rights infringements given below. The other obviously similar example concerns the period leading up to the 1939 Soviet invasion of Finland. Prior to invasion, the Russians had demanded that the Finns cede territories to the USSR in the interests of ensuring that the Russians would be able to defend Leningrad from a possible future German attack. As Rodin writes: 'These demands were clearly in violation of Finland's sovereignty as a neutral state, but there does not seem to be any question as to the genuinely limited nature of the Soviet Union's intentions. The demands were made on the basis of clear and obvious security concerns. What is more, the Russians offered the Finns compensation totaling roughly twice the territory they proposed to take and even after the Soviet Union had overcome Finnish resistance in an eventual invasion, they adhered roughly to their initial territorial demands' (Rodin, *War and Self-Defense*, p. 136n).
87. Mapel, 'Realism, war and peace', p. 72.
88. Mapel, 'Realism, war and peace', pp. 72–3.
89. Also known in the literature as the 'stranded hiker'.
90. Feinberg, 'Voluntary euthanasia and the inalienable right to life', p. 102.
91. Feinberg, 'Voluntary euthanasia and the inalienable right to life', p. 102.
92. Feinberg, 'Voluntary euthanasia and the involuntary right to life', p. 103.
93. Loren E. Lomasky, 'Compensation and the bounds of rights', in John W. Chapman (ed.), *Nomos XXXIII: Compensatory Justice* (New York: New York University Press, 1991), 13–44 at p. 31.
94. Janna Thompson, *Taking Responsibility for the Past*, p. 46.
95. Frederick Lugard, cited by Cheedy Jaja in the context of an exposition of Thomas Hobbes's account of colonialism. See Jaja, 'Hobbes's theory of colonialism and the African colonial experience: structural and programmatic affinities', *American Philosophical Association Newsletters* 97 (1998), available at http://www.apa.udel.edu/apa/archive/newsletters/v97n2/black/hobbes.asp/.
96. Strong arguments against the possibility of the use of lethal force against not only (to use Judith Jarvis Thomson's terminology) Innocent Threats but *also* Innocent Bystanders have been put forward by Michael Otsuka ('Killing the innocent in self-defense', *Philosophy and Public Affairs* 23 (1994), 74–94) and David Rodin (*War and Self-Defense*). Rodin's arguments are consonant with Otsuka's in terms of personal self-defence and self-preservation, and in this

limited area I am inclined to agree with both of them. However, Rodin goes on to develop an argument which is broadly hostile to the plausible justification of national self-defence, and which is certainly hostile to the justifiability of the current universal ascription of national self-defence to states. I am sympathetic to this latter claim, but dispute the former, based on two arguments: (*a*) the extent to which the analogy between individual and national self-defence breaks down based on the assumed presence of a police-style authority in the former case but not the latter, and (*b*) the extent to which national self-defence can be characterised not, in fact, as self-defence at all (where the self is presumed to be either the individual or the community), but *other-defence*, whereby the others one is protecting are one's family and friends, to whom one is partial in a way which many political philosophers increasingly acknowledge as legitimate. Crucially, some see such partiality to *others* as (at least potentially) legitimate when it would not be legitimate were it applied to oneself. I think it may be possible to extend this partiality to the community as a whole, but leave this as an open question. Either way, one's own survival may not be the justification for one's actions at all. For a critique of Rodin's argument see Jeff McMahan, 'War as self-defense', *Ethics and International Affairs*, 18 (2004), 13–18.

4

Compensation for Historic International Injustice

4.1 INTERNATIONAL COMPENSATORY JUSTICE

It was previously observed that it is difficult to consider the history of international relations without becoming readily aware of the scale of international historic injustice. This chapter addresses the question of the effects of this injustice, in asking whether current generations have obligations to pay compensation for historic wrongs. The idea that one political community can cause injury to another in such a way as to give rise to claims for reparation is not a new one, although historically such reparations have tended to reflect the superiority of military victors rather than any coherent account of compensatory justice. Having accepted the principles of just international interaction, which hold that states have (at least) minimal duties of non-intervention in relation to non-nationals, it follows that states can act unjustly in relation to non-nationals and, accordingly, that such actions can be harmful. It is in such circumstances that issues relating to compensatory justice emerge. Compensation necessarily refers to some kind of harm or loss. Questions of compensatory justice arise when we feel that a given entity has suffered in some regard, and that this loss should be made up. As such, a claim that compensation should be made necessarily means a departure from the common law principle of 'risk bearing', which holds that losses should generally lie where they fall.[1] Cane describes the principle as follows:

> The shifting of a loss – or making one person compensate another for some misfortune – involves an alteration of the *status quo* and so it involves administrative expense. Therefore (it is usually asserted), the onus is on those who wish to shift a loss to justify the shift. Unless there is some good reason for shifting a loss, it should be left to lie where it falls.[2]

In saying that one agent has a duty to compensate another, we maintain that there are reasons of justice why the loss should be shifted from the latter to the former. The standard account of rectificatory justice outlined in Chapter 2 gives one such compelling reason for such a redistribution of loss.

In circumstances where one individual has wrongfully caused another to incur a loss, it seems straightforward to hold the wrongdoer responsible for her actions and require her to shoulder the loss herself. Thus, we require that she compensates the victim of her actions, by acting in such a way so as to improve her victim's circumstances, and thus erase the loss. Why do we require her to act in this way? The answer is that we think it is unfair if the loss is not transferred. As stated in Chapter 2, insofar as we are holding wrongdoers responsible for paying for the costs of their harmful actions, rectificatory justice and distributive justice are perfectly complementary.

Such a claim concerning the fairness of shifting a loss need not only be made in connection with losses incurred as a result of others' malfeasance.[3] Distributive justice is centrally concerned with the fair distribution of benefits and burdens. The idea of compensating individuals for losses, or other deficiencies, recurs repeatedly in a range of different accounts of what constitutes a fair societal distribution. Luck egalitarians, for example, maintain that individuals should be compensated when they suffer the effects of undeserved, unpredictable 'brute luck', but not when they suffer losses as a result of deliberately exposing themselves to certain kinds of risk. Elizabeth Anderson goes so far as to argue that, for luck egalitarians, 'the fundamental aim of equality is to compensate people for undeserved bad luck – being born with poor native endowments, bad parents, and disagreeable personalities, suffering from accidents and illness, and so forth'.[4] The idea is that there is something unfair about the loss caused by bad brute luck being borne exclusively by those individuals who happen to be unlucky rather than by society as a whole; and conversely, that it would also be unfair to make other members of society pay for losses for which particular individuals are responsible.

As Chapter 3 made clear, international libertarians do not believe that principles of distributive justice extend across state boundaries. The international libertarian vision of the world is one which rejects patterned redistribution across national boundaries, and instead maintains that political communities should be able to exercise self-determination in shaping their own futures. The fact that distributive principles do not extend across different peoples means that there will inevitably be inequalities between modern day states, for a range of different reasons. Some of these reasons will be matters of chance, to do with levels of natural resource holdings, geographical location, and so on. Others will reflect decisions which previous generations within different communities have made. International libertarians do not hold that any of these kinds of historical reasons for difference are cause for concern from the perspective of justice. As such, their default position on losses is that they should lie where they fall, unless they result from wrongful harm, defined in terms of violations of the principles of just international interaction. Chapter 6 examines the question of the circumstances under which it is reasonable to hold a political community collectively responsible for the actions of its leaders; for now it is sufficient to maintain that international libertarians can accept the claim that the standard account of rectificatory justice, which holds wrongdoers accountable for the costs of their actions, applies to international relations. They do not, however, seek to rectify inequalities between political communities which arise in the absence of wrongdoing, whatever their cause. An 'international luck egalitarian' would presumably seek to compensate political communities who were the victims of bad brute luck, such as being harmed by an unpredictable natural disaster, for example, but international libertarians are not committed to compensating for the effects of bad luck. If the victims of the natural disaster are reduced below some minimal threshold of well-being, then it may be that non-nationals have duties of assistance to them, but otherwise the loss is left to lie where it falls. If this means that later generations have a lower standard of welfare than they would have enjoyed if the natural disaster had not taken place then this is certainly unfortunate, but it is not unjust.

The situation, however, becomes more complicated when one confronts situations where wrongful harm is not rectified. Suppose that it is still clearly the case that a given political community is being harmed as a result of a past infringement of the principles of just international interaction. Those morally responsible for the commission of the wrongful action in question are now dead. What should happen to the extant loss? Should it be shifted to another party or parties, such as, perhaps, the descendants of those responsible for the injustice in question? Or should it stay with the community which was historically wronged, and be seen as their bad luck – unfortunate, but not unjust? In this chapter, I argue that present day parties who are benefiting from the act in question may face compensatory duties to rectify historic injustice. It is important to appreciate that this is a controversial argument given the background international libertarian account of distributive justice. The conclusion need not be controversial for many theorists who are broadly egalitarian in a domestic context. Any loss stemming from injustice clearly looks to be arbitrary from a moral point of view. Domestic egalitarians are likely to compensate such a loss, along with other morally arbitrary deficiencies, in the short term, and, as Chapter 2 argued, such losses are unlikely to have lasting effects across generations in any case, as a result of periodic redistributions of resources. But in a broadly libertarian context it is indeed controversial, as it seems to contravene the common libertarian principle that one can only owe obligations to others as a result of one's own voluntary actions. I challenge this principle in Section 4.4. Before this argument is presented, however, it is necessary to examine the question of what it means to say that present day parties are benefiting, or being harmed, as a result of the effects of historic injustice. Section 4.2 is concerned with the type of counterfactual which is involved in assessing whether or not individuals or groups have been harmed by a given act of injustice. I outline the common way in which such calculations are normally made, but reject this as inappropriate for the task of assessing the harm caused by historic acts of injustice, particularly in relation to exploitation. I then describe an alternative form of counterfactual.

Although in what follows I do argue that it is theoretically possible that present day parties may possess compensatory duties as a result of temporally distant wrongdoing, this does not mean that an acceptance of the rectificatory project means that we need to determine whether compensation be paid for each and every recorded instance of international injustice. The key issue here concerns the net effect of historic injustice. The question we face is whether modern day states can be said to be in a state of moral equilibrium with one another in relation to historic wrongs. By a 'moral equilibrium' I mean a situation where it does not seem as if any given party has particularly gained or lost relative to other as a result of injustice. Such a situation can come about in two ways. The first is simply the case where the effects of injustice are no longer significant. Imagine the situation within a modern day, industrialized state, characterized by high levels of education, equality of opportunity, and social mobility. It seems implausible to maintain that, for example, most of the income differentials in such countries are likely be the result of historic events (such as a civil war 500 years ago) rather than more recent domestic interaction. The situation might be rather different, however, if society is not homogenous in, for example, ethnic terms, and there are clear characteristics which separate the descendants of victims and oppressors. If social mobility is, in such cases, linked to membership of particular ethnic groups, then historic injustice may continue to cast a shadow. We can assume that the redistribution of wealth within domestic societies will lessen the importance of historical injustice, whether this be through state action or the workings of markets, only insofar as different groups tend to be affected equally by these mechanisms. One may make a similar point in relation to international injustice. Inequalities between political communities are generally harder to overcome than inequalities within communities, and are often self-perpetuating. The point can be seen by considering those examples of historic injustice which involve the physical removal of property. It is one thing for there to be an unjust appropriation of property within a particular sphere of distribution; the property in question remains within the system and is likely to be redistributed again in the future, by one mechanism or another. But the case where resources are literally removed from one sphere and incorporated into another seems rather different. The point here is simply that one should not assume that the passage of time will necessarily wipe out the effects of historic injustice – it may do so, but it may not. Imagine, for example, a case where one state wrongs another at a critical stage in its industrial development. This might confer a competitive advantage upon the wrongdoer in terms of international trade at a vital moment, allowing it greater bargaining power in terms of the shaping of institutional rules governing further interaction. Thomas Pogge argues that 'large inequalities, once accumulated, have a tendency to intensify' within the global economy.[5] If these inequalities initially obtained as a result of wrong doing, then the lasting effects of injustice will be profound. In many cases, the effects of injustice will no longer be significant, but this cannot be taken for granted.

The second way a moral equilibrium between different parties may be said to come about is if all parties involved have both harmed and been harmed in roughly equal measure. This point may be made on a theoretical and a practical level. Theoretically, it is possible that the effects of two harms may serve to cancel each other out. Thus, if A harms B, causing ten units of damage, and B harms A, also causing ten units of damage, then we may reasonably conclude that there is no need for either side to pay the other compensation.[6] Of course, it is unlikely that many parties will be in this precise situation of equivalence, but it is also unlikely, in a large number of cases, that we will be able to say who has actually gained and who has lost as a result of historic injustice. This practical objection is related to the epistemic difficulties a number of authors have identified with attempts to rectify historic injustice. It should be noted that these difficulties are likely to be more pronounced in some cases than in others within an international context. It does indeed seem likely that, given the nature of interaction between, say, the United Kingdom and France (and, significantly, the degree to which this interaction has resulted in intermingling of the two populations, as with, for example, the influx of Normans into the predominantly Anglo-Saxon English population at the time of the Norman Conquest) it is going to be impossible plausibly to maintain that one community is suffering from historic injustice more than the other. Although this might in fact be the case, practical limitations on our knowledge mean that any attempt to draw up a balance sheet will inevitably prove arbitrary from a moral point of view. When nations are located in close geographical proximity and have developed at roughly the same time, such a situation is likely, though not certain, to be the norm. Arguments for compensation for injustice in such cases are likely to allude to relatively recent acts, when an equilibrium is disturbed by one (or more) state's aggressive foreign policy. Thus, within a west European context, arguments relating to compensation for historic wrongs today typically centre around the Second World War.

But there are other kinds of international relations which do not fit this pattern: most notably, those between the colonial powers and their former territories. Such relations have typically taken place over much shorter periods of time, and our knowledge of the history of these relations is frequently fairly substantial. In such cases, the historic losses suffered as a direct consequence of injustice tend to be one-sided, as the power differentials between the different nations, and the limited extent of their historical interaction, make it harder to argue that any kind of equilibrium has been reached. In such cases, one cannot assume that each community has historically harmed the other to equal degree, since colonies have never been in a position to act in a reciprocal way towards their masters or former masters.

The real world context of this question, then, is provided by two closely related arguments which historians of colonialism have addressed. The first of these concerns the development of the West. In simple terms, the question is whether the West has benefited from colonialism. The second question concerns the West's former colonies, and asks about the effects of colonialism on present day generations. Are people still in fact suffering as a result of ancient wrongs, or might it be that they have even benefited from the fact that they were treated in a way which we now recognize as being unjust? These questions of the lasting legacy of historic injustice, both in terms of harm suffered and benefit gained, lie at the heart of this chapter. As we shall see, what it means to speak of 'harm' and 'benefit' is complicated, and frequently misunderstood.

4.2 IDENTIFYING THE MORALLY RELEVANT COUNTERFACTUAL

What does it mean to say that a group of people is entitled to compensation as a result of a given act of injustice? In simple terms, it must be maintained that the group in question is still suffering in some sense from the act of injustice in question. The whole point of compensation is to provide counterbalancing benefits to offset losses. What is required here is some notion of a counterfactual. Superficial accounts of compensatory justice define this counterfactual very simply, as being the state of affairs which would have obtained had the act of injustice in question not occurred. In this section, I show that this formulation of compensatory justice, as it stands, is inadequate. It is indeterminate as to the nature of the counterfactual to which it appeals, and its most conventional interpretation leads to unacceptably counter-intuitive outcomes. In particular, I argue that the conventional account of compensatory justice is inadequate when it comes to considering a particular kind of injustice that has characterized a great deal of international history, which is best described as non-consensual exploitation.

Let us accept that circumstances can arise where it is appropriate for one community to pay compensation to another. The paradigm case concerns instances where one community injures another, which is to say both that it harms (or, we might say, damages the interests of) the other, and acts unjustly in so doing. As Chapter 3 suggested, some notion of injustice or wrongdoing is important here to distinguish what we might think of as rights-violating actions from actions which set back another party's interests, but do so in a legitimate way (through, for example, fair competition). This is still a long way from maintaining that any historic actions give rise to contemporary compensatory duties, for we still need an account of what it is to suffer as a result of historic injustice. It is often suggested that, whatever we think about colonial practices themselves and the motives of those who perpetuated them, it does seem as if they have been beneficial in the long run, in that current day members of the former colonies now enjoy a better standard of life than they would do had colonialism never occurred. Let us call this the Counterfactual Observation. A version, in relation to the descendants of slavery, is put forward by Ellen Frankel Paul:

> If not for the slave trade, most of the descendants of the slaves would now be living in Africa under regimes known neither for their respect for human rights, indeed for human life, nor for the economic well-being of their citizens. The typical denizen of one of these states, I dare speculate, would envy the condition of the black teenage mother on welfare in one of this country's worst inner cities. Starvation, war, tribal depredations, infant mortality, disease, and hopelessness are the standard condition of many regions of Africa, for example, Ethiopia and Somalia.[7]

The observation is sometimes presented as a defence of the colonial practices themselves, whereby it is suggested, by implicit or explicit reference to some kind of consequentialist reasoning, that the ends justified the means. In this crude form, the argument is manifestly inadequate even on simple consequentialist grounds. When we are considering the consequences of an action, we cannot (for example) simply measure the amount of utility at one particular point in time, such as the present day, and compare it with the amount of utility at the point in time directly before the action occurred to determine whether the action was justified or not; we need to give consideration also to other time periods which were affected by the action. So it might be, for example, that present day members of nation X are indeed better off in the current day than they would have been had colonial practice Y never occurred, but that this overlooks the fact that in the intervening period the members of nation X suffered tremendously, meaning that the total amount of utility measured across time is less than it would have been had Y never occurred. In such cases, the observation that colonial practices have proved beneficial in the long run *to present day nationals* need not lead one to the conclusion that the end justified the means, or that the practices were, in a wider sense, beneficial. But there is one sense in which it is commonly felt that the Observation is important, and this concerns the issue of contemporary compensation for historic wrongs. How can a claim for compensation be advanced for an event which has actually benefited the person making the claim?

The problem here concerns the role that counterfactual reasoning is normally understood to play in calculating appropriate compensation. As stated, claims for compensation must, by definition, refer to some kind of loss or harm. The purpose of compensation (ideally, at least) is to cancel out this loss. It is far from the case that a loss necessarily gives rise to an entitlement to compensation, but in order for there to be an entitlement it is a necessary condition that there be a loss of some kind. Thus Goodin articulates the common understanding of compensation when he writes that, 'Compensation is supposed to provide the "full and perfect equivalent" of what was lost, and so to restore completely the *status quo ante*.'[8] This reference to the restoration of the *status quo ante* can be misleading, as it is, in fact, generally accepted that the situation which should be brought about is not the equivalent of the state of affairs before the injustice was perpetrated, but the state of affairs which *would* have obtained had the unjust action not occurred. Thus Nickel writes that, 'Compensatory justice requires that counterbalancing benefits be provided to those individuals who have been wrongly injured which will serve to bring them up to the level of wealth and welfare that they would now have if they had not been disadvantaged.'[9] The claim, then, is that we need to devise a *counterfactual* account of how the victim would have fared had the offence never been committed. This is Nozick's account of full compensation:

> Something fully compensates a person for a loss if and only if it makes him no worse off than he would otherwise have been; it compensates person X for person Y's action A if X is no worse off receiving it, Y having done A, then X would have been receiving it if Y had not done A. (In the terminology of economists something compensates X for Y's act if receiving it leaves X on at least as high an indifference curve as he would have been on, without it, had Y not so acted.)[10]

This is what is normally meant when it is claimed that individuals or groups are entitled to compensation. Insofar as they have suffered as a result of an act of injustice, they will be compensated to the extent that they are moved to a position equivalent to their counterfactual position. Now the problematic nature of the Counterfactual Observation becomes clear. How can a claim for compensation be made by a party who has actually benefited as a result of injustice?

In fact, for some, it now begins to look as if the entire project of compensating for historic injustice is conceptually flawed. A number of writers have referred to a variant of the Counterfactual Observation in relation to compensating for ancient wrongs, termed the non-identity problem. Typically, such approaches take their lead from Derek Parfit's writing on personal identity in *Reasons and Persons*.[11] The idea is that unjust actions can make a difference to who actually exists in later time periods, since they affect the circumstances in which procreation takes place. Each individual grows from a particular pair of cells, an ovum and a spermatozoon. If their parents had mated at a different time, it is almost certain that a different pairing of spermatozoon and ovum would have taken place, resulting in a different person. Were it not for the acts of injustice in question, present day individuals would not exist. So how can they claim that they have been harmed?[12] There are a number of possible responses from the viewpoint of international compensatory justice. The first is to place emphasis on the group membership of the individuals who are to be compensated, and claim that it is the group which has suffered rather than the component individuals of the group.[13] Although it might be true that there is a sense in which individual members of the group have benefited from the historic act in question, it might be possible to claim that it, *qua* group, has suffered. This is evidently a way around the non-identity problem which is particularly accessible within an international context, given that the entities we are dealing with are continuous political communities. It is not an unproblematic response, since these communities are nonetheless composed of individuals, and one may reasonably question how it can be that a collective is worse off even though all its members individually have benefited.[14] I return to the issue of group membership in Chapter 6, where I outline a model of harm to collectives which is not vulnerable to the non-identity problem. However, I do not, in fact, believe that the account of counterfactuals I give in this section is susceptible to the objection. Insofar as it generates counterfactuals in a nonprobabilistic fashion, it is able to make reference to a counterfactual state where the individuals who claim compensation exist, but where the unjust action did not occur. This move is controversial, philosophically speaking, in terms of certain understandings of personal identity and possible worlds.[15] Should my account be rejected for such reasons, however, I should stress that my argument here is not dependent on my providing a solution to the nonidentity problem. I am very dubious, in fact, as to whether we should allow the non-identity problem to play any role at all in our theorizing over what should actually happen in the real world. The conclusions of the non-identity problem in the field of compensatory justice are so counter-intuitive as to be absurd.

Consider the following example. I negligently disregard the safety of my factory. One night, the factory blows up, and leaks a chemical into the water supply. If pregnant women drink this water, their children will suffer physical defects for the rest of their lives. These defects will not be so serious as to mean their lives are not worth living, but they will cause regular pain and inconvenience. Two pregnant women do drink the water. They conceive their children twenty minutes apart. The first child is conceived five minutes prior to the factory exploding. The second child is conceived fifteen minutes afterwards. When the factory explodes, the parents of the second child are sufficiently disturbed by the noise that they interrupt their intercourse. This seemingly makes a difference as to whether a given individual exists, since it is highly unlikely that precisely the same conjunction of spermatozoon and ovum would have occurred had this disturbance not taken place. So it looks as if the first child conceived will be entitled to compensation for my culpable negligence, but the second one will not, since she would not exist had my factory not exploded. Analogous examples are routinely given in the literature on the rectification of historic injustice in order to support the conclusion that compensation need not be paid in the real world for historic injustice. Generally, one might note, it is one of a list of reasons why compensation need not be paid, although if the non-identity objection holds, then it is seemingly sufficient in itself to rule out the compensation claim. Is it really plausible to think that, in the factory case, compensation should be paid to the first child but not to the second? Would anyone actually propose such a course of action in the real world? The suggestion seems positively offensive if one considers, for example, real world environmental catastrophes, such as the 1984 Bhopal disaster, or the 1986 Chernobyl disaster. Children who were conceived in the locality of the Union Carbide pesticide plant in Bhopal or the Chernobyl nuclear power plant following the disaster may, in a sense, be said to owe their existence to these disasters. But would anyone seriously argue that, in the event of their suffering health problems, they should not be compensated on account of the non-identity problem? My view is that the non-identity problem can be resolved, but even if one rejects the following account, it does not necessarily follow that one should conclude that compensation should not be paid. It may be that we should see the problem as a paradox of philosophical interest until such a point as it can be properly explained, should such a thing be possible, but not something which should guide actions in the real world. In any case, the controversy over identity is emphatically not the context in which real world debates relating to historic injustice take place. When the political opponents of reparations argue that former colonies have benefited from colonialism, or that the descendants of slaves are now better off than they would be had their ancestors not been forcibly taken from Africa, they are not referring to Chapter 16 of *Reasons and Persons*. They are instead making an argument about such factors as GDP, economic development, the rule of law, and quality of life. It is to this real world debate that my argument is primarily directed.

How, then, should the Counterfactual Observation be addressed? As has been seen, in asking whether modern day parties have been harmed by injustice, we make reference to some kind of counterfactual account of how they would be had the injustice not occurred. This is a complicated matter. It raises two related problems in particular, one of which has received rather more critical attention than the other. The first problem concerns the effects of the unjust act. How are we to judge how the victims of injustice would have fared had the unjust act not occurred? The second concerns the characterization of the unjust act itself. In terms of the first problem, the difficulty is that we clearly cannot know for certain how the victim of injustice would have fared had the unjust action not taken place. Suppose I lock Pedro in my cellar for an hour. It is possible that, had I not done so, Pedro might have gone to the shop and purchased a winning lottery ticket, having chosen his numbers at random. It is, therefore, possible that my actions mean that Pedro is millions of pounds worse off than he would have been had I not acted unjustly. It is also possible that Pedro might have been struck by a bolt of lighting and been killed. Perhaps my actions have saved his life. Which is the relevant counterfactual to employ? The standard way of answering this question is to say that we ask what is the most probable outcome, in the absence of my action. Thus Kershnar writes:

> The purpose of the relevant counterfactual is to determine those effects that result from the injuring act. To do so, the relevant possible world should include the condition of a person wrongfully injured in the actual world in the most similar world in which the injuring act did not occur... Hence, we determine the conditions on the relevant possible world by assuming that the conditions in it are identical with those in the actual world up until the time of the injury, *and then envisioning the most probable outcome if the injuring act had not occurred.*[16]

Thus, for Kershnar, the criterion for identifying the relevant possible world is that of probability. It is unlikely that Pedro would either have been killed or have become a millionaire; it is much more probable, let us suppose, that he would have gone home for a nap. On the probability account, this is the approach which should be employed. This also reflects the standard version of the non-identity objection, which, as A. John Simmons notes, involves 'a tacit assumption that a significant injustice *necessarily* alters subsequent conditions for the conception of offspring.'[17] This is normally interpreted as meaning that had the act of injustice not taken place, it is highly unlikely that a given sperm would have fertilized a given egg. But it is not *impossible* that this could have occurred, nonetheless. We could tell a hypothetical story whereby the same sperm united with the same egg, even if conditions for conception were different. Even if the act of injustice meant, for example, that the parents of a given child were relocated from one area to another, and were unlikely to have met had the act of injustice not taken place, we cannot say, for certain, that this could not have happened, even if we have to tell an extremely implausible story in order to describe how it could have happened. What is clear is that such a story would not be the most likely outcome, in the absence of the unjust action. It is not the most probable counterfactual, in the absence of injustice. But is this in fact how we use counterfactuals within compensatory justice?

It is useful here to look at the account of harm to others put forward by Joel Feinberg. In his article, 'Wrongful life and the counterfactual element in harming', Feinberg writes of harming as having two components: '(1) it must lead to some kind of adverse effect, or create the danger of such an effect, on its victim's *interests*; and (2) it must be inflicted wrongfully in violation of the victim's *rights*.'[18] Feinberg contrasts this particular notion of harm with the broader, ordinary use of harm referring to any state of adversely affected interest, whatever its cause. Certainly, insofar as we are here concerned with the unjust actions of agents, it is this prior sense of harm which is relevant. Feinberg holds that it is a necessary condition for A to be said to harm B that the 'counterfactual test' is met. In its original formulation, this reads as follows:

> B's personal interest is in a worse condition (usually but not always lower on the interest graph) than it would be in had A not acted as he did.

This is contrasted with what Feinberg calls the 'worsening test' (not a necessary condition for showing harm) which requires that:

> B's personal interest is in a worse condition (lower on the interest graph) than it was before A acted.

The point here is obviously significant for our purposes. Feinberg is maintaining that a person can be harmed by an action even though that person is better off than they would have been had the action not been performed. He cites cases of causal overdetermination, where the harm a victim suffers as a result of an act of injustice is actually less than the harm they would have suffered had the offender not so acted (for example, a businessman is injured in an accident caused by the reckless conduct of his taxi driver, but as a result misses an aeroplane flight which in fact crashes).[19] Feinberg suggests that we consider a 'doubly counterfactual' formulation in such cases.[20] Is it necessarily the case that there is no possible world whereby the businessman is neither harmed by the taxi driver nor dies in the plane crash? It seems not: we can imagine a world where the car accident does not occur, but where the businessman does not catch the plane for some other reason, or where the plane does not crash. It may well be clear that 'the most probable outcome if the injuring act had not occurred' would be that the businessman would indeed have caught his plane. Yet this is not the counterfactual we choose to use in our everyday experience of compensatory justice. It is certainly clear that the taxi driver would not be able to use the fact of the aeroplane's crash as a defence against the charge of negligence. The fact that his actions, in all probability, saved the businessman's life does not affect his compensatory duties. As various writers note, it is commonplace to accept that an individual can be owed compensation when an unjust act illegitimately sets back one of her interests, even if the action in question does not cause her a net harm.[21] James Woodward makes such a claim:

> ...people have relatively specific interests (e.g. in having promises kept, in avoiding bodily injury, in getting their fair share) that are not simply reducible to some general interest in maintaining a high overall level of well-being and...many moral requirements function so as to protect against violations of such specific interests. That an action will cause an increase in someone's overall level of well-being is not always an adequate response to the claim that such a specific interest has been violated.[22]

For some, this claim is sufficient to allow the rectificatory project to resist the non-identity problem. So Cécile Fabre writes:

> ...the fact that someone has not been harmed overall by a particular act does not preclude the possibility that he has been harmed along a particular dimension. Thus, even if existing Maoris have not been harmed overall by the act of dispossession of which their ancestors were victims, they may nevertheless have been harmed by it....[23]

The important point for our current purposes is the claim that when it comes to the identification of the morally relevant counterfactual, we do not in fact necessarily look to the most probable outcome in the absence of the act of injustice. Instead, it may be possible to construct a different counterfactual, in order to calculate what compensation is owed in response to a violation of a specific interest. To be clear, in some cases it might be highly improbable that this situation would ever have come about, but it still constitutes the morally relevant counterfactual.

This is evidently significant in terms of claims relating to colonialism. In general terms, the conventional account of compensatory justice is inadequate for dealing with questions relating to exploitation, insofar as this involves using other agents as means to one's material ends, in ways which contravene their rights. As the Counterfactual Observation observed, it may often be the case that exploitative actions leave the victims of injustice better off than they would have been had the act of exploitation never occurred. Consider the familiar dilemma faced by many critics of the business practices of multinational corporations. Such companies seek to cut costs and maximize profits by employing extremely cheap labour in developing countries. Defenders of such practices point out that the position of the workers in question is actually improved by the presence of these companies, in that the people who work for them are actually better off than would be the case if these companies were not present.[24] But this does not seem to be the relevant counterfactual to consider in cases of exploitation. This can be understood by thinking about the second of the problematic aspects of the identification of the morally relevant counterfactual: the characterization of the unjust act. What, exactly, do we mean when we say 'the act of injustice did not occur'?

There is more than one just counterfactual to an act of injustice than the simple non-performance of the act in question. Instead, the act might be performed in a different, just way.[25] If I steal an item from a shop, I act unjustly. One account of the unjust act not occurring describes the case when I do not pick up the object at all. Another account describes the case when I pay for the item. The characterization of the injustice, in some cases, is deeply significant. Consider the following example. A is an impoverished farmer in a rural area with no dependents, who barely scrapes by and manages to grow enough food to support himself. B is a wealthy entrepreneur, who has recently acquired a (rather dangerous) underground diamond mine. He has no desire to go and mine the diamonds himself, so he kidnaps A and forces him to work in his mine for five years. At the end of this period, B has made a huge sum of money. He releases A, who returns home. During the course of his captivity, A has been taught a number of new skills, which allow him to get a better job. Does B owe A compensation? We would surely think so. But how is this to be measured? I would suggest that the relevant counterfactual here to the exploitation of A is not the possible world whereby B does not approach A at all, and consequently leaves his diamonds unmined, but rather that whereby A agrees to come and work for B in return for a fair wage, which reflects the dangerous nature of the work he is undertaking and, perhaps, the vast wealth which he is generating for A.[26] To be clear, this does not simply mean that B pays A the wage he would have earned had the transaction been consensual. We use this point as the counterfactual baseline, and then see how much worse off A is in the real world, given not just his wealth but his general well-being. B may well owe A massive amounts of compensation for the suffering he has undergone relative to this baseline. The point here is that identifying the relevant counterfactual means that B cannot offset the benefit which accrues to A incidentally in the course of his exploitation. This outcome fits in with the account of compensatory justice which requires that we look to a counterfactual whereby the act of injustice did not take place. However, it does not assume that the only way this can come about is by nothing resembling the unjust act taking place, as a result of the agent who acts unjustly not acting at all. Instead it suggests that the relevant counterfactual is that whereby the act of injustice does not take place because the agent acts in a similar way, but does so in accordance with justice. Both of these alternatives represent a just action. In one case, the agent does not interact with others. In the other, she interacts in a justifiable way.

It is my contention that it is this latter approach which is most useful when considering historic injustice such as colonialism. As a matter of fact, there has been a considerable degree of interaction between nations. The relevant counterfactual world is one in which this emerged as a result of consensual cooperation, in accordance with the principles of just international interaction, rather than by unjust actions on the part of the developed world. Once this is understood, we have a test for assessing whether modern day political communities are suffering or benefiting from historical injustice. In opposition to the Counterfactual Observation, the question which needs to be asked is: 'Would current generations be better off had historic interaction between colonial powers and their colonies been characterized by consensual and non-exploitative relations?' The important point here is quite how different this question is from that which is normally asked, which is along the lines of 'Would current generations be better off had there been no interaction between colonial powers and their colonies?' It should be clear that the baseline in the former case is much higher than the baseline in the latter case. Insofar as this is not recognized and the latter baseline is the one which is employed, a significant conceptual error is typically made in political debate on this issue.

In the above example, the relevant counterfactual was identified largely through intuitive deduction. It was suggested that it was simply unfair in cases of exploitation to apply the conventional account of counterfactual harm and benefit. This approach reflects Sher's account of how the relevant counterfactual should be identified. He argues for a normative conception of the morally relevant counterfactual, whereby what is considered is what the victim of injustice *should* have in a rectified world. He points out that it is not in fact necessarily the case that we believe that victims of injustice should be entitled to what they would have in a rectified world, to the extent that this overlooks the actions which they would have to perform in the rectified world to gain these entitlements; actions which they have not, in fact, performed. Sher uses the example of a student who is unjustly denied a place in law school. Had this not occurred, then the student would have become a prominent lawyer with a high degree of prestige and a high salary. Instead, he allows himself to be discouraged by his rejection and does not reapply the next year, and so has a far inferior life. Sher suggests that there are two reasons why we might not feel that he should be entitled to compensation relative to what he would in fact have had in the just world.[27] The first of these refers to what Sher calls 'the degree to which one's entitlements in a rectified world are generated anew by one's own actions there.'[28] Obviously, it would require a great deal of hard work to become a successful lawyer. Consider the following example. Three men, A, B, and C are all diamond miners (this time, of their own free will). Again, they have no family. One day, A is kidnapped, and held prisoner for twenty years. The format of his prison is somewhat unusual, as he is kept in a luxury hotel, with access to a wide range of recreational activities. He is released after twenty years. In the course of these twenty years, B and C have become very rich through working in the diamond mine. However, they have had to work exceedingly hard to earn this money – the work involves a huge amount of physical effort. Assuming that all three are in equally good health, their different lifestyles notwithstanding, there does seem to be something unfair about the suggestion that A is entitled to the level of resources he would have had he not been kidnapped. Certainly he is entitled to something, but in the absence of the backbreaking effort of the other two, it does not seem to be the full equivalent of what he would otherwise have had.[29]

The second way in which entitlement seems to come into the picture concerns the subsequent actions of victims of injustice. Sher's point is that one of the reasons that the well-being of a victim might be inferior to that which she would have had in a world where no injustice had taken place may not be because of the 'automatic effects' of the act of injustice, but rather because of omissions for which they, and not the act of injustice, are responsible. An extreme example will make the point: suppose that one day, when I am walking to the shops, I encounter my childhood nemesis, the boy who bullied me at school. Reverting to type, he trips me up and I fall over. As a result of this, I decide that the world is against me, and I elect to spend the rest of my days skulking in my house brooding upon my misfortune, instead of pursuing my successful career as a popular circus performer. Now, in such a case I have been treated unjustly, but the vast majority of the blame for the difference between my actual and counterfactual positions seems to lie at my door. The suggestion is that I have allowed a trivial incident to blight my life; in short, I should have got over it. Thus the difference between actual and counterfactual worlds is down to my omissions, and the normative counterfactual – what I 'should' have – is not the same as what I would actually have had the unjust action in question never occurred.

So far, all this seems correct. Sher, however, goes on to link this explicitly to compensation for historic wrongs, claiming:

> Where the initial wrong was done many hundreds of years ago, almost all of the difference between the victim's entitlements in the actual world and his entitlements in a rectified world can be expected to stem from the actions of various intervening agents in the two alternative worlds. Little or none of it will be the automatic effect of the initial wrong itself. Since compensation is warranted only for disparities in entitlements which *are* the automatic effect of the initial wrong act, this means that there will be little or nothing left to compensate for.[30]

The first point to make about this claim, as Simmons notes, is that it does not necessarily say that automatic effects of injustice *cannot* last over long periods of time, simply that the necessary conditions of entitlement in fact become harder to satisfy the more time passes.[31] Furthermore, while Sher's claim about the likely effects of historic injustice may seem convincing within a domestic setting, it is not clear that the same can be said for the kind of international injustice currently under consideration. First, as was pointed out in Section 4.1, there are reasons to suppose that the effects of international injustice may be hard for victims to counter, in that it is hard to acquire alternative entitlements once one has been unjustly deprived of large quantities of one's natural resources and/or is at a competitive trading disadvantage relative to other nations. Secondly, we should be careful when blaming the lingering effects of historic injustice on the omissions of the victims not to underestimate the profound impact which injustice can have upon its victims, even when they do make reasonable efforts to 'get over' its effects. Of relevance here are Jeremy Waldron's comments as to the significance of historic wrongs to national and group identity.[32] Insofar as international injustice compromises the self-determination of a people, it can have a profound effect upon the national identity of members of the nation, and may indeed prejudice the ability of the nation to govern itself subsequent to the act of injustice.[33] A great deal of colonial practice was aimed explicitly at subjugating pre-existing ideas of communal identity; often, traditional cultural practices and traditions were repressed and identifiable communities were split asunder. Insofar as the ability of nations to adapt and prosper following the colonial period has been a result of colonial practices, the extent to which they should be deemed responsible for their omissions must be accordingly limited. Finally, it should be pointed out that the first claim identified above, whereby one only acquires entitlements through actual performance of actions, has only a limited amount to say in relation to circumstances of exploitation, given that the objection is that the victims of injustice have not received their due deserts for actions they have indeed performed. I would suggest that the combination of these three observations limits the extent to which we should feel that the passage of time means that the automatic effects of justice are necessarily lessened.

Finally in this section, we may note that this approach does allow for the application of Simmons's response to the non-identity problem. As has been stated, Simmons denies that it is necessarily true that significant acts of injustice which affect individuals' interaction make a difference as to who it is that exists. His claim is that it is possible for the same offspring to be conceived in a counterfactual state where the act of injustice did not take place as in the real world; it is just highly unlikely. Thus, we could imagine situations where the same sperm ends up uniting with the same egg, meaning that the same person is conceived in both the real world and the possible world, which in turn allows for the assessment of loss and subsequent claims for compensation to be made in relation to historic injustice. Sher has criticized this conclusion, arguing that, 'even if we substitute a criterion that *does* allow possible worlds that lack the original wrong but nevertheless contain the victims' current descendants, the relevance of such worlds to compensation will remain problematic if they are sufficiently remote from the actual world'.[34] Sher's concern here is with very serious acts of injustice which involve social upheaval and the relocation of persons, such as the slave trade or the Holocaust. If we imagine a world where these injustices did not take place, so as to construct a counterfactual for compensatory purposes, then it seems as if we will have to tell very improbable stories as to what could have happened in order to have the same parents conceiving the same children. Sher argues that there is no single obvious way to construct such counterfactuals, which means that it is hard to see why we should afford moral weight to whatever narrative we devise. Given that individuals will seemingly be due differing amounts of compensation depending on the precise counterfactual which is set up, Sher's concern is that whether people are owed compensation may be 'radically indeterminate'. It is not immediately clear how much weight to attach to this objection. Compensatory justice frequently has to deal with serious indeterminacy. Suppose a healthy young child suffers an accident which leaves her with a serious mental disability, which will prevent her ever gaining paid employment. How are we to compensate her for her loss of earnings, given that we have no idea what profession she would have followed? We obviously cannot know what is the correct counterfactual to employ, but we are nonetheless required by justice to make the best approximation we can. Regardless, we might note here is that such worries typically do not apply to cases of the kind that we are examining. Given that our counterfactual includes a similar form of interaction to the real world, but holds that it should in fact have been just in character, it is much more straightforward to describe a counterfactual where the same parents conceive the same children. It is, of course, highly improbable that they would have conceived the exact same individuals in the counterfactual world as they did in the actual world, but, as the earlier argument maintained, we do not need to rely on probabilistic outcomes here.

In conclusion, in this section I have accepted the claim that, to assess harm following injustice, it is necessary to compare the current day with some kind of counterfactual. This is done by imagining a possible world where no injustice occurred. However, there are many such possible worlds, as there are many possible kinds of interaction between the victim and offender which do not involve injustice. One possible world is the world where the act of injustice simply did not take place, understood in terms of an absence of interaction between victim and offender, and a projection as to what would most likely have happened is made on the basis of probability. However, it has been shown that this approach can, in some cases, result in wildly unintuitive outcomes, both in terms of its use of probability and the way it characterizes the act of injustice. Such counterfactual reasoning does not take account of actual actions which have been performed, and entitlements which have been generated. In cases where the victim and offender have had frequent interaction following the act of injustice, the best way to characterize the morally relevant counterfactual is by reference to a possible world where all the interaction between the relevant parties was just and consensual. If an act of injustice has truly not had lasting consequences, this possible world should now be very similar to the real world. But if injustice has had a significant causal effect on the subsequent interaction of the two parties, even though the victim has not reacted unreasonably to the injustice in question, we may well find that, relative to the morally relevant counterfactual, present day parties have either gained or lost as a result of historic injustice. Section 4.4 is concerned with this situation.

4.3 COUNTERFACTUALS AND RELATIONAL JUSTICE

This approach to the assessment of morally relevant counterfactuals can be used to cast some light on a dispute within the literature on international justice. As noted previously, in *Political Theory and International*

Relations Charles Beitz argued that, given (*a*) the character of Rawls's relational account of distributive justice, and (*b*) the empirical reality of the international economic order, Rawlsian principles of distributive justice should be applied not (as Rawls would have it) within particular societies, but across national boundaries to the world as a whole. Thus Beitz claimed that 'the membership of the original position should be global rather than national because national societies are not, in fact, self-sufficient; the system of global trade and investment, organized within a structure of international institutions and conventions, constitutes a scheme of social cooperation in Rawls's sense.'[35]

Beitz's conclusion here has been challenged by Brian Barry and Christopher Brown, who both argue that regardless of the extent of interdependence, interaction between states lacks the right character to make the global system the kind of scheme of social cooperation to which Rawls refers. As Brown argues,

> ...even making allowances for subsequent deepening of interdependence since the late 1970s when Beitz wrote, it remains the case that the present world system cannot plausibly be defined as a co-operative venture for *mutual advantage* which...is the definition of society Rawls employs to get his schema under way. Possibly parts of the advanced industrial world could be seen in this way – the European Union for example – but it would be a particularly enthusiastic neo-liberal who argued that this applies across the board to all interactions between rich and poor. The alternative view that the rich are exploiting the poor makes it difficult to argue that the kind of reciprocity involved in Rawls's definition of a society can apply at the global level.[36]

Brian Barry argues in similar fashion:

> Beitz's argument for extending the Rawlsian difference principle is in essence that the network of international trade is sufficiently extensive to draw all countries together in a single cooperative scheme. But it seems to be that trade, however multilateral, does not constitute a cooperative scheme of the relevant kind.[37]

Whether these criticisms are sufficient in undermine Beitz's account of cosmopolitanism in *Political Theory and International Relations* is an open question.[38] Caney argues that Beitz's own theory only requires that groups of people be 'interconnected in some way, even if that interconnection is not mutually beneficial or cooperative': thus Beitz writes, 'the requirements of justice apply to institutions and practices (whether or not they are genuinely cooperative) in which social activity produces relative or absolute benefits of burdens that would not exist if the social activity did not take place'.[39] Leaving this issue to one side, let us focus on the claim that principles of distributive justice apply if and only if interaction and interdependence has a particular cooperative character. This claim leads to a problematic conclusion when we consider unjust forms of international interaction, such as colonialism. It appears to be the case that if political communities are interdependent upon one another as a result of just interaction, then their interdependence constitutes mutually advantageous cooperation, and transnational principles of distributive justice apply to them. But insofar as their relations have been characterized by exploitation, that is, by injustice, no such entitlement to a fair share of the product of the societies is created. The outcome is that present day states owe less to other states because they treated them wrongly in the past than they would do had they acted in accordance with the principles of justice.

The insight which the foregoing account of compensatory justice provides is that the question to be asked is not whether international relations *are* characterized by mutually beneficial cooperation. Instead we should ask whether, given contemporary levels of development, historic interaction between nations *should* have been characterized by mutual cooperation. If the relevant counterfactual here is one whereby historic interaction was not in fact exploitative but was consensual, and if we hold that mutually beneficial cooperation is the condition which triggers duties of distributive justice, then it may well be that, historically, colonies were wronged by being excluded from the domestic sphere of distributive justice. So if, for example, one is an egalitarian at a domestic level, one would presumably have to conclude that an injustice was done to historic colonies when resources were not redistributed so that all individuals in both the colonial powers and the former colonies had an equal distribution of resources. If this is indeed the case, then modern day compensatory duties to non-nationals may be colossal.[40]

4.4 BENEFITING FROM INJUSTICE

We have established the morally relevant sense in which modern day parties might be said to be benefiting or suffering as a result of historic international injustice. It still remains to be shown, however, that anything follows from a recognition that this is indeed so in a given case. This section examines the question of whether agents can acquire moral obligations as a result of involuntarily benefiting from the unjust actions of others.[41] As such, it retains the current methodological assumption of treating modern day agents as innocent third parties in relation to historic injustice. I start by considering David Miller's article 'Distributing responsibilities'[42] which focuses on the distribution of duties of assistance, in cases where it is accepted that someone ought to provide assistance to those in need but where it is controversial upon whom the costs of assistance should fall. Miller proposes four morally relevant forms of connection with the victims of injustice which can give rise to moral obligations to assist; I propose that benefiting from events which led to the plight of those in desperate need, however involuntarily, constitutes an additional morally relevant form of connection. I proceed to argue that moral agents can possess compensatory obligations as a result of involuntarily benefiting from injustice even when the victims of injustice do not need to be lifted above some minimal threshold level of well-being.

4.4.1 Benefit and Duties of Assistance

In 'Distributing responsibilities', David Miller seeks to address what he calls 'the problem of remedial responsibility', which he defines as follows:

> To be remedially responsible for a bad situation means to have a special obligation to put the bad situation right, in other words to be picked out, either individually or along with others, as having a responsibility towards the deprived or suffering party that is not shared equally among all agents.[43]

As we have seen, Miller's account of just international interaction adopts further principles which both forbid exploitation and establish duties of assistance in terms of resource transfers. In *On Nationality* he outlines a theory of basic rights with correlative obligations regardless of nationality. These are principally conceived of as rights to forbearance, 'but may also include rights to provision, for example in cases where a natural shortage of resources means that people will starve or suffer bodily injury if others do not provide for them'.[44] As such, the kinds of 'bad situation' he has in mind are those where individuals or groups are below some minimal threshold of well-being, such as Iraqi children who are malnourished and lack access to proper medical care. In such cases, Miller supposes that it is not in question whether the situation requires a remedy, given that it is possible that a remedy could be given; the interesting question is who it is that should do the remedying (in the absence of an institutional mechanism for formally assigning responsibility). His aim is to find a principle, or set of principles, for assigning this responsibility 'which carries moral weight, so that we can say that agents who fail to discharge their remedial responsibilities act wrongly and may properly be sanctioned.'[45] His methodology here makes explicit reference to our existing intuitive beliefs as to who it is that properly bears these responsibilities: his aim is to 'lay out principles for distributing responsibilities that we hope will command widespread agreement'.[46] He considers four different approaches that seemingly find support in the real world: based upon causal responsibility for the occurrence of the condition, on moral responsibility for the occurrence of the condition, on capacity for remedying the condition, and on communal obligations to the affected party or parties. He concludes that no single approach can give a full account of who should remedy the situation in any given situation – using a single principle results in intuitively unpalatable outcomes. Instead, he argues for a 'connection theory', whereby any of the four relations listed above may establish a sufficiently strong link between parties to allocate remedial responsibility. Which principle is to be invoked in a given case will depend upon its particular characteristics, so that 'when connections have to be weighed against each other, we can do no more than appeal to our shared moral intuitions about which is the stronger.'[47] In this section I accept the idea of the connection theory, but argue for a fifth possible ground for the acquisition of remedial responsibility, specifically that of receiving benefits from the occurrence in question. My claim is that it is possible to think of cases where this form of connection seems intuitively to give rise to remedial responsibilities, even though other forms of connection, as listed by Miller, are also present.

Consider the following example. Four people, A, B, C, and D live on a remote island, each one possessing one-quarter of the land. All four are entirely self-sufficient, and their landholdings are separated by high fences. There is little or no contact between the four. The only crop which will grow on the island is the extremely versatile Polychrestos plant, whose root can be used to produce a wide variety of different dishes, as well as providing raw materials for clothing and other household essentials. The Polychrestos plant's root grows underground and is harvested each autumn, and must not be disturbed at any other part of the year. Although this means that the size of the crop will only be revealed at harvest time, the climate on the island is extremely constant, and the island's underground river distributes water evenly throughout the island's soil. Nonetheless, the Polychrestos plant is a high maintenance crop; and the size of the underground portion of the plant therefore is strictly correlated to the amount of care the overground portion of the plant receives. In order for each person to support herself, she must produce 200 kilos of root per year. A is a very hard-working, industrious type, whose agricultural efforts, from dawn to dusk each day, mean that she produces 700 kilos per annum, allowing her to eat very well and produce a wide range of leisure products. B, C, and D are rather laid-back in their approach to agriculture, and work just five hours a day to produce the minimum 200 kilos a year. After a year of this, however, D, a rather unsavoury character, decides she does not want to work even five hours each day. Unknown to all the others, she diverts the underground river away from B and C's sections of land, so that her land receives all of their water, boosting, she hopes, her own crop considerably. When harvest time comes, there are a number of surprises. A harvests her regulation 700 kilos. C's land has had no water, and consequently she has no crop. She is destitute, despite her efforts over the past year. It also emerges that D (no water engineer) has in fact diverted the water away from her own land as well as that of C, and B, far from having a failed crop, has been the beneficiary. To her surprise, she harvests 400 kilos. D is also destitute, and in rage and despair hangs herself with a rope fashioned from the last of the previous year's Polychrestos crop. This leaves the problem of C. Without her year's produce, C will die unless A and B provide her with the necessary 200 kilos. How should the remedial responsibilities be distributed? There appear to be no ties of community between the individuals, and neither is either causally or morally responsible for C's fate – that responsibility, in both senses, lies with D. This seems to leave us only with capacity – who is better placed to remedy C's situation? Either A or B could transfer the necessary 200 kilos to C, while retaining at least 200 kilos themselves, but evidently A's extra level of resources mean that her capacity is the greater. As such, on Miller's account, A has the greater connection to C and bears the remedial responsibility. Yet such a conclusion seems intuitively objectionable. Miller notes of the capacity approach that, 'its exclusive focus on the present necessarily blinds it to historical considerations'[48] – it does not consider how the resources which are to be redistributed came about. In this case, D's actions conferred benefits upon B. Should we not hold that B's improved position, which has come about as a direct result of C's worsened position, constitutes just the sort of 'morally relevant relation' between parties which might be considered when we ask who should bear remedial responsibilities?

Thus, one could formulate the following claim in relation to remedial responsibilities:

If the events which cause agent C to fall below the morally relevant threshold confer benefits upon agent B, then the fact of the receipt of these benefits, however involuntary, establishes a morally relevant connection between C and B, which may give rise to remedial obligations on the part of B.

It is key that the claim only states that receipt of benefits *may* give rise to remedial obligations. As with Miller's four other forms of morally relevant connection, in cases where more than one party is relevantly connected to the suffering agent we must use our moral intuitions to determine either which party bears the primary responsibility, or how the costs should be shared amongst different parties. My claim in this section is simply that benefiting constitutes a fifth form of morally relevant connection to go alongside Miller's existing four, which may give rise to remedial responsibilities in certain circumstances.[49] This improves the existing typology in two ways. The first is that it responds directly to the problems that Miller cites with the capacity problem, in that it identifies a class of resources which may be available for remedying a situation – those which have arisen elsewhere as a result of that situation – which do not have a problematic history, in that it is hard to link them to their present owners by any kind of desert claim. But furthermore, there are independent moral reasons for supposing that some such resources should be redistributed. It is not so much that they represent a class of neutral resources which can be safely redistributed, as that, insofar as they represent the 'fruits of injustice', they may be seen as distortions within the overall scheme of distribution. This can be seen by examining Miller's account of when it is that different relations amongst the four he identifies become relevant in determining remedial responsibility. It is not always the case that this allocation of responsibility should turn on, for example, the extent to which different parties can effectively remedy the situation, and the costs they will bear in doing so. Thus in some cases there are 'independent moral reasons' for assigning remedial responsibility to a particular agent, and this applies most obviously when A is morally responsible for P's injury, when there may be two such reasons. These essentially stem from the idea of rectificatory (or corrective) justice. The first of these is that:

> Where A has unjustly benefited from the injury he has inflicted on P – he has stolen something of P's or exploited him, for example – then if A is made to compensate P by returning what he has taken or in some way undoing the damage he has inflicted, then this will help to cancel out A's unjust gain, and so restore justice between them.[50]

Second, even if A has not benefited from his actions, he has wronged P, and owes P compensation. Our concern here is with the first of these reasons. We need not think that the only circumstances where a party enjoys an 'unjust gain' are those whereby she gains as a result of acting unjustly. In a legal context, for example, the category of 'unjust enrichment by subtraction' within the law of restitution is principally concerned with those circumstances whereby injustice in distribution arises despite the absence of wrongdoing; in the case, for example, of a mistaken payment.[51] It is possible to see the changes in distribution that emerge as a result of injustice as (to use Nickel's term) 'distortions' in the overall scheme of distribution, even if the party who has benefited has acted legitimately and has not committed any wrongdoing. Such cases may be seen as falling squarely within the preserve of corrective justice, defined by Nickel as, 'the matter of people having those things that they deserve and are entitled to, or otherwise ought to have.' He further claims that compensation serves justice by preventing and undoing actions that would prevent people from having those things'.[52] Such an approach claims that compensation serves an Aristotelian conception of justice as the maintenance of an equilibrium of goods between members of society.[53] If corrective justice is seen in this way, then, as Coleman writes, 'rectification... is a matter of justice when it is necessary to protect a distribution of holdings (or entitlements) from distortions which arise from unjust enrichments and wrongful losses. The principle of corrective justice requires the annulments of both wrongful gains and losses.'[54] The claim here, then, is that insofar as a third party directly benefits from unjust action and the victim suffers, a distortion in the fair scheme of distribution is created. Insofar as pinning remedial obligations on benefiting third parties seeks to correct this distortion, it appears that we have independent moral reasons for the allocation of responsibilities.

One further complication must be noted at this point. So far, reference has been made to benefits which have been *conferred* on B. The aim here is to identify the extent to which B's improvement, which has the occurrence of the act of injustice as a necessary component, may be seen as an automatic effect of the act of injustice. In the Polychrestos case above, the improvement in B's position was precisely of this kind; she can have no claim to her extra 200 kilos based on anything approximating desert. But the situation is more complicated when a third party benefits from an injustice, in that her position is better following the injustice than it would have been had the injustice not occurred, but part of the reason for this difference stems from her own actions. For example, suppose that, in the preceding example, B could tell that her Polychrestos plants were becoming healthier and growing faster. She wrongly supposes this to be a result of her own efforts, and is inspired by her progress to redouble her efforts, with the consequence that she produces 600 kilos of produce. Now, if we measure the degree of her benefit by simply comparing the current situation with the counterfactual situation where the unjust diversion of the river did not occur, we would conclude that B has benefited to the tune of 400 kilos, and this is the relevant amount which would be available for redistribution. Yet this seems unfair. The problem is again that of specifying the morally relevant counterfactual. As in Section 4.2, this is not done by crudely comparing what has happened with what would have happened and subtracting the one from the other, but rather looks at the extent to which the actions of the parties who have benefited from injustice have created new entitlements for themselves. It is the automatic effects of the act of injustice which ground remedial responsibility.

4.4.2 Benefit and the Effects of Injustice

It has been argued that the receipt of benefits – however involuntary – stemming from an act of injustice can confer remedial obligations upon a moral agent. The arguments put forward so far, however, apply only to a particular kind of remedial responsibility, namely responsibility for fulfilling duties of assistance. In such cases, it is a given that assistance should be given by someone, given an acceptance of the relevant further principle of just international interaction; the question is who it should be. But such 'bad situations' are not the only ones which may be thought to be in potential need of remedy. What of 'bad situations' where one party is wronged and harmed by another, but not so badly harmed as to fall below a minimal level of welfare sufficient to bring duties of assistance into play? Might a third party which benefits from the injustice in such cases potentially acquire compensatory obligations? In speaking of 'victims of injustice' here, I mean to refer to people who have been both wronged and harmed by the actions of another agent or agents. The 'bad situation' here is not defined in terms of some independently derived minimal level of welfare, an absolute criterion, but in relation to the morally relevant counterfactual as outlined in Section 4.2. If we assume that the harm suffered is not sufficient to bring the victim below our welfare threshold, then why should we believe that anyone not responsible for causing the harm should have obligations to remedy it?

The question is whether, within an account of distributive justice which is generally happy to allow individuals to suffer losses without requiring that others pay compensation to make up for their losses, such as international libertarianism the fact that an innocent third party has benefited from another's wrongdoing gives us a good reason to shift some or all of the victim's losses to the third party. It is my belief that we lack a coherent set of principles to answer this question. For example, having just cited a common law principle, it is interesting to see how different branches of legal theory cope with the problem. Mention has already been made of the concept of unjust enrichment under the law of restitution, according to which, it is maintained, the law protects one person from being unjustly enriched at another's expense. This seems clearly applicable to the present case, and yet the extent to which claims may be made under this general principle are (broadly speaking) limited to cases where one party has either freely accepted a particular benefit or has possession of or legal title to a particular item of property or sum of money to which another party has a strong moral entitlement. For reasons which will be discussed later, moves to claim that an agent might acquire obligations through the involuntary receipt of a benefit in kind are severely restricted. In the area of criminal law, a different approach is often taken to the subject of possessing stolen goods. If I have been given or have bought for a cheap price an item of stolen property in good faith, I may reasonably be said to have benefited from an act of injustice. The question of what should happen next varies for different kinds of property, and in different legal jurisdictions. In some cases, the beneficiary has to return the item, receiving no compensation even if she has purchased it in good faith. Clearly, this might leave the (one-time) beneficiary of an injustice paying the greatest price for the injustice, and being worse off than she was prior to the injustice. In other cases it is the victim who is held liable for these costs, and the beneficiary keeps the property in question.[55]

Given the variable legal treatment of the issue, we must look to its theoretical underpinning. The most common way that moral agents are said to acquire compensatory obligations is through what is sometimes called 'the fault principle'. In broad terms, this is the idea that those who are responsible for injuring other parties bear a moral responsibility to compensate the victims of their actions, precisely because it is their fault that the injuries in question occurred. Once it is established what would compensate the injured party, the guilty party has a moral obligation to so act, insofar as they are able to do so. Evidently, this is the understanding of moral responsibility discussed by Miller in the previous section, and, as before, it seems clear that this should generally be the primary response to acts of injustice and is in most cases the ideal response. What of circumstances, however, where the parties who were actually responsible for the act of injustice do not or cannot fulfil their obligations? For some writers this is the end of the matter, and any suggestion of the acquisition of compensatory obligations without fault is simply unacceptable. Thus O'Neill writes:

> ...some laissez faire liberals are dubious about rights to compensation except where the individuals who inflicted wrong are identifiable and obliged to compensate for the injuries they inflicted. On such views rights to compensation are symmetrical with rights to punish, in that they are absent when there is no wrongdoer, or no identifiable wrongdoer. Just compensation presupposes an injuring as well as an injured party.[56]

As it stands, such a position is too strong, as it rules out the possibility that non-offenders may acquire compensatory obligations through prior agreements that one party will cover another's losses in the event of them suffering particular harms. This may be either as a result of a contractual arrangement, as in the case of buying insurance, or simply as a result of a promise or commitment, such as when a government sets up an agency to compensate victims of crime for their injuries. Such schemes are not normally seen as justifiable if they actually allow the offender to escape responsibility, but rather act as a safety net to compensate victims should they not receive their due from the offender. Thus, for example, car insurance should not protect one from a conviction for dangerous driving, nor from subsequent claims for damages, but covers one for accidental harm one causes and for any harms one may suffer through accident or the fault of others. This is simply a case of a special obligation, of the same nature as a promise. As such, the obligation is essentially voluntaristic.

The issue becomes controversial, then, when it is claimed compensatory obligations can be acquired involuntarily. The question of the involuntary receipt of benefits has been explicitly invoked in the context of discussions of the normative justifications of reverse discrimination as a compensatory response to injustice. A frequently cited example comes from the writing of Judith Jarvis Thomson. She concedes that practices of reverse discrimination in hiring impose costs upon the (say) white males who are affected by them, but she argues that this is not necessarily unjust:

> ...of course choosing this way of making amends means that the costs are imposed on the young male applicants who are turned away. And so it should be noticed that it is not entirely inappropriate that those applicants should pay the costs. No doubt few, if any, have, themselves, individually, done any wrongs to blacks and women. But they have profited from the wrongs the community did. Many may actually have been direct beneficiaries of policies which excluded or downgraded blacks and women – perhaps in school admissions, perhaps elsewhere; and even those who did not directly benefit in this way had, at any rate, the advantage in the competition which comes of confidence in one's full membership, and of one's rights being recognized as a matter of course.[57]

The principle at stake seems to be that, by benefiting from an act of injustice, one can acquire obligations towards the victims of that injustice. This is not an uncontroversial conclusion, and it has been strongly criticized by Robert Fullinwider. Fullinwider claims that the passage cited above reflects a particular moral principle, 'he who benefits from a wrong must help pay for the wrong'.[58] Fullinwider claims that this is 'surely suspect as an acceptable moral principle', suggesting that only 'he who wrongs another shall pay for the wrong' is justifiable as a principle of compensatory justice.[59] To illustrate his case he uses the following example:

> While I am away on vacation, my neighbour contracts with a construction company to repair his driveway. He instructs the workers to come to his address, where they will find a note describing the driveway to be repaired. An enemy of my neighbor, aware, somehow, of this arrangement, substitutes for my neighbor's instructions a note describing *my* driveway. The construction crew, having been paid in advance, shows up on the appointed day while my neighbor is at work, finds the letter, and faithfully following the instructions paves my driveway.[60]

It is clear that in this case the neighbour is a victim of his enemy's unjust act, and has a valid claim against him. But what is to be done in the absence of the enemy? Fullinwider rejects the conclusion, which he believes follows from the principle of compensatory justice he attributes to Thomson, that I am obliged to pay my neighbour for his driveway, contending that to do so would constitute an act of moral supererogation; a laudable act certainly, but not one which is required by a moral obligation. The key point for Fullinwider is that the receipt of the benefit in this case is *involuntary*. Perhaps the situation is different with regard to those who willingly accept benefits stemming from injustice: 'If I knowingly and voluntarily benefit from wrongs done to others, though I do not commit the wrong myself, then perhaps it is true to say that I am less than innocent of these wrongs, and perhaps it is morally fitting that I bear some of the costs of compensation.'[61] But those who involuntarily receive benefits bear no compensatory obligations.

This takes us to the heart of the issue. Is Fullinwider right about the involuntary receipt of benefits? It seems to me that he is not, and that the power of his example derives from a confusion over how extensive compensatory obligations stemming from injustice should be.

So let us return to the driveway. The crucial question here seems to stem from my attitude towards my newly resurfaced driveway. Let us suppose that the driveway cost my neighbour £500. I have not, however, benefited financially, as the resurfacing has added no value to my property.[62] But let us also assume that I have indeed derived overall benefit from the experience, in that I prefer my new driveway to my old one. This is not to say, of course, that I would necessarily have been willing to pay £500 to have it resurfaced. Let us suppose that, had the driveway resurfacer knocked on my door the day before and offered to resurface my driveway for £500, I would have refused.[63] Asking me to pay £500 in this circumstance does seem unfair, since to do so would leave me worse off than I would be had the whole experience not taken place. I would, in truth, have become the victim of the piece. But this is not the only alternative open to us. Imagine that the driveway resurfacer had in fact offered to do my driveway for £200. This is considerably below the going rate, and I may well have leapt at the opportunity. If this was indeed the case, and I am correspondingly (at least) £200 better off on the basis of my own evaluation, then is it unreasonable to say that I should pay £200 to my neighbour? After all, I am still benefiting from the whole transaction; to use economic terminology, I am on a higher utility curve than before. We may well think that I do not (necessarily) owe my neighbour £500, but it does not necessarily follow from this that I owe him nothing at all. Certainly I am innocent of wrongdoing towards him at this point. But might it not be that our moral relationship, the balance between the two of us, will be altered if I materially benefit from my neighbour's unrectified experience of injustice without making any effort to offset his losses?

Fullinwider's example seems initially powerful due to its 'all or nothing' character. One can have compensatory obligations to X, however, without having an obligation to compensate X fully. Thomson's point in relation to affirmative action, if it is to succeed, must be that the situation of white males even after policies of affirmative action have been put into place is better than it would have been had past and recent injustice not occurred; they derive a net benefit from their social position even when such policies have been enacted. Clearly, the principle 'he who benefits from a wrong shall pay for the wrong', which Fullinwider initially attributes to Thomson, is a nonsense, given that the benefit one receives from the wrong might be marginal, whereas the cost of paying for it might be monumental. So the compensatory obligations of the beneficiaries of injustice can be limited to paying compensation up to the point where they are no longer beneficiaries of the injustice in question. Nor is it necessarily the case that a beneficiary need pay anything at all, given that other parties (most notably, the agent responsible for the act in question) may have prior obligations which fully compensate the victims, leaving no work for the beneficiary to do.[64] Insofar as the receipt of benefits does give rise to a principle, it can only be as demanding as, 'she who benefits from a wrong may have obligations to (help to) pay for the wrong, insofar as doing so does not leave her worse off than had the wrong not occurred'. Interestingly, this follows closely a parallel argument within the literature on political obligation over the extent to which the involuntary receipt of benefits provided by the state can ground obligations to obey the law. Jonathan Wolff, for example, disputes the extent to which this can be the case on the basis that, for some people, the benefits the state provides are not worth the price the state extracts: i.e. acceptance of political obligations. Thus he writes concerning the fairness account of political obligation:

> ...a revised account does not appeal to the idea that the mere receipt of benefits is sufficient to create obligations...Rather obligations are generated for an individual only if an individual receives a *net* benefit according to his or her subjective scale of valuation.[65]

It is my contention that compensatory obligations can be generated in a similar fashion. Moral agents can have obligations to compensate victims of injustice if they are benefiting and the victims are suffering from the automatic effects of the act of injustice in question. It is crucial to the argument that the losses and benefits in question arise from injustice, which is to say wrongdoing by other agents.[66] The individual's duty not to benefit from another's suffering when that suffering is a result of injustice stems from one's moral condemnation of the unjust act itself. In consequence, a duty to disgorge (in compensation) the benefits one gains as a result of injustice follows from one's duty not to so benefit. My claim is that taking our nature as moral agents seriously requires not only that we be willing not to commit acts of injustice ourselves, but that we hold a genuine aversion to injustice and its lasting effects. We make a conceptual error if we condemn a given action as unjust, but are not willing to reverse or mitigate its effects on the grounds that it has benefited us. The refusal undermines the condemnation. The belief that certain acts are wrong and should not be performed on account of their harmful consequences commits one to endorse the application of rectificatory justice to seek to undo the effects of injustice, insofar as doing so does not render oneself a victim, by lowering oneself below the morally relevant counterfactual. Being a moral agent means being committed to the idea that justice should prevail over injustice. Losses which others suffer as a result of the unjust actions of other persons cannot be dismissed as arbitrary or simply unfortunate: they create distortions within the scheme of fair distribution. If no one else is willing or able to make up these losses, then the duty falls to those who are benefiting from the distortions in question.[67]

It is useful here to consider Janna Thompson's work on the nature of apologies for historic wrongs. Thompson's query is what it means to say that one is 'sorry' that a particular event occurred. She identifies what she calls, 'the apology paradox': if we owe our existence to a given act of injustice, and if we are happy that we are alive, how can we meaningfully say that we regret the act of injustice that brought our very existence about? And if we do not regret the act of injustice, how can we apologize for it? Thompson argues that we need to reinterpret what we are actually doing when we apologize for historic injustice:

> Many people feel uncomfortable or even apologetic about benefiting from an injustice even when they had no responsibility for it. They are sorry that the good things they now possess came to them because of a past injustice. They do not regret that they have these things, but that they came to have them in the way they did. An apology could be interpreted as an expression of this kind of regret. So interpreted it is not, strictly speaking, an apology *for* the deeds of our ancestors or an expression of regret that they happened. Rather, it is an apology *concerning* deeds of the past, and the regret expressed is that we owe our existence and other things we enjoy to the injustices of our ancestors. Our preference is for a possible world in which our existence did not depend on these deeds.[68]

The claim here is not that we should regret our own existence, insofar as it stems from historic injustice, but that we should regret the fact that our existence is a result of unjust rather than just actions. We would prefer a world where both we existed and where our ancestors had not acted unjustly. But if we accept (as I think we should) all that Thompson says, are we not obliged in fact to do rather more than simply regret the fact that the world is as it is, and issue an apology in recognition of this fact? If we actually wish that we were in a different kind of world, and think that such a world would be more just than our current world, surely it follows that we should seek to make our world more similar to the counterfactual world in question? Thompson specifically refers to 'our existence and other things we enjoy'. But while we obviously cannot alter the fact that we have come into existence, we do have control over those 'things we enjoy' which are transferable resources. Suppose that, through the intervention of an unknown enemy, the estate of A's parents is left to B in their will rather than to A, as A's parents had intended. A would surely be entitled to feel aggrieved if B expressed her sorrow at what had taken place, and expressed the wish that they lived in a counterfactual world where the event had never happened, while still retaining the estate. My point is not just that B's expressed sentiments seem empty; it is that they are incompatible with her subsequent actions. If our moral condemnation of injustice, our regret that injustice has occurred, is to be taken seriously, it must be matched by action to remedy the effects of injustice, insofar as they persist as the automatic effects of injustice. We are right to feel guilty at benefiting from others' misfortune, precisely because this suggests that we have not fulfilled our compensatory obligations.

One final point in this section. In 'Superseding historic injustice', Jeremy Waldron refers to what he calls the 'contagion of injustice'.[69] The interdependence of different parties, both domestically and internationally, and their involvement in, for example, market transactions makes it likely that many people may, to an extent, have benefited as a result of a given act of injustice. It follows from the preceding argument that such people may collectively possess a duty to put the situation right, insofar as doing so does not leave them worse off than if the injustice had not occurred. So it might well be argued, for example, that the West as a whole has benefited from the injustices of the colonial period, and so even those countries which did not directly act as colonial powers may have compensatory duties in the current day. When considered at a domestic level, the likelihood that many and diverse innocent third parties may have benefited from a given act of injustice may in some cases make the fulfillment of the ensuing duties onerous, and at times practically impossible. This might well be thought to provide an argument for an automatic, government-sponsored scheme for compensation for the victims of crime. But this notwithstanding, we might nonetheless think that some duties may appear more pressing to some beneficiaries of injustice than to others. This relates to the earlier claim that recognizing one's duties amounts to a condemnation of the previous act of injustice, and a kind of determination that injustice should not prevail. It seems to me that the parties who should feel this most strongly are those people who were intended to benefit from the act of injustice. Consider, yet again, the example of the driveway. Suppose that the purpose of the evil note leaver was not only to harm my neighbour, but also to benefit me specifically. Insofar as I have in fact benefited from his actions, he has achieved his aim and injustice, as it were, has triumphed. This is true not only in the sense that a distortion in the fair scheme of distribution remains, but also in the sense that what has resulted is the precise unfair distribution which the perpetrator of injustice intended. This has relevance in an intergenerational context, in that it is often a principal aim of those who seek to gain unfair advantage to improve the prospects of their descendants, and relevance in an international context, as frequently the motivation for international wrongdoing is to benefit one's nation, understood as a historic community which exists through time. There is, then, a sense in which it might not be wholly accurate to see some innocent persons or groups as genuinely third parties in relation to injustice. Their position is more involved or implicated than this. It is not a necessary condition of having these duties that it was intended that we benefit from the act of injustice, but it may be that we can see our moral duties more clearly when this is indeed the case.

4.4.3 From Theory to Practice – Problems of Measuring Benefit

It has been claimed that insofar as moral agents have benefited from the wrongdoing of others, they may have obligations to compensate the victims of this wrongdoing. Thus far, the calculation of what constitutes a benefit has been presented as either uncontroversial, as in the Polychrestos case, or as being subjective in that it depends upon the extent to which the putative beneficiaries believe that they have themselves benefited, as in the driveway case. That calculations of advantage will often turn upon the subjective preferences of those concerned does undoubtedly have complications for the application of the theory. It suggests that it would be very difficult to ground legal rights to compensation in a variety of such cases, as is demonstrated by existing laws on unjust enrichment. Seeking restitution in a legal context simply because another has been unjustly enriched at one's expense is difficult in the absence of free acceptance of the benefit in question, because of the problem of subjective devaluation. This is an argument based upon the premiss, 'that benefits in kind have value to a particular individual only so far as he chooses to give them value. What matters is his choice.' So what constitutes a benefit is up to the individual and is an inherently subjective manner: 'Some people like their poodles permed. Others abhor permed poodles.'[70] Only in the case where one party actually receives money can it be taken for granted that she has benefited, since its nature as a medium of exchange is taken to mean that is beneficial by definition: 'Where the defendant received money, it will be impossible on all ordinary facts for him to argue that he was not enriched. For money is the very measure of enrichment.[71] To refer to the previous example; one could not hold the owner of the new driveway legally liable for the costs to his neighbour, because there is no way for an external agent to determine the degree of benefit the owner has received. There is nothing inherently unreasonable about his claiming that he has received no benefit from the experience whatsoever, and in fact preferred the driveway as it was. Even if it is the case that the resurfacing has unambiguously added to the value of his property, he still has to live with his unfavoured driveway until such a time as he sells his house, and it is quite conceivable that this experience might make him worse off overall, even if he eventually receives a higher price for his property. So it may be that, even if one accepts the moral force that attaches itself to benefiting from injustice, there is no way that rights stemming from such obligations can, in many cases, be written into the law, since defendants would simply have to claim that they did not consider themselves to have received benefit to avoid legal obligations. Two things follow from this. First, and most obviously, the topic becomes more a matter of moral than legal obligation, unsuitable for codification into positive law. Benefiting from historical injustice may not present a sound way to ground claims against an unwilling putative beneficiary due to the problem of subjective devaluation. But there is no problem with claiming that moral agents must honestly ask themselves to what extent they have themselves benefited from injustice, and assess their moral obligations accordingly. This is not, of course, to say that the question is not a matter of public policy, but simply that it becomes a moral and a political question, of what ought to be done in policy terms, rather than of what one has to do in order to fulfill one's legal obligations. When the beneficiaries are not individuals, with particular likes and dislikes, but collective entities such as peoples or corporations, it may in any case be easier to make an objective assessment of well-being, and hence of advantage and disadvantage, by reference to material considerations. Such entities will have to debate and decide upon the actions they think it is right to pursue given their circumstances.[72] Given the weakness of international law, and the extent to which it reflects the interests of powerful states, this is the only way the compensatory element of the rectificatory project is likely to get off the ground in any case.

Second, it might be that a discourse of 'rights to compensation' on the parts of victims is simply misplaced in this context, and we should instead be moving towards a duty-based model, where initiatives of compensatory justice gain momentum not from the political protests of victims, but from critical reflection by benefiting moral agents as to the provenance of their advantages. It was precisely this duty-based approach to the rectificatory project that was endorsed in Chapter 1. It was noted that Onora O'Neill argues that, 'Only the weak and powerless have reason to make the perspective of recipience and rights their primary concern.'[73] Insofar as those who have benefited from injustice are not the weak and powerless, the duty-based approach is surely the way they should approach the rectificatory project.

One final point arises. Throughout this chapter, I have sought to depict the involuntary beneficiaries of injustice as innocent third parties, even if their advantage was the motive of the wrongdoer. This is the correct way to address the problem in a purely theoretical sense. Throughout, the beneficiaries of injustice have been presented as if they have only just received the benefits in question. A and B, we might imagine, are considering C's plight as they survey their freshly harvested Polychrestos crop. The surprised owner of the repaired driveway has just come home from work and is trying to work out what to do next. In such cases, the beneficiaries in question truly are innocent third parties. But, if it is accepted that they at this point have rectificatory obligations to others, then they are innocent only insofar as they act reasonably promptly to fulfill the said obligations. A third party which benefits from injustice but does nothing to repair the plight of the victim, when it is clear that no other party is likely to act, is not an innocent bystander; she is acting unjustly in relation to the victim and so becomes a wrongdoer herself. Fullinwider states the principle succinctly in outlining the case against his own position:

> Possession of illicit benefits undermines one's claim to 'innocence'. The wrongful possession serves the same function as personal fault, it makes one liable to pay appropriate compensation.[74]

This argument is of great significance when it comes to considering real world compensation claims, precisely because they typically respond to acts of injustice which have already occurred, sometimes some distance in the past, and for which no one has paid compensation. In such cases, the argument is not simply that an innocent third party has moral obligations towards victims still feeling the effects of the act of injustice. It further holds that the third parties are themselves guilty of compounding the act of injustice by withholding due compensation, which is to say that they have acted unjustly to the victim and so may owe them compensation over and above that which would have been required had they acted correctly initially. This suggests an alternative vision of historical injustice; instead of seeing it as something which fades with time, perhaps we should see its continued non-rectification as a perpetuation of the injustice itself, locking successive generations into compensatory obligations which, in their turn, are not met. This possibility will be discussed in Chapter 6, when the methodological assumption of innocence is relaxed. At the very least, it suggests an urgent need to consider the source of our present-day advantages – and to consider at what expense to others they were procured.

NOTES

1. See Jules L. Coleman, 'Justice and the argument for no-fault', *Social Theory and Practice* 3 (1974), 161–80 at p. 161.
2. Peter Cane, *Atiyah's Accidents, Compensation and the Law* (London: Butterworths, 1993), p. 355.
3. Bernard Boxhill argues that community membership is sufficient to ground obligations of compensation to victims on the part of the community as a whole. Such a commitment is, he maintains, implicit in the community's social contract; so he writes, 'The case for rights of compensation depends ... on the fact that the individuals involved are members of a single community, the very existence of which should imply a tacit agreement on the part of the whole to bear the costs of compensation', Boxhill, 'The Morality of Reparation', in Gross (ed.), *Reverse Discrimination* (Buffalo: Prometheus, 1977), 270–8 at p. 272.
4. Elizabeth Anderson, 'What is the point of equality?', *Ethics* 109 (1999) 287–337 at p. 288.
5. See Thomas Pogge, ' "Assisting" the global poor', in Deen K. Chatterjee (ed.), *The Ethics of Assistance: Morality and the Distant Needy* (Cambridge: Cambridge University Press, 2004), 260–88 at p. 265.
6. The issue of apology for wrongdoing is conceptually distinct. We would normally think that two parties who have wronged each other to equal degree should each apologize for their actions.
7. Ellen Frankel Paul, 'Set-asides, reparations, and compensatory justice', *NOMOS XXXIII: Compensatory Justice*, 97–139 at p. 119. One may take issue with Paul's rather sweeping claims concerning contemporary Africa, and, indeed, the United States.
8. Goodin, 'Compensation and redistribution', p. 145.
9. James W. Nickel, 'Preferential policies in hiring and admissions: a jurisprudential approach', in Barry Gross (ed.), *Reverse Discrimination* (Buffalo: Prometheus, 1977), 324–47 at p. 327.
10. Nozick, *Anarchy, State, and Utopia*, p. 57. Nozick goes on to qualify this by noting that Y should compensate X for how much worse off Y's action would have made a reasonably prudently acting X.
11. Derek Parfit, *Reasons and Persons* (Oxford: Clarendon Press, 1984), pp. 351–5.
12. Stephen Kershnar points out that this only poses a problem insofar as we assume that it is, in fact, a good thing to come into existence. He implies that, although there might be exceptions in terms of extreme disabilities, this is normally the case, given that, for example, many of the descendants of slaves are 'flourishing'. Kershnar, 'Are the descendants of slaves owed compensation for slavery?', *Journal of Applied Philosophy* 16 (1999), 95–101.

13. This is a solution which is suggested, to some extent, by James Fishkin in 'Justice between generations', in John W. Chapman (ed.), *Nomos XXXIII: Compensatory Justice*, 85–96. His putative model is complicated by the fact that he is considering compensation for slavery within the United States. The relevant group to be compensated, therefore, is modern day African Americans, understood as the descendants of slaves brought to America from Africa. Fishkin suggests that it is precisely because of the lingering effects of slavery that there is such a recognizable group within the United States of today. Difficult questions as to the identification of the set of descendants to be identified and the distribution of compensation within this set would, of course, have to be addressed. One might think, however, that the case is more straightforward in an international context (or, at least, in some international contexts) where communities are more readily identifiable and separable.
14. In particularly strong cases of group loyalty, it might be possible for individuals plausibly to maintain that they would prefer not to have existed if the alternative would be the avoidance of some particular harm to the group; which is to say their own personal identity is less important than their membership of the group. This seems theoretically possible, but is unlikely to be widespread in practice.
15. It rejects, for example, the account given by George Sher of the 'branching criterion' of personal identity across possible worlds. See 'Transgenerational compensation' (*Philosophy and Public Affairs*, 35 (2005) 181–200, at p. 187). One might note that Sher's account here gives rise to even more counter-intuitive outcomes than the probabilistic account, as discussed later in this section, since it holds that no individual can be compensated for an event which occurred prior to the point where she began to exist as a person, even if this event had no effect on which sperm unites with which egg, since there is no possible world where it is both true that she exists and the event did not take place (p. 186). Sher's argument in this article rejects his earlier position in Sher, 'Ancient wrongs and modern rights', *Philosophy and Public Affairs* 10 (1980), 3–17. In what follows, I defend the broad thrust of Sher's earlier position against some of his later criticisms.
16. Kershnar, 'Are the descendants of slaves owed compensation for slavery?', pp. 97–9 [my emphasis].
17. Simmons, 'Historical rights and fair shares', p. 178n.
18. Joel Feinberg, 'Wrongful life and the counterfactual element in harming', in *Freedom and Fulfillment: Philosophical Essays* (Princeton: Chichester, 1992), 3–36 at pp. 3–4. Feinberg is using 'interests' here in a similar way to that employed by Nozick previously in terms of indifference curves. Thus he writes, 'despite the diversity of component interests in any person's interest-network, and their different degrees of importance to one's overall good, our concepts seem to commit us to the view that interests can be summed up or integrated into one emergent personal interest' (pp. 4–5).
19. Feinberg, 'Wrongful life and the counterfactual element in harming', p. 8.

20. Feinberg, 'Wrongful life and the counterfactual element in harming', p. 11.
21. Kershnar, pp. 95–6.
22. James Woodward, 'The non-identity problem', *Ethics* 96 (1986), 804–31 at p. 809.
23. Fabre, *Justice in a Changing World*, p. 143.
24. Of course, this claim is controversial, as it may be argued, for example, that the presence of such companies prevents the development of indigenous industries, whose profits would be retained by national members, which would work to the advantage of the national community in the long run. Or it might be more generally argued that, although the individual workers are better off in material terms, this is not true of their overall interests.
25. See M.A. Roberts, 'The non-identity fallacy: harm, probability and another look at Parfit's depletion example', *Utilitas* 19 (2007), 267–311 at pp. 277–84.
26. Of course, what we understand by a 'fair wage', i.e. a non-exploitative wage, is deeply controversial. Our view on this will be determined by our stance on the nature of exploitation, as discussed in Chapter 3.
27. These objections mirror similar points made by Waldron, who notes that some of the events in counterfactual states 'are exercises of human choice rather than the inexorable working out of natural laws' ('Superseding historic injustice', p. 9). It should be stressed that the claim here is not that no compensation is owed; the question rather concerns how much compensation is to be paid. Clearly the student is entitled to some compensation.
28. Sher, 'Ancient wrongs and modern rights', p. 12.
29. This may not be obvious if one assumes that the compensation is being paid by the same agent who was responsible for the kidnapping in the first place. But imagine instead that we are asking what degree of compensation A should receive from a general compensation fund, paid collectively by society as a whole to victims of injustice.
30. Sher, 'Ancient wrongs and modern rights', p. 13.
31. Simmons, 'Historical rights and fair shares', p. 171n. Sher acknowledges this point at the end of his article when he suggests that ancient wrongs to Native Americans and African Americans may be atypical in that they have made it very hard for the descendants of the (originally) injured parties to acquire alternative entitlements.
32. Waldron, 'Superseding historic injustice', p. 6.
33. This is not to say that the opposite cannot occur, in that political injustice can create politicized identities and empower agency within wronged. groups. The point is that one cannot assume that harms will not be long lasting.
34. Sher, 'Transgenerational compensation', p. 187.
35. Charles Beitz, 'Cosmopolitan ideals and national sentiment', p. 595. In this article Beitz revises his earlier position, claiming that he need not show that international society actually does have this character, but merely that it is feasible that an international society could do so.

36. Brown, *Sovereignty, Rights and Justice: International Political Theory Today*, p. 173.
37. Barry, 'Humanity and justice in global perspective', p. 531.
38. As stated previously, Beitz's later work relies on a non-relational, rather than a relational, account of distributive justice. Beitz, 'Cosmopolitan ideals and national sentiment', p. 595.
39. Caney, *Justice Beyond Borders*, p. 110; Beitz, *Political Theory and International Relations*, p. 131.
40. This claim has been articulated in terms of a particular account of the circumstances of justice, based on mutually advantageous cooperation, but other international libertarians, who give different accounts of when different individuals are governed by the same principles of distributive justice, may also be vulnerable to this critique. So, for example, accounts which are based on the coercive power of the state must look at the extent to which, historically, members of other political communities were forcibly coerced, and determine whether the character of this historical interaction was sufficient, at that point in time, to give rise to distributive duties to non-nationals which were unfulfilled.
41. I use 'involuntary' here, and throughout, to indicate that the benefits in question are not voluntarily acquired or accepted, in that they are conferred upon those who receive the benefits without an exercise of the will on the part of the beneficiaries.
42. David Miller, 'Distributing responsibilities', *Journal of Political Philosophy* 9 (2001), 453–71.
43. Miller, 'Distributing responsibilities', p. 454.
44. Miller, *On Nationality*, p. 74.
45. Miller, 'Distributing responsibilities', p. 454.
46. Miller, 'Distributing responsibilities', p. 454.
47. Miller, 'Distributing responsibilities', p. 469.
48. Miller, 'Distributing responsibilities', p. 461.
49. This is now accepted by Miller – see *National Responsibility and Global Justice*, pp. 102–3.
50. Miller, 'Distributing responsibilities', p. 470.
51. See Andrew Burrows, *The Law of Restitution* (London: Butterworths, 1993), pp. 16–23.
52. James W. Nickel, 'Justice in compensation', *William and Mary Law Review* 18 (1976), 379–88 at p. 382.
53. For discussion of this in a legal context, see Lon L. Fuller and William R. Purdue Jr., 'The reliance interest in contract damages', *Yale Law Journal* 46 (1936), pp. 52–96. See also Ellen Frankel Paul's discussion in 'Set-asides, reparations and compensatory justice', pp. 98–104.
54. Jules L. Coleman, *Markets, Morals and the Law* (Cambridge: Cambridge University Press, 1988), p. 185.
55. Saul Levmore, 'Variety and uniformity in the treatment of the good-faith purchaser', *Journal of Legal Studies* 16 (1987) pp. 43–65. Levmore attributes the

wide variety of practice he identifies in the treatment of good-faith purchasers of stolen goods to the existence of uncertainty or reasonable disagreement about the behavioural effects of alternative legal rules: 'some reasonable people might favor the innocent owner, some might prefer the innocent purchaser, and others might split between the two on the basis of time passed, place of purchase, or both' (p. 57).

56. Onora O'Neill, 'Rights to compensation', *Social Philosophy and Policy* 5 (1987), 72–87 at p. 77.
57. Thomson, 'Preferential hiring', p. 152. This position, insofar as it relates to the benefit acquired by a group rather than by individuals, obviously raises important questions as to the distribution of compensatory burdens within the benefiting group, which Thomson only addresses fleetingly. For criticism, see Hardy E. Jones, 'On the justifiability of reverse discrimination' in Gross (ed.) *Reverse Discrimination*, pp. 348–57. Others have questioned the extent to which all white males do in fact benefit from their racial identity. For defence of the proposition, see Charles R. Lawrence III and Mari J. Matsuda, *We Won't Go Back: Making the Case for Affirmative Action* (Boston: Houghton Mifflin Company, 1997). For opposition, see Gertrude Ezorsky, *Racism and Justice: The Case for Affirmative Action* (Ithaca: Cornell University Press, 1991), pp. 83–4.
58. This is the version of the principle given in Fullinwider's 1980 book, *The Reverse Discrimination Controversy* (Totowa, New Jersey: Rowman & Littlefield, 1980). It replaces the more commonly cited 'he who benefits from a wrong shall pay for the wrong' from his 1975 article, 'Preferential hiring and compensation', *Social Theory and Practice* 3 (1975), pp. 307–20.
59. Fullinwider, 'Preferential hiring and compensation' in Steven M. Cahn, *The Affirmative Action Debate* (New York: Routledge, 2002), 68–78 at p. 75.
60. Fullinwider, 'Preferential hiring and compensation', pp. 75–6.
61. Fullinwider, 'Preferential hiring and compensation', p. 76. This point mirrors the legal doctrine of free acceptance. See Birks, *An Introduction to the Law of Restitution* (Oxford: Clarendon Press, 1989), p. 265.
62. Perhaps I rent my house on a long-term lease. Or perhaps the re-surfacing has been cosmetic rather than structural. I am grateful to Hillel Steiner for helping to clarify this point.
63. Fullinwider assumes this to be the case: 'Presumably I valued other things more dearly than having my own driveway repaired; otherwise I would have done it myself', *The Reverse Discrimination Controversy*, p. 39.
64. Generally, it seems to me that we should see the obligations of offender to victim as conceptually prior to any compensatory obligations other parties might have. O'Neill argues that only when compensation is forthcoming from offender to victim can restitution, in the sense of the restoration of the moral relationship between the parties, occur. As such, compensation is always a second-best response to an incidence of injustice. Thus, there is a temptation to introduce lexical priority here, and hold that third parties only acquire

compensatory obligations when offenders cannot or will not fulfill their own obligations. However, some may prefer to extend Miller's 'connection theory' into this area, and maintain that this is only a presumptive priority. It is quite possible to think of circumstances where relatively minor wrongs could have massive consequences, in that one party could lose and a third party could gain huge amounts, but where the offender makes no material gain at all, or even an overall loss (should, for example, her plans go awry). It is not necessarily clear that the offender should foot all of this bill, even if she is able to, when such an obvious distortion has entered into the distributive scheme. Nonetheless, even Fullinwider's revised formula, 'he who benefits from a wrong must help pay for a wrong' is far too strong here, as in many cases of wrongdoing when a third party benefits, the entire burden of compensation will fall on the wrongdoer.

65. Jonathan Wolff, 'Political obligation, fairness and independence', *Ratio* 8 (1995), 87–99 at p. 96. This point can be used in the context of Nozick's famous account of the community public address system, whereby it is claimed that one has an obligation to contribute a day's labour to the system on the grounds that one has benefited from it, even though one voted against its institution. See *Anarchy, State, and Utopia*, pp. 93–5. The burden becomes less onerous if the proviso that one receives *net* benefit is included, which is to say that one has benefited even after doing one's day of service. Nozick's initial example has such force because we imagine the possibility of an individual who has indeed benefited from the system, but not to the extent that he would receive a net benefit from having listened to the system and provided a day's labour.

66. Nothing in this argument, therefore, should necessarily be taken as providing support for the idea that one can acquire obligations to others simply by benefiting from their actions. The key idea in this Section is that one is benefiting *from injustice* specifically; as such, my argument does not, for example, depend upon the version of the fair play account of political obligation which is based on the involuntary receipt of benefits. For an account of such a view, see George Klosko, *The Principle of Fairness and Political Obligation* (Lanham: Rowman & Littlefield, 1992); for criticism, which I need not reject, see Daniel McDermott, 'Fair-play obligations' *Political Studies* 52 (2004), 216–32.

67. A complementary argument to this can be found in Axel Gosseries's account of 'moral free-riding', in Gosseries, 'Historical emissions and free-riding', *Ethical Perspectives* 11 (2004), 38–62.

68. Janna Thompson, 'The apology paradox', *The Philosophical Quarterly* 50 (2000), 470–5 at p. 475.

69. Waldron, 'Superseding historic injustice', p. 11.

70. Birks, *The Foundations of Unjust Enrichment* (Wellington: Victoria University Press, 2002), p. 95.

71. Birks, *The Law of Restitution*, p. 109.

72. It should be noted here that the fact that the extent to which an agent benefits from a given action will, to a large extent, depend upon the subjective

preferences of the agent does not necessarily mean that an agent cannot be mistaken concerning the degree of benefit which they have in fact received. Suppose it is the case both that (*a*) I prefer, in aesthetic terms, my old driveway to my present driveway, and that (*b*) the new driveway adds considerably to the value of my house. If I am not aware of (*b*), then it may be that I have in fact gained a net benefit from the act of injustice, but mistakenly believe that I have not. (Of course, it is still possible that even though I am ignorant of (*b*), my dislike of my new driveway is so great that I am not compensated by the increase in my property's value, and so have not benefited overall.) In such a case, I do possess compensatory obligations to my neighbour, even though I am not aware of it. Whether or not I am culpable here, in moral terms, depends on whether we think I am negligent in failing to be aware of the true nature of the lasting effects of injustice. Evidently, in keeping with the spirit of the rectificatory project, I do believe that moral agents face a duty actively to scrutinize the nature and provenance of their place in the world.

73. O'Neill, 'Rights to compensation', p. 84
74. Fullinwider, *The Reverse Discrimination Controversy*, p. 37.

5

Restitution and Inheritance

5.1 THE INHERITANCE MODEL OF RECTIFICATORY JUSTICE

The focus of Chapter 4 was the harm-based account of compensatory justice. The two questions which were addressed concerned the identification of harm to current individuals as a result of historic actions and the attribution of responsibility for the redress of any such harm. Calculation of harm, it was argued, required the use of counterfactual comparison, though not necessarily in the simple way that counterfactuals are often understood. Chapter 5 takes as its theme what has commonly been thought of as an alternative way of justifying the rectificatory project. This focuses on the issue of the inheritance of entitlement to property. The suggestion is that present day individuals or groups may be entitled to property currently in the possession of others as a result of inheriting a claim to the property in question. The most straightforward way in which this could be said to occur is via the misappropriation of a given piece of property. If A steals X (where X is an item acknowledged to belong to B) from B, and B then dies, leaving all her property to C, then it might well be thought that C has a moral entitlement to the restitution of X. In common parlance we need make no reference to counterfactuals here – the suggestion is simply that A has something that belongs to C – and so should give it to her. Nor need this necessarily depend upon the fact that A was the guilty party in the misappropriation of X. Suppose that A also dies, leaving all her property to D. We may concede that D is blameless, that she has done nothing wrong, but nonetheless maintain that she is in possession of an item of property to which she is not entitled. This model fits in with the methodological assumption of this part of the book that treats current generations as innocent third parties in relation to historic injustice.

The argument can be taken further by expanding the range of property under question to include not just misappropriated possessions (including, significantly, land), which were once legitimately in one individual or group's possession and subsequently misappropriated, but items (or, slightly more abstractly, sums of money) to which individuals acquired entitlements despite not having originally possessed them. The example most commonly used in this context concerns the wages which should have been paid to slaves in North America. Such payments might be viewed in cash terms, or as particularized shares in the property of the agents who should have paid the wages.[1] Potentially, this could be taken further, to refer to compensation payments which should have been paid to victims of injustice in general.[2] The previous chapter even suggested that, on some accounts of distributive justice, exploited nations in the colonial period might have been owed an equal share of the resources of the nation responsible for their exploitation. As will be argued later, the nature of the possession in question is often crucial in determining the effects of the passage of time.

This chapter, then, examines the inheritance account of the rectificatory project in an international context. Specifically, I seek to defend the inheritance account from a number of objections which have been recently raised against it by Janna Thompson and Jeremy Waldron. These may be broadly described as external or internal to an acceptance of the normative justifiability of inheritance *per se*. The first, external series of objections suggests reasons why a given society should not endorse (at least) substantial transfers of valuable resources from members of one generation to another by means of inheritance, understood in terms of rights to bequest. The second, internal series of objections suggest that descendants of victims should not be able to claim title to the possessions of their ancestors after significant periods of time even if one believes that inheritance is generally justifiable. My claim in what follows is that while these may be good reasons to reject the idea that present day parties can inherit entitlements to property misappropriated in the distant past in a domestic context, they do not necessarily apply in an international context when we think about what one political community owes to another. In particular, international libertarians have very good reasons to take the inheritance account seriously, given that their account of distributive justice explicitly rules out generational redistribution across national boundaries. I argue that in resisting cosmopolitan accounts of international distributive justice, advocates of the principles of just international interaction are committing themselves to serious scrutiny of the provenance of their property holdings. If they are in possession of property to which non-nationals can plausibly claim to have inherited entitlements, this property should be returned.

5.2 THE JUSTIFIABILITY OF INHERITANCE

It has been suggested that the key question which the rectificatory project has to answer in the present day is *distributive* – whether there should be a transfer of resources between extant, present day parties. This means that it is impossible to evaluate the normative desirability of the rectificatory project without a consideration of how it fits into theories of distributive justice, and this is particularly so in the case of the inheritance model. The issue is simple – does the theory of distributive justice in question leave room for the restitution of misappropriated property? The nature of the foundation of the property right is crucial to the inheritance model. In what follows, I will first acknowledge reasons why such a foundation – in historical entitlement accounts of property – may arouse suspicions among political philosophers, before showing why such concerns do not necessarily apply within the particular context of the international rectificatory project.

The inheritance model rests on the idea that moral title to property stems from historical entitlement. The entitlement in question is derived via inheritance, by tracing a line of descent, defined in terms of consensual transfer, from a legitimate owner of the relevant property. As such, it depends upon the normative justifiability of the practice of inheritance, and, as Chapter 2 stated, this justifiability has been repeatedly called into question by contemporary theorists. As Thompson notes, 'Inheritance rights can be criticized from most of the moral perspectives that have dominated Western thought in the last 200 years.'[3] Thompson singles out three perspectives in particular from which inheritance rights appear problematic: consequentialism, egalitarianism, and desert. There are a wide variety of approaches to resource distribution which may be considered under the label of 'consequentialism', but the most obvious candidates focus on efficiency and/or some understanding of utility. On Thompson's account, the consequentialist critique concentrates on the potential inefficiency of allowing rights of bequest, since, 'those who inherit wealth are not necessarily the most efficient users of it, and their hold on resources hinders other people from reaching their productive potential and thus making a contribution to the welfare of their society'.[4] This much, evidently depends on the outcomes of an empirical investigation into the practical effects of permitting inheritance, as well as the particular model of consequentialism being employed, although the claim does have obvious plausibility.

The perspectives from equality and desert seem more straightforwardly inimical to the practice of inheritance. It seems clear that allowing individuals to acquire potentially very large shares of resources simply as a result of who their parents were goes against principles of distribution which suggest that either, on the one hand, reward for effort and/or achievement or, on the other, equality should be the index used to order the allocation of resources. And so it seems that, if we endorse one of these indices, we should reject the inheritance model of the rectificatory project. Theories of distributive justice which afford central roles to either equality or desert are described by Nozick as 'patterned', in contrast to his own historical entitlement theory, insofar as they specify 'that a distribution is to vary along with some natural dimension, weighted sum of natural dimensions, or lexicographic ordering of natural dimensions.'[5] As Chapter 2 argued, equality can be seen as either an end-state or a historical principle of distributive justice. Desert is an explicitly historical distributive principle.[6] The problem here in both cases is with the transfer of property. It looks as if transfers of resources from one individual to another are likely to disrupt the distributive pattern in question, unless the state steps in and forcibly redistributes property to restore the pattern. Evidently, it is precisely this form of pattern-disrupting transfer which is involved in intergenerational bequests.[7] So insofar as one seeks to block the practice of inheritance to preserve a distributive pattern, one will not be interested in the inheritance account of the rectificatory project. The resources which are being claimed will simply be confiscated by the state and redistributed. There can be no inheritance of entitlements if there is no entitlement to inheritance.

Things change dramatically, however, when we address the issue from an international libertarian perspective. International libertarians reject the extension of principles of distributive justice across international boundaries. Whatever their domestic principles of distributive justice, and however inimical to the practice of inheritance they might be within political communities, they do not call for a generational redistribution of property across national boundaries. Even if they accept that individuals within the polity should not be entitled to inherit differential shares of resources compared to their co-nationals, owing perhaps, to their acceptance of egalitarianism as a principle of domestic distributive justice, for example, they also accept that it is legitimate for different generations across the world to inherit differential shares, depending on their national identity. This suggests that the inheritance account of the rectificatory project may have compelling force at an international level. If community A is in possession of an item which was historically misappropriated from community B, why should we not say that members of B are entitled to the return of that property, as they have inherited an entitlement to it? Clearly a response which simply maintains that inheritance is morally unjustified does not have force here. International libertarians may, indeed, seek positively to justify the practice of national inheritance by reference to the some of very indices which are used to criticize inheritance within a domestic context. Take consequentialism, for example. If the consequence in mind is something like efficiency, it will not be hard to find theorists in favour of the principle of holding states responsible for their own levels of resources and thus not engaging in patterned redistribution, subject, perhaps, to a duties of assistance-based proviso that they should not fall below some minimum threshold level of well-being. A standard example is provided by David Miller. He imagines two countries starting out from equal natural resource allocations:[8] Affluenza, where the citizens share an ethos of consumerism, depleting their natural resources at a rapid rate; and Ecologia, with a widespread commitment to sustainable development. His suggestion is that, in the future, the two will be unequal, with Ecologia possessing more resources than Affluenza. Does this mean that there should be a redistribution of resources from Ecologia to Affluenza? He suggests not:

> ... there would be little incentive for any state to behave in the responsible way that the citizens of Ecologia... have decided to behave if the result is that the resources that have been conserved are then transferred away to states that follow no such policy. In my simple example Ecologia... could expect to lose only half of their savings; but if a global equalization policy was applied in a world of many states, any one state that tried to conserve per capita resources... would find that it lost almost everything that it had saved – so no state would make the attempt.[9]

In other words, the consequences would be disastrous. Furthermore, the consequentialist argument against domestic inheritance suggested that the practice prevented resources from being used by those who would use them most efficiently. Rawls puts forward a similar argument to that of Miller, again looking at two imaginary societies which start on an equal footing and choose to follow divergent paths: one deciding to industrialize and increase its rate of (real) saving, the other preferring a more pastoral and leisurely society. The result of this is that, decades later, the first country is twice as wealthy as the second. Rawls sees no problem with this, and no role for redistribution. He writes:

> Assuming, as we do, that both societies are liberal or decent, and their peoples free and responsible, and able to make their own decisions, should the industrializing country be taxed to give funds to the second? According to the duty of assistance there would be no tax, and that seems right; whereas with a global egalitarian principle without target, there would always be a flow of taxes as long as the wealth of one people was less than that of the other. This seems unacceptable.[10]

Rawls does not tell us directly *why* this seems unacceptable. There seem two obvious candidates. We might believe that the outcome is unacceptable for consequentialist reasons. Or we might hold that it is *unfair* to the first country. The latter approach is more in keeping, evidently, with Rawls's general philosophy, although it raises the difficult issue of to whom precisely redistribution would be unfair, once we are thinking of societies whose resource levels stem not from their own decisions, but those of previous generations.[11] Regardless, it is clear that insofar as international libertarianism rejects international redistribution across generations, it is content to condone the transmission of resources from one generation to the next within an international context, regardless of how particular communities divide up their resources internally. As such, the inheritance account of the rectificatory project cannot be dismissed out of hand by reference to the unjustifiability of inheritance. This is a clear case where the argument relating to rectificatory justice is substantively different at an international level than at a domestic level. It is true that the inheritance model is of limited importance within domestic societies, given the prevalence of forward-looking accounts of distributive justice (in ideal theory, at least). But one cannot assume that it is equally insignificant in the international arena, insofar as the accounts of international distributive justice put forward by many theorists and the great bulk of the population are backward-looking in character.

Is this enough to settle the question in favour of the inheritance model? Not quite. Two significant objections to the inheritance model remain. Both of these derive from the fact that, when we are dealing with historical misappropriation of property, the property in question has been out of the possession of its original owners, and of their heirs, for a lengthy period of time. This creates two potential challenges to the claim that the property should be restored. The first of these maintains that the fact of dispossession means that the entitlement to the property in question has lapsed. The second rests upon indeterminacy as to the identity of the rightful owner of the property in question. In the remainder of this chapter, each of these will be considered in turn.

5.2.1 Property and Possession (1)

Jeremy Waldron puts forward the first objection to the inheritance model of the rectificatory project as the 'main difficulty' which this approach faces. His claim is summarized by Janna Thompson as holding 'that considerations that justify ownership of property tell against the claims of descendants'.[12] He starts by asking, 'Are we sure that the entitlement that was originally violated all those years ago is an entitlement that survives into the present?'[13] This is obviously the central question the inheritance model faces. One response to this, which holds that the entitlement does not survive as inheritance *per se* is unjustifiable, has already been rejected within an international libertarian perspective. But this is not Waldron's point. Rather, he is suggesting that the fact that the property has been in someone else's possession for a prolonged period of time means two things: both that the heirs to the property have lost their entitlement to it, and that the current possessors of the property have gained an entitlement to it.

Why should this be the case? For Waldron, the answer is to do with the nature of property rights. Waldron is generally sceptical of historical entitlement theories. Consistent with his approach in other writings,[14] Waldron rejects accounts such as that of Locke which rest upon the notion of mixing one's labour with an unowned object in order to acquire a property right in it and suggests that, if an account of historical entitlement is to work, it will have the following character:

> If we abandon Locke's image of the mixing of labour, the most plausible account of initial acquisition goes like this. An individual, P, who takes possession of an object or a piece of land and who works on it, alters it, and uses it, makes it in effect a part of her life, a pivotal point in her thinking, planning and action... If any defense of historical entitlement is possible, it is going to be something along those lines.[15]

This account of the nature of entitlement is extremely sensitive to physical possession of the property in question. If someone is without her property for some period of time, and learns to live without it, the entitlement lapses. Waldron gives a stark account of the implications of this view, as the following striking passage makes clear:

> If something was taken from me decades ago, the claim that it now forms the center of my life and that it is still indispensable to the exercise of my autonomy is much less credible. For I must have developed some structure of subsistence. And that will be where my efforts have gone and where my planning and my practical thinking have been focused. I may of course yearn for the lost resource and spend a lot of time wishing that I had it back. I may even organize my life around the campaign for its restoration. But that is not the same thing as the basis of the original claim. The original entitlement is based on the idea that I have organized my life around the use of this object, not that I have organized my life around the specific project of hanging on to it or getting it back.[16]

This does not, of course, mean that the act of misappropriation was just. Nor, surely, does it mean that there are not reasons why the object should now be returned. It is simply that, on Waldron's account of what makes entitlement legitimate, the entitlement in question has, technically, faded. As such, distributive justice does not require the object's restitution. Conversely, the entitlement now resides with whoever has the property in her possession. On the assumption that it is now central to her life, it is now, on Waldron's account, her property. This does not happen overnight, of course – the property needs to be in another's possession for some considerable time. Waldron is aware of the troublesome implications of this argument, not least in terms of the moral hazard which it creates for wrongdoers to hang on to their ill-gotten gains so as to gain a property entitlement over it.[17] But this might seem less troubling if we imagine a situation where we are thinking of the descendants of the wrongdoer, or of other third parties, rather than the miscreant herself. For Waldron, entitlements fade with time when property is not in our possession – and this means that others can acquire entitlements.

This argument poses a powerful challenge to the inheritance model. Waldron's argument here is similar to that which is made by libertarians such as David Schmidtz and Loren Lomasky, who base their account of current day property rights not in historical entitlement, but rather on the role which property holdings play within individuals' lives, allowing them to form stable plans, and be secure in their transactions with others. The key point here concerns the perceived weakness of historical entitlement theories of property rights. The most famous contemporary historical entitlement theory, of course, is that of Robert Nozick. His conclusion that individuals can come to have absolute property rights over previously unowned resources through applications of the principles of justice in acquisition, transfer, and rectification has been subjected to severe criticism, as I shall go on to discuss. Thus, Schmidtz argues that 'Nozick has a theory of just *transfer*, not a theory of just *distribution*.'[18] For Schmidtz, we are 'fated to live in a world of background injustice' – we are not able to rectify historic injustice so as to fit in with some just initial distribution, and so must just make the best of what we have. His view of what this means seems to consist of leaving everything where it currently is. Lomasky expresses this view explicitly:

> Neither the persons nor property holdings that would have characterized an ideal world are now actualisable. The option that is available to us is to respect the interest in project pursuit of actual persons by refraining from encroachment on their property holdings.[19]

All of this, it must be understood, is dependent upon the idea that historical entitlement theory is intrinsically flawed. If one were able to provide a convincing account of property rights based on historical entitlement, then it seems as if the inheritance model would again be significant. My argument in this section is that this is precisely what international libertarians are able to do. Again, it is a mistake to take an argument from the domestic sphere, in this case, the weakness of historical entitlement theory, and assume that the same problems bedevil it in an international context. If we replace the foundational unit of historical entitlement theories, and speak of the entitlements of *collectives* rather than *individuals*, a host of problems associated with the domestic variant of the argument disappear. So my claim here is twofold. First, it is possible to build a historical entitlement theory within international libertarianism which is significantly stronger than domestic historical entitlement theory. In what follows, I sketch such a plausible alternative view. I should note here that although this model challenges Waldron's rejection of historical entitlement theory, it is crucially limited in that it does not extend to granting absolute property rights over territory. I take it that the issue of rights over territory is, in fact, Waldron's main concern in 'Superseding historic injustice' – my argument is that there are significant non-territorial claims which international libertarians can advance within the terms of the inheritance account, and that Waldron's arguments do not undermine such claims. Second, my belief is that international libertarianism is, in fact, best understood as *being* a theory of historical entitlement. The best responses that international libertarians can give to cosmopolitan challenges, on this view, are grounded in property rights. This does not amount to an endorsement of international libertarianism; it is merely the claim that this is its strongest form. If this is right, then the inheritance model of the rectificatory project is of great significance for international libertarians.

It should be made clear once again in this context that international libertarianism should not be seen as a description of what domestic libertarians think about international distributive justice. As stated before, writers whom I describe as 'domestic libertarians' are in fact characteristically cosmopolitan in their accounts of distributive justice, since they premise their accounts on the rights and entitlements of individuals rather than groups. So the argument is not that the same principles which regulate the interaction of individuals should also regulate the interaction of states. Instead, I suggest that international libertarians hold that certain principles which are thought by some to be appropriate to the regulation of interpersonal conduct are in fact more appropriate to the regulation of international conduct. This position does not rest upon a mistaken 'domestic analogy' whereby individuals and groups are assumed to be relevantly similar, so that what is right for one, at a domestic level, is characteristically also right for the other, at an international level. Clearly, the writers whom I describe as 'international libertarian' are often far from libertarian in their domestic principles of justice. My argument, if anything, is a case of a domestic disanalogy.

5.2.2 International Libertarianism and Historical Entitlement

Nozick's argument concerning distributive justice in *Anarchy, State, and Utopia* is summarized in his famous claim that, 'liberty upsets patterns'.[20] The force of his famous Wilt Chamberlain argument stems from the central role seemingly played by the free and voluntary choices of individuals – if I am entitled to a set of resources, why should someone come and interfere with the use I make of them? The central idea at the heart of Nozick's argument is that individuals should be allowed to do whatever they like (other than positively cause harm to others) with what they rightfully possess. For an institution such as the state to fail to protect the property rights of individuals is to fail to respect their autonomy. For some, this element of his argument is appealing. The problem comes when we ask where the entitlements he describes come from. The challenge for libertarians is to move from the intuitively plausible premise of self-ownership, in relation to one's own body and talents, to a position whereby one's use of one's body and talents has generated property rights over external objects. As we have already seen, Nozick outlines three principles by which property holdings should be judged: justice in acquisition, transfer, and rectification.[21] In fact, nearly all the work is done by the first principle: justice in acquisition. Nozick claims that it is possible to acquire (effectively) absolute property rights over property. Once such absolute rights are granted, relatively little argument is needed to justify the principle of justice in transfer and of rectification. Quite how these rights are to be established, however, is a vexed issue. As Steiner argues:

> Historical entitlement conceptions of property rights avoid the error correctly attributed to competing conceptions which 'treat objects as if they appeared from nowhere and out of nothing' and were not the products of personally owned labour. But historical entitlement conceptions attend insufficiently to the fact that natural resources are, precisely, objects which appeared from nowhere and out of nothing. And it is thus not surprising that the Achilles' heel of such conceptions can almost invariably... be located in their accounts of the right to initial appropriation, from which all other historical entitlement-based property rights logically derive.[22]

Wolff expresses a similar concern:

> Libertarianism presupposes that individuals have strong rights to property. But everything that is now owned is constructed out of materials which, once, no individual owned. How can initial appropriation be justified?[23]

Nozick is scathing of some of Locke's attempts to account for initial acquisition, but himself presents only a self-confessedly incomplete account of justice in acquisition.[24] As Waldron notes, Nozick retains, 'the form of a Lockean approach – insisting that an adequate theory of justice must be founded on some principle of unilateral acquisition – without telling us much about the content of that principle or how it might be justified.'[25] The account he does give, which relies on a reformulated Lockean proviso, requiring that the appropriation of property should leave others at least as well off as they were prior to the act of appropriation, has come in for a great deal of criticism. Many writers have argued that historical entitlement accounts fall down as a result of the failure of the principle of justice in acquisition to demonstrate the plausibility of the absolute property rights on which they depend. J.W. Harris's critique is typical when he speaks of historical entitlement theorists' 'dogmatic insistence on a supposedly uncontestable and supra-temporal concept of ownership':

> Ownership just must comprise, not merely unlimited use-privileges and control-powers, but also unlimited powers of transmission. Original appropriation, at whatever past date it occurred, must have involved that concept of ownership. No normative argument need be supplied to establish these preconceived conceptual truths. It follows that the fostering of human autonomy becomes private property's supreme virtue.[26]

I want here to consider three arguments that have been advanced against the libertarian account of the acquisition of property. The first of these concerns the ownership of raw materials. G.A. Cohen has strongly criticized Nozick for the fact that he assumes that all raw materials are originally unowned.[27] He claims that, 'far from establishing that premiss, he does not even bother to state it, or show any awareness that he needs it'.[28] The assumption is very important as it is necessary if appropriation of resources in accordance with the reformulated Lockean proviso is to be legitimate. Cohen posits an alternative, whereby we regard natural resources, prior to appropriation, as jointly owned. This makes a big difference, since, as Cohen notes, under joint ownership what each individual might do with the resources in question is subject to collective decision. Cohen accepts that the appropriate procedure for deciding on use in such cases may be hard to define, 'but it will certainly not be open to any one of the joint owners to privatise all or part of the asset unilaterally, no matter what compensation he offers to the rest'.[29] If the raw materials which have been used do not become the absolute property of the appropriating individual, then there is no reason to suppose that she acquires absolute property rights over the object she has created or transformed. This need require no denial of self-ownership: it may be admitted that people own their talents, and are entitled to sole ownership of the fruits of their talents. But they have combined their talents with something to which others have an entitlement, and this at least suggests that the property rights they have (if any) over the finished item in question are not absolute.[30] An interesting facet of the disagreement over ownership of the earth's resources is that it might be thought that there is no immediate way in which it can be resolved, short of recourse to some intuitive belief.[31] Cohen makes the point in a hypothetical form: *if* Nozick is wrong about initial ownership, his argument falls. As Exdell notes, 'the doctrine that land and resources are collectively held stands as the most prominent rival to Nozick's theory',[32] but all that Nozick really does to address it is to shift the burden of proof, of plausible argument, onto the collectivist camp:

We should note that it is not only persons favouring *private* property who need a theory of how property rights legitimately originate. Those believing in collective property, for example those believing that a group of persons living in an area jointly own the territory, or its mineral resources, also must provide a theory of how property rights arise; they must show why the persons living there have rights to determine what is done with the land and resources there that the persons living elsewhere don't have (with regard to the same land and resources).[33]

There is the suggestion of an impasse here.

Second, Nozick's account of the reformulated Lockean proviso has been forcefully criticized. The perceived problem lies in Nozick's use of counterfactuals. Locke's original formulation held that individuals may legitimately appropriate goods from the state of nature 'where there is enough, and as good left in common for others'.[34] Such a formulation is obviously deeply problematic in a context of scarcity of natural resources in general, and of land in particular. Thus, Nozick argues instead that appropriation can be justified insofar as it does not make other individuals worse off. A system of private property makes people better off than they would be if no appropriation had taken place, and thus provides them with new, different opportunities. But, as the argument of Chapter 4 makes clear, questions of harm and benefit necessarily make reference to counterfactuals. Nozick seems only to consider two possible states: one where individuals appropriate resources and acquire absolute property rights, and one where there is no appropriation of resources at all, and a tragedy of the commons ensues. However, as Cohen points out, there are other possible counterfactuals here.[35] Imagine a world where there are two individuals, A and B. Suppose A appropriates all the land, and pays B to work upon it. It may well be that this improves B's position, relative to the counterfactual world where neither appropriates the land, and thus neither can be secure in the expectation that they will be able to harvest any crops they grow, and so grow no crops. But there are other possible worlds we might consider. What if, instead of A appropriating the land, B does so, and is more efficient than A, resulting in a higher yield of crops? What if A and B agree to own the land collectively, and both work upon it, sharing the produce between them? If B's position in these two counterfactual states is better than in the world where A appropriates all the land, it seems as if the reformulated Lockian proviso has not been met.

Third, we might look at the charges of atomistic individualism which have been leveled at the libertarian account of historical entitlement. These focus not on the raw materials which are involved in an act of appropriation, but on the question of who it is that is doing the appropriating. The suggestion is that, in many cases, it is not plausible to maintain that the act of transformation or creation which is the basis for the property entitlement is the result of the actions of a single individual. Charles Taylor speaks of the 'atomism' of the libertarian account, and sets it against the Aristotelian concept of man as a social animal; not self-sufficient, but dependent upon a wider community: for Aristotle, the polis.[36] Harris provides an eloquent account of the objection:

> Locke, Mill and Nozick all posit individual appropriators. Perhaps the scope of the creation-without-wrong argument is drastically reduced by the social character of labour... in the real world productive labour is (and doubtless always has been) social, for the most part, in two respects. Most productive work is not carried on by isolated individuals; and, even when it is, the materials upon which it operates are not the spontaneous gift of nature, but rather the product of other people's labour. It was upon the social character of labour that... Proudhoun founded his argument that all men are entitled to arithmetically equal shares in all accretions to social wealth.[37]

From this perspective, it is hard to think of many productive acts which do not owe a great deal to the efforts of others. It is not only the physical efforts of those involved in a given act of production, such as the workers in a factory, which are included here; it is also necessary to consider the background to the productive act, the extent to which techniques and working practices are shaped by the past experiments and insights of one's predecessors. Even what seem to be, on the surface, relatively pure individualist acts of creation, such as the production of art, are seen in terms of the cultural context in which artists are located, and which they reflect, whether they embrace it, or define themselves in opposition to it. This may be taken to apply equally to intellectual property: even when no raw materials are involved in the creation of a 'mental product', the prior actions of others in the field have presumably played a contributory role.[38] Libertarians who claim to be autarkic, apart from the social matrix and responsible for (and therefore entitled to) the fruits of their labours, are in fact parasitic on the efforts of others. It is a matter of debate how far such an argument need be taken. On the one hand are socialist arguments that see all wealth as a social product which belongs equally to all members of society as a whole. This is not too distant from Rawls's discussion of the benefits of social cooperation in *A Theory of Justice*.[39] Alternatively, we might see the point of these observations as a justification for the limitation of property rights following transformation or creation. Thus, for example, we might see the issuing of a patent right, affording a limited degree of ownership over an invention for a specified period of time, as a fair compromise between the input of the individual most closely associated with the invention and the prior efforts of other members of the community.[40] In either case, the conclusion drawn is that the historical entitlement account fails to show why individuals should be afforded absolute property rights when they are not solely responsible for production.

How does international libertarianism fit into all this? I suggest that if we replace the individual with the collective, these objections lose a good deal of their force. As such, the international libertarian account can provide more convincing responses to these challenges than the domestic variant. Let us first consider the issue of the appropriation of natural resources. International libertarians can justify national ownership of the raw materials which go into production by making one assertion and leaving one question open. The assertion is the claim that states are entitled to the exclusive use of resources within their territories. The question which is to be left open is that of how they themselves come to possess these territories legitimately. This is evidently a crucial question and will be addressed later in the chapter.

The claim that states are entitled to exclusive use of their natural resources is one that commands the support of those I have labeled international libertarians. The claim is nonetheless extremely controversial within philosophical circles and is expressly denied by cosmopolitans such as Beitz, Pogge, Steiner, and Barry. Thus Brian Barry, for example, specifically argues in favour of 'the principle that natural resources are the joint possession of the human race as a whole'.[41] In doing so, however, he is forced to acknowledge the strength of existing support in the real world for the principle of national sovereignty over natural resources. This has the backing of international law: it is a convention 'reinforced by international declarations such as votes of the United Nations General Assembly in 1970, 1972, and 1974 to the effect that each country has "permanent sovereignty over natural resources" within its territory'.[42] Nor does this necessarily reflect only the will of powerful, resource-rich states: he notes that, 'as far as I am aware, no body of opinion in either the North or the South is averse to the principle that each country is entitled to benefit exclusively from its own natural resources'.[43] As such, it is an appropriate assumption for us to accept within this book's commitment to double practicality: it reflects the beliefs of real world actors engaged in contemporary politics.

The suggestion, then, is that allocating exclusive sovereignty over the natural resources within a given territory to the community in rightful possession of the land in question answers the question of who owns the resources in question prior to their being used in productive processes, and so allows for a resolution to the aforementioned impasse.[44] In fact, and significantly, the national sovereignty assumption is compatible with *both* intuitive responses to the question of original world ownership. Those who believe it was originally unowned can still endorse the claim that communities have come to own particular territories, and thus have collective control over the resources contained therein.[45] And advocates of universal world ownership may accept the suggestion that, given real world constraints and for ease of administration, resources should be allocated to particular communities in keeping with the principle of national sovereignty. This point is made by Exdell, who writes:

> One may take the view – as have many socialists – that the earth's land and resources are held by mankind. If one could have one's way, American wheat and Arabian oil would be divided equitably for use by the world's population. Unfortunately one cannot have one's way. Given the state of mankind's political institutions, there is presently no hope of establishing this form of distribution and management. The best we can do, therefore, is to affirm the doctrine of collective holdings within political communities. We come closer to the requirement of serving the good of all men if nations act on the principle that resources under their control are jointly held by all their citizens and not by private individuals.[46]

As Exdell presents it, this is still a non-ideal solution as it does not solve the problem of the arbitrary distribution of (at least some) resources. The fact of the inegalitarian distribution of natural resources stands as a significant challenge to this element of international libertarianism. Cosmopolitans stress that some individuals are born within states with a greater supply of natural resources than others. Thus, Beitz argues:

> ... natural resources are distributed unevenly over the earth's surface. Some areas are rich in resources, and societies established in such areas can be expected to exploit their natural riches and to prosper. Other societies do not fare so well, and despite the best efforts of their members, they may attain only a meager level of well-being because of resource scarcities.[47]

Clearly, the place of one's birth is arbitrary from a moral point of view. Can legitimating such unequal distributions of resources be just?

There are three possible responses to this. The first is simply to say that this kind of inequality does not matter. This is the position of Walzer, who is untroubled by international inequalities *per se*.[48] He makes the point in relation to Richard Arneson's suggestion that his theory would not require the international redistribution of resources, even in circumstances of extreme inequality. Walzer simply accepts the claim. He argues:

> If international inequalities have no *international* reason ... then indeed no injustice is involved. Consider the comparison between victims of earthquake and fire in this part of the world and men and women untouched by disaster in some other part. We should be 'morally troubled' if the second group doesn't help the first, but not because the comparison itself is troubling or the earthquake unjust. Arneson's inequality is very much like a natural disaster (though its explanation would presumably involve a mix of natural and social causes: climate, resources, political culture, and so on).[49]

So, the first international libertarian response is to deny that inegalitarian holdings of natural resources matter from the viewpoint of distributive justice. The second is to cast doubt upon the extent to which they matter even from the viewpoint of equality itself. Inequalities in resource holdings need not be problematic if one does not believe that the differential distribution of natural resources is necessarily significant in different cultures' economic development. This is the view of John Rawls. Rawls claims, citing David Landes's book *The Wealth and Poverty of Nations*,[50] that since 'the crucial element in how a country fares is its political culture – its members' political and civic virtues – and not the level of its resources, the arbitrariness of the distribution of natural resources causes no difficulty.'[51] Thus, while some resource-poor countries, such as Japan, are rich, some resource-rich countries, such as Argentina, suffer serious difficulties.[52] Admittedly, as this account stands, it is a *non-sequitur*. Even if the level of natural resources is not crucial in how a country develops, it may still be a significant factor, whose inegalitarian distribution is morally worrying. Earlier in the book, however, Rawls goes further, explicitly describing political culture as the determinant variable in the wealth of nations:

> I believe that the causes of the wealth of a people and the forms it takes lie in their political culture and in the religious, philosophical, and moral traditions that support the basic structure of their political and social institutions, as well as in the industriousness and cooperative talents of their members, all supported by their political virtues.[53]

This claim is very controversial, and a number of writers have noted that Rawls here is taking a rather definite stance on what is still thought by most to be an open controversy in development economics, which Niall Ferguson has called 'economic history's version of the nature-nurture debate'.[54] Certainly, it is unfortunate that Rawls's treatment of the subject is so cursory. However, the claim that levels of natural resource holdings simply do not matter to a nation's level of development is supported by a number of authors. For example, Joseph Heath writes:

> There is essentially no correlation between the domestic supply of natural resources and the wealth of a nation, simply because the two have nothing to do with one another. The only exception is oil, which appears to be the example that set Beitz and Pogge off on the wrong track. Oil trades at artificially high prices because it is cartelized. If one looks at any other example (e.g. diamonds, gold, nickel, molybdenum, fresh water, agricultural land) it should be clear that resource endowment does not translate into wealth in any direct way. (In fact, many have argued that the industrial revolution occurred in England precisely because its *lack* of domestic resources encouraged manufacturing.)[55]

The question is extremely complicated, and becomes more so once we start considering factors such as geographic location as being variables which may help or hinder assistance.[56] It is sufficient for our current purposes to note that an advocate of this view, or of that associated previously with Walzer, need raise no objection to national sovereignty of resources. An acceptance of this view also provides a response to the second domestic critique of historical entitlement theories. Insofar as inegalitarian holdings of natural resources does not affect a given people's ability to develop, it looks as if by dividing the world up into sovereign, self-governing communities, each with control over a given territory, we have afforded each community 'enough and as good' as one another.

The third possible response need not take a strong line on the importance of natural resources. This position acknowledges the unfairness of the world's unequal resource holdings, and so accepts the argument that resource rich countries should pay some degree of compensation to those who do not have the same initial endowments. The full account of what is owed on such an account is undoubtedly complicated, and it seems as if a position will have to be taken on the question of the relative importance of natural resources to national productivity, but nonetheless, it seems theoretically possible to come up with an account of what is owed by whom to whom. The key point, again, is that the distributive obligations associated with such an account will be limited, with a cut-off point. Once a given community has its fair share of resources, the suggestion is that it can use them in whatever way it sees fit (subject, perhaps, to showing sufficient concern for the effects of their actions on contemporaries in other polities and future generations, both domestically and internationally).[57]

Once this account of national sovereignty is accepted, we have the necessary elements for a plausible account of initial acquisition. Natural resources, to which the nation has a legitimate claim, are transformed via the efforts of nationals, either singly or in concert. The issue of property entitlements within the nation is left as an open question. Whether the property in question is held by the nation in common, and perhaps allocated temporarily to individuals, or whether individuals within the polity have strong entitlements to the property in question is something which need not be addressed for our current purposes. An answer would presumably require a judgement to be made on many vexed issues within the literature on historical entitlement accounts of property, such as a thoroughgoing account of the reformulated Lockean proviso, and consideration of the relevant benchmark against which the well-being of one's fellow citizens should be judged. But this does not affect the claim that, whatever these questions and answers may be, they apply within a domestic, national context.

It should be clear that this account provides a response to the domestic variants of the critique from atomism. This is a good example of how international libertarianism does not fall foul of the domestic analogy, in that its provisions actually serve to undercut the domestic variant. The point which is made by the critics of domestic libertarianism is that the property which results from societal production belongs, in at least some sense, to the community as a whole, rather than the particular individuals who happen to end up with it. This point can be perfectly happily accepted by international libertarians, who can hold that the nation as a whole has some entitlement to the fruits of social production. However, some national property holdings now seem vulnerable to an international version of the critique from atomism. Granting exclusive property rights to nations still seems to rest upon an assumption of autarkism; but rather than of individuals, it is in this case an assumption of the separateness of nations, of separate schemes of social cooperation and production.[58] Clearly, given cosmopolitan arguments in relation to global interdependence as cited previously, such arguments are controversial. It is clear that a great deal of contemporary production is international in nature: some products may have their origins not only in different countries but in different continents. Again, two points may be made by way of response. First, insofar as there is international production, which involves the interaction of different communities as well as different individuals, we might think that the requirements of justice simply require that the exchanges which pave the way for international production should be fair. If the terms of the exchange are not exploitative, and if the resources involved in the exchange are legitimately owned by the parties to the exchange, there is at least a prima facie case for endorsing the subsequent property holdings. The international libertarian can insist that the kind of interdependence and interaction involved is different in character from that involved in domestic production. As such, non-nationals may contribute, in a sense, to production, but they do not gain entitlements if their contribution is fairly rewarded.

The second defence of particular property holdings available to the international libertarian account claims that global interdependence is a relatively recent phenomenon. Even if we think that some forms of contemporary production, in some areas of the world, are genuinely international, we need not think that this is universal; either in terms of extending to all modern day production, or (in particular) in applying to historic production. Even if one felt that some contemporary production could not be fairly exclusively allocated to a given nation, this is surely not characteristic of a great deal of historic production. In order for the objection from atomism to have force here, we must really believe that particular forms of production in the past were genuinely international, taking raw materials and labour from different nations, so that the different nations in question genuinely cooperated. It might instead be maintained that the vast majority of historic production did not have this character, but rather was concentrated within relatively small communities, or at most within national groups. At some points, to be sure, particular nations may, for example, have been parts of much larger empires, and so it may be fair to say that particular outputs were manufactured, in some sense, by the empire as a whole. But this is still not the same as making an argument concerning *global* interdependence. In such cases, we might say that the entitlement is shared between the constitutive parts of the empire who contributed to the production. But this does not legitimate appropriation of the property in question by quite different parties at a subsequent date, nor undermine the joint, continuing entitlement to the property of those who contributed to its manufacture. It might be, for example, that we hold that certain art works are owned jointly by a number of Central or South American nations, as members of historic empires which pre-date the arrival of European settlers. The cooperative nature of the manufacture does not lessen the property entitlement – it just means that it is held more widely.

Finally, it is necessary to return to the question which was left open at the beginning. I have argued that international libertarianism is capable of sustaining a plausible historical entitlement account of property rights. This is based on the assumption of national sovereignty over natural resources, and I suggested reasons why this assumption need not be seen as problematic. But this still leaves open the question of how a nation comes to acquire its territory. This is a crucial issue for the rectificatory project, and its resolution importantly qualifies its outcome. My assumption here is that it is possible to identify many contemporary territorial holdings which we are happy to endorse as legitimate. So, how are territories legitimately acquired? The most obvious candidate theory is that of first occupancy; however, it is unlikely that this will solve the problem. Quite aside from the open question of why first occupancy should confer entitlement,[59] it is obvious that many of the holdings we would consider legitimate do not rest upon it. It is commonplace within the literature to note that the history of land holdings is one of dispossession after dispossession. Thompson, for example, writes:

> Nations and individuals who now exist are not, for the most part, the original occupiers of their territory or their heirs, but have displaced others, often by conquest... In every area of the world, wave after wave of invaders have expropriated land and political control from existing occupants. As a result, virtually no nation can establish that it has a historical title to the territory it occupies. In fact, we know that most cannot make this claim.[60]

First occupancy, then, seems unlikely as the foundation for legitimate territorial entitlement. As such, it seems to me that the best alternative is to endorse Thompson's claim, following Michael Walzer, that it is some account of sustained possession which grounds territorial claims. I leave it as an open question as to quite how this is to be worked out in terms of the amount of territory which might be fairly occupied by a given number of people in conditions of scarcity, and of the form of political sovereignty which must be exercised over the territory in question,[61] and note the suggestions of David Lyons that this is likely to change with time, meaning that property holdings which were legitimate at one time can become less so in the future.[62] But it does seem right to say that if the claim to property is based on sustained possession, then the entitlement to the territory itself is likely to disappear in the absence of said possession (or, at least that another party may gain entitlement to it on the same basis).[63] In relation to land, then, it appears that Waldron's objection does have force. How long it takes for one entitlement to fade and another to grow is a desperately difficult question which I will not attempt to answer here, except to observe that we can witness cases at either end of the spectrum, and can at least talk about them in a relatively straightforward fashion. This does leave, of course, a wide range of disputed territorial claims in real world politics, including cases of recurrent invasions and reinvasions, and cases where different nations are intermingled, and lay claim to the same territories. I do not think that the theory of possession can provide much of an answer to such questions. Tamar Meisels cites Miller's remark that, 'People of liberal disposition...will throw up their hands in despair when asked to resolve the practical problems that arise when...two nationalities make claim to the same territory, as for instance in the case of the Jews and the Palestinians in Israel.'[64] The technical answer is that, in real-world disputed situations, both parties are likely to have, if not necessarily equally valid claims, then claims of some validity, and so the solution reached will have to be essentially political. One would hope for a fair compromise, although one would doubtless expect an outcome which reflected the economic and military strength of the parties to the bargaining procedure.

Three qualifications need to be attached to the above argument. First, it must be stressed that this applies only to the territory itself, and to the resources which naturally accompany it. My claim is that national entitlements to territory are qualitatively different from other national entitlements: as such, the nature of the property rights are different in each case. It is a category mistake to take arguments derived from the impermanence of territorial entitlements and apply them in other contexts. Secondly, this argument only really applies to the physical space the land fills and to the *natural* resources specifically which fill this space. Insofar as a nation has laboured on a given piece of land and has improved it, we might suppose that its members have generated entitlements which will not fade with their title to the geographical space the land itself fills.[65] As such, present day nationals may still have legitimate claims to restitution stemming from the inheritance model in relation to the historic misappropriation of their ancestors' land. It is just that this claim will not necessarily require the literal return of all the land in question. Thirdly, I have so far been discussing *moral entitlements* to property. But there is, of course, another sense in which an agent can be said to have a property entitlement, and this is when a right is conferred upon the agent by an institution with the appropriate jurisdiction. We might point out that current international property holdings (controversial cases, perhaps, aside) are institutional as well as moral entitlements. Since the development of international law, it might be suggested that a line has been drawn in relation to the previously insecure nature of national property holdings, and the current state of play has been formalized by its recognition in international law. The changed nature of the international community may provide a new way for nations to acquire territory, if their existing holdings can be said to have been approved by humanity as a whole, insofar as their views are expressed through international institutions. Such recognition may ground a more substantial claim to ownership of territory.

My conclusion, then, in this section, is that it is possible to develop a plausible account of historical entitlement within an international context. Again, this conclusion is conditional, and does not serve as an authoritative rejoinder to cosmopolitan theorists. But I would suggest that it has important implications for international libertarians who resist resource redistribution across national boundaries. The claim is that such people have to take historical entitlement seriously. The weaknesses of the domestic historical entitlement model cannot be assumed to apply to the international variant.

5.2.3 Property and Possession (2)

With our international historical entitlement account in hand, let us return to Jeremy Waldron's supersession argument. I have argued that international libertarians do, *contra* Waldron, have a plausible account of historical entitlement. As such, they need not accept Waldron's claim that entitlements to property necessarily fade with time when they are out of an agent's possession. But it is still the case that other individuals build expectations and life projects around them. So Waldron writes:

> For better or worse, people build up structures of expectation around the resources that are actually under their control. If a person controls a resource over a long enough period, then she and others may organize their lives

and their economic activity around the premise that that resource is 'hers', without much regard to the distant provenance of her entitlement. Upsetting these expectations in the name of restitutive justice is bound to be costly and disruptive.[66]

What we now have is a suggestion that there are independent moral reasons why we should override historical entitlement. The argument now holds that the centrality of the resource to the agent controlling the resource is so great that we should override the owner's legitimate title. What to make of this argument? First, it should be noted that it is not necessarily true that misappropriated property will be this important to its current possessor. It is not hard to think of cases where an agent may possess property *without* it playing a central role in her life. She may have forgotten she possesses it, it may be of little or no use to her, she may have a great deal of the kind of property in question – more, in fact, than she needs. So, at the very least, the burden of proof rests upon the possessor to demonstrate why the resource is so important to her that the owner's entitlement should be overridden.

What if this can indeed be shown? There are two broad responses available in relation to the life projects argument. One is simply to ignore it, and insist that property rights, properly acquired, cannot be overridden for the sake of other desirable goals. This is the approach taken by Murray Rothbard, who launches a vigorous defence of the rights of heirs of the victims of injustice.[67] If something legitimately held in the past was misappropriated, it must simply be returned – that is the nature of a property entitlement.[68] This, I would suggest, is the option most in accordance with international libertarianism. That there might be damage to legitimately conceived life projects is unfortunate, but the principles of just international interaction do not mandate international redistribution to preserve such projects. It should, of course, be noted that it might be possible to carry out the rectificatory project in such a way as to limit this sort of damage. If it takes place over a substantial period of time, then the current possessors of misappropriated property will presumably be able to adapt their life projects to reflect the fact that they, or indeed their children, will eventually lose the property in question. Restitution need not operate as a bolt from the blue.

Alternatively, one could seek to develop an integrated theory of restitution which was sensitive to existing life projects, and saw them as trumps which, *in certain cases*, could stop the return of misappropriated property. If this is the preferred solution, then two points should be made. The first is that this does not pose a general objection to the rectificatory project. Instead, it calls for an empirical investigation of the centrality of the holdings, both to the current possessors *and* to the putative claimants. It should be noted that this inquiry will *not* have to adopt Waldron's limited conception of centrality to life projects. The context of that conception was his grounding of property rights, which we have supplanted, and so the investigation would, and should, be able to include cases which Waldron rejects, such as where a group do not have possession of a holding but have organized their lives around the campaign for its return. This suggests the second point: that refusing to return misappropriated property risks fetishizing existing life projects. Although it may be true that taking holdings away from one group will damage their life projects, there is likely to be a positive outcome as well, in that the new recipients will be able to develop new, more expansive, and more valuable life projects. Depending on the overall patterns of holdings, the loss to the first group may be far outweighed by the benefit to the second. Imagine two nations, M and N. M is very rich, and N rather poor. Average GDP per person is 1,000 units in M, and ten units in N. Two hundred years ago, M stole resources from N. The return of these resources would cost each member of M five units, meaning that their average GDP would fall to 995 units each, whereas the average in N would rise to fifteen. Now, it is true that both the inhabitants of M and of N have learned to live within their respective means – but can it really be suggested that it would be wrong to return N's holdings because N's people have learned to live without them, and because the people of M are accustomed to having them? The background justification for respecting life projects is a concern for autonomy. But there is more to autonomy than the ability to fulfill one's projected life plans – there is also the matter of what resources one has available in formulating these plans. On any reasonable interpretation, restitution in this case serves to further the ends of autonomy overall.

5.3 INHERITANCE AND INDETERMINACY

We now turn to the final objection to the inheritance account. This concerns the claim that there is a problem, in relation to historic wrongdoing, in determining who, if anyone, is the rightful heir of misappropriated property in the possession of others in the present day. Janna Thompson draws upon Waldron to cast doubt upon the right of descendants to reclaim misappropriated possessions, referring to his 'indeterminacy thesis'. She portrays Waldron as saying that, for descendants to have a right to demand property that was taken from their forebears, 'they have to be in a position to demand what they would have received from their forebears if the injustice had not been done'. The problem is that there is no way of knowing what, if anything, this might be:

Where human choice is involved, there is no fact of the matter. Even our best guesses about what people will do are often confounded. If victims of injustice had not been dispossessed, they might have disposed of their possessions in some other way. They might have gambled them away, made a bad investment, given them to someone else, or used them for their own projects. Even immediate descendants of victims have no right to assume that the property of their forebears would have been passed on to them if the injustice had not been done. The further the injustice recedes in time, the more choices that could have been made by intervening generations, the less credible this assumption.[69]

Possibly the most important element of the inheritance account, and one which a number of theorists have misunderstood, is that it need not rely upon counterfactual calculations. The problem with Thompson's presentation of this problem is that it introduces counterfactual speculation in an area where it is not required. Waldron himself differentiates between the harm-based and the inheritance-based accounts, and acknowledges that the latter model does not face the same objections as the former, noting that:

> On this model, the rectification of injustice is a much simpler matter than the approach we discussed in the previous section. We do not have to engage in any counterfactual speculation. We simply give the property back to the person or group from whom it was taken and thus put an end to what would otherwise be its continued expropriation.[70]

Thus, Thompson is misapplying the indeterminacy thesis. The thesis appears in an earlier section of 'Superseding historic injustice', where Waldron is considering a different issue, the claim that current day individuals have been *harmed* because they have not received property that they would have, in fact, received had a historic injustice not occurred. The claim that current day individuals have inherited an entitlement to property currently in another's possession does not require that this be so. There is in fact only one area in this case where Waldron acknowledges that counterfactual judgements are necessary; namely, in relation to the question of who inherits the entitlement, and this element of indeterminacy will be addressed in due course. But this is much less problematic than the objection Thompson attributes to him.

To illustrate the point, let us consider an example where there is not just uncertainty as to whether subsequent generations would have inherited items of property but near-certainty that they would not, despite a clear intention on the part of the owner to bequeath the property. Imagine a situation where we have an offender (O), guilty of stealing an object (X) from a victim (V). Even though O misappropriates X, so that X is physically in O's possession, V retains her entitlement to X. It belongs to V regardless of O's actions. Now, suppose that V dies, but that before she does, she makes a will, leaving all her possessions to her descendant, V1. In her will, she makes explicit reference to X and makes it clear that she is bequeathing her entitlement to X to V1. It seems that what is at issue here has nothing to do with counterfactuals. O has something which now belongs to V1. It did belong to V, but she has transferred her title to the property from herself to V1. We would surely want to say that V1 has inherited an entitlement to X, given the assumption that we consider the practice of inheritance itself to be legitimate. There is no reason to appeal to counterfactual reasoning to justify V1's claim against O. In fact, as the following examples will show, counterfactual reasoning can lead to different, and intuitively undesirable, outcomes.

First, let us imagine that V always kept item X in a particular building. One day after O's theft of X, the building is destroyed by a fire. Had X been *in situ* in its original location, it would certainly have been destroyed. As such, V1 cannot claim that, had X never been stolen, she would have inherited it. Yet we would not say that her entitlement to X is any the less. O still faces a moral obligation to return it.

In this example, the loss of the article in the counterfactual world cannot be said to be the fault of V. So further, imagine that V is an inveterate gambler. Before her death, she puts all the property she possesses on number thirteen on the roulette wheel at Monte Carlo. She loses everything, and dies destitute, unable to leave a penny to V1 – save for her entitlement to X. Had she been in physical possession of X at the time, she would certainly have sold it in order to increase her stake. In fact, before the bet, she writes directly to O, begging her to sell X and place the money, in V's name, on the ill-fated thirteen. O refuses. In the counterfactual world where O's misappropriation did not take place, V1 would not have inherited X. In the counterfactual world where O latterly acted justly and returned the misappropriated property to V, or acted according to her instructions, V1 would not have inherited X. But her entitlement remains nonetheless. There is no good reason to think that V's actions meant that she lost her entitlement or that O's actions meant O gained the entitlement, or, indeed, that V's actions meant that the Monte Carlo casino gained them.

The inheritance model of restitution, therefore, does not hold that current day parties may claim an item if they can prove that they would have inherited it had an act of injustice not occurred. Rather, it simply holds that it is possible to inherit an entitlement to an object even if that object is not physically in the possession of the bequeather. For so long as the item in question is not returned to its rightful owner, an injustice is perpetrated against that owner, whether she was herself the original victim of the original act of misappropriation or not.[71]

This still raises an important question, of course, as to what should happen in cases where the entitlement in question is not explicitly bequeathed. Waldron suggests that this has, at least, the potential for the reintroduction of indeterminacy and counterfactual speculation, noting that in restoring property to the victim's successors 'we are already setting off down the counterfactual road, reckoning that this is what the proprietor's wish would have been had she had control of her property'.[72] But there are reasons to suggest that such a reckoning need not be overly problematic. First, it might be the case that, in many cases, we are happy to say that the entitlement in question has – *as a matter of fact* – been bequeathed. If A leaves all of her property to B, then there is no reason that her entitlements to property not in her possession should not be deemed to be included in the bequest – regardless of whether or not they were stipulated in the will. Secondly, even in the absence of any bequest at all, there are good reasons to assume that the direct descendant or descendants of the victim should be deemed her heirs. As Thompson notes, 'We assume, in the absence of any reason to believe the contrary, that children and spouses are the rightful heirs of the deceased.'[73] In such cases, the burden of proof lies upon others to show why this should not be the case. In the absence of justified claims of this kind, what are constructed are, in Steiner's terms, 'ancestral-chains-of-individual-persons'.[74] With each passing generation the same assumption is made, and the entitlement is passed on. We need not take the claim that present generations inherit the entitlement 'from' the original victims as meaning anything other than that the entitlement has passed down the line in this fashion. In this context, there is no reason for indeterminacy to pose a problem. If A begets B, who begets C, who begets D, who begets E, then the entitlement X simply passes along the line from A to B to C to D to E.

The model, then, claims that there is no conceptual difficulty with present day individuals inheriting entitlements from distant ancestors, if we accept that they are entitled to inherit property *per se* in this fashion. However, indeterminacy still poses a problem for the rectificatory project, as we are unlikely to find such unbroken chains very often in the real world. In an international context, it is more likely that we will know that resources were taken from a given nation by members of another nation, without necessarily knowing who specifically owned the resources in question at the time, and, in all probability, not knowing who the legitimate heir of the victim now is. This is not simply a problem of the lack of empirical knowledge of which individual has an entitlement to X. There is also likely to be what I shall call a *diffusion* of entitlement. The preceding examples have, for reasons of clarity, assumed a linear descent of entitlements from one generation directly to the next, whereby each generation has been represented by a single individual.

But this is not necessarily how inheritance works in the real world. Suppose that A has four children, B1, B2, B3, and B4, and leaves her property to the four equally.[75] Each of them, in turn, has two children, leaving us with C1–8. Who is to inherit the entitlement which we were confident in awarding to C in the previous example? The obvious answer seems to be that the entitlement is shared between all the C's. But if this continues for a large number of successive generations we may well, practically speaking, lose track of who is and who is not entitled to X.

I do not wish to resist the broad thrust of this argument. My response to indeterminacy in this context again reflects the international perspective of the book. My claim is that, in circumstances of these kinds, we have two good reasons to claim that the entitlement passes to the political community as a whole. The first, and most important, of these is based upon the claim that the nation has on the property. It was suggested in the earlier discussion of international libertarianism that accepting the principle of national sovereignty over natural resources would limit the property rights which individuals are able to claim over the fruits of production, since (*a*) they contain natural materials collectively owned by the nation and/or (*b*) they are the result of the efforts of many members of the nation. This being the case, it seems legitimate to contend that the entitlement reverts to the nation in the absence of a clear line of descent from the victim of misappropriation. This is, of course, entirely compatible with the common law practice that holds that the estates of those who die without heir revert to the state.[76] Secondly, in many cases it seems likely that the victim would *want* her property to go to her community, at least in cases where community membership is important to its members. Of relevance here is Thompson's discussion of Loren Lomasky's concept of 'lifetime-transcending interests'.[77] Thompson uses this idea, that stresses the legitimate interests which individuals have in states of affairs after their death, to justify limited inheritance practices, across two generations, as the expression of love and concern for one's immediate descendants. She feels that this only applies to two generations, as people, 'are not likely to be unduly disturbed by the possibility that their distant descendants may fail to receive [bequests] (at least in a society where individuals are not likely to be disadvantaged by injustices that happened many generations ago)'.[78] It seems to me that this argument is most plausible if it is considered within the context of a given community. It may well be that people are not overly concerned as to whether their property goes to people who happen to be related to them a long way down the ancestral line. But they still may reasonably prefer it if the property in question remained within their own community. This is particularly the case when we consider that the alternative is presumably that the property remain within another community – specifically, that of those responsible for the act of injustice in the first place! Feelings of solidarity and identification with others are typically strengthened when communities are collectively victims of injustice. It is common to stress the extent to which victims of injustice, who receive no redress during their lifetimes, wish that they may be vindicated eventually. I would suggest that we see this desire as indicative of a legitimate lifetime-transcending interest, which maintains that one's community should receive one's property in lieu of one's heirs.

Once it is accepted that the proper holder of the entitlement is the nation rather than an individual within the nation, there is no more work for the concept of inheritance to do – the entitlement is held in perpetuity by the nation. This is a point frequently acknowledged within the literature in relation to property which is *initially*, at the time of misappropriation, held in common. Thus, for example, Simmons notes in the context of Native American land claims that the property in question was taken by Native Americans, at the time of its misappropriation, to be tribal and not individual property. So he notes:

> If the property was thus held jointly, so were the relevant rights to rectification of injustice; and then, of course, the death of individual Native Americans was irrelevant to the question of persisting historical rights, as was the question of inheritance of rights (since the tribe as a whole never died, in at least many actual historical cases).[79]

What is not normally discussed are the mechanisms by which a nation can come to be in this position even if the property in question apparently belonged to an individual at the time of misappropriation. Once this is properly understood, the potential scope of the inheritance model becomes far more extensive. Indeterminacy actually ends up strengthening the position of the national community seeking the restitution of property, as it emerges as the sole, legitimate heir to the property in question.

This brings to a close my discussion of the second way in which present day generations may be connected to historic wrongdoing in a relevant sense. Both this chapter, on restitution, and the preceding chapter, on compensation have operated within the methodological assumption that present day agents are innocent third parties in relation to historic injustice. In the following chapter, which focuses on the idea of responsibility, this assumption is relaxed.

NOTES

1. For related discussion, see Simmons's treatment of particularized shares in 'Historical rights and fair shares', pp. 161–3.
2. Kershnar, 'Are the descendants of slaves owed compensation for slavery?', p. 99.

3. Thompson, *Taking Responsibility for the Past*, p. 109.
4. Thompson, *Taking Responsibility for the Past*, p. 109.
5. Nozick, *Anarchy, State, and Utopia*, p. 156.
6. For an example of an account of property entitlement founded on desert, see Stephen Munzer, *A Theory of Property* (Cambridge: Cambridge University Press, 1990).
7. See Hillel Steiner, 'Justice and entitlement', *Ethics* 87 (1977), 150–2.
8. This assumption is presumably unnecessary if one accepts Rawls's view of the role natural resources play in a people's development.
9. David Miller, 'Justice and global inequality', p. 194.
10. Rawls, *The Law of Peoples*, p. 117.
11. Samuel Freeman suggests that it is indeed fairness that is at stake here, maintaining that it is appropriate to hold the members of the pastoral society responsible for their decisions (*Justice and the Social Contract*, p. 312). He does not address the question of fairness to subsequent generations, raised in Cécile Fabre, *Justice in a Changing World* (Cambridge: Polity, 2007), p. 104.
12. Thompson, *Taking Responsibility for the Past*, p. 111.
13. Waldron, 'Superseding historic injustice', p. 15.
14. See Jeremy Waldron, *The Right to Private Property* (Oxford: Oxford University Press, 1988), Chapters 6 and 7.
15. Waldron, 'Superseding historic injustice', p. 18.
16. Waldron, 'Superseding historic injustice', pp. 18–19. Waldron does acknowledge that this argument may not apply to cases where the dispossessed entity is a tribe or community, and where the holding in question is particularly important to its sense of community. His point here is that certain cultural traditions are particularly resilient, so that it is, in fact, plausible to suggest that the return of the holding is central to the community's way of life *as it is lived in the current day* (pp. 19–20).
17. Waldron, 'Superseding historic injustice', pp. 15–16.
18. Schmidtz, *Elements of Justice*, p. 209.
19. Lomasky, *Persons, Rights, and the Moral Community*. p. 146.
20. Nozick, p. 160.
21. Nozick, *Anarchy, State, and Utopia*, p. 151.
22. Hillel Steiner, 'Liberty and equality', *Political Studies* 29 (1981), 555–69 at pp. 567–8.
23. Jonathan Wolff, 'Libertarianism', in Edward Craig (ed.), *Routledge Encyclopedia of Philosophy* (London: Routledge, 1998), available at http://www.rep.routledge.com/article/S036/.
24. 'I am as well aware as anyone of how sketchy my discussion of the entitlement conception of justice in holdings has been.' *Anarchy, State, and Utopia*, p. 230. As Waldron acknowledges, Nozick can get away with this insofar as his primary purpose is to criticize the argument of *A Theory of Justice*, rather than substantively articulate an alternative theory *à la* Rawls: as such, his account stands as 'a sketch of a plausible alternative view' (Waldron, 'Superseding historic injustice', p. 18.)

25. Waldron, 'Superseding historic injustice', pp. 17–18.
26. J.W. Harris, 'Inheritance and the justice tribunal', in Stephen R. Munzer (ed.), *New Essays in the Legal and Political Theory of Property* (Cambridge: Cambridge University Press, 2001), 106–37 at p. 125.
27. Locke made the opposite assumption, in opposition to Filmer's patriarchal theory of property ownership descending from Adam, repeatedly stressing that God has given the earth to all men in common.
28. G.A. Cohen, *Self-Ownership, Freedom, and Equality* (Cambridge: Cambridge University Press, 1995), p. 84.
29. Cohen, *Self-Ownership, Freedom, and Equality*, p. 84.
30. Steiner argues in this fashion in 'Liberty and equality': 'The...insight...of some conceptions of socialism...is that, in a normative social order, economic decision making and individual liberty are indissolubly linked through the institution of property rights. Each person's possession of a veto on the initial allocation of property eliminates the possibility of his being exploited, by minimizing the number of non-contractual enforceable obligations to which he is subject. Such an arrangement is, recognizably, a form of socialism' (pp. 568–9).
31. It is not even clear to me that people do have intuitive beliefs on this issue, given the complexity of ideas relating to joint ownership. What is more common is to find writers simply asserting one position or the other to be the correct one.
32. John Exdell, 'Distributive justice: Nozick on property rights', *Ethics* 87 (1977), 142–9 at p. 147.
33. Nozick, *Anarchy, State, and Utopia*, p. 178.
34. John Locke, *Two Treatises of Government*, Peter Laslett (ed.) (Cambridge: Cambridge University Press, 1988), p. 288.
35. Cohen, *Self-Ownership, Freedom, and Equality*, pp. 79–83.
36. Charles Taylor, 'Atomism', in Taylor, *Philosophy and the Human Sciences: Philosophical Papers 2* (Cambridge: Cambridge University Press, 1985), 187–210 at p. 189.
37. J.W. Harris, *Property and Justice* (Oxford: Oxford University Press, 1996), p. 202.
38. See Seana Valentine Shiffrin, 'Lockean arguments for private intellectual property', in Munzer (ed.), *New Essays in the Legal and Political Theory of Property*, 138–67 at p. 140n.
39. Rawls, *A Theory of Justice*, p. 4
40. This is not to say that this is how patent rights generally *are* justified, which seems more often to be the result of straightforward consequentialist reasoning.
41. Brian Barry, 'Humanity and justice in global perspective', p. 534.
42. Barry, 'Humanity and justice in global perspective', p. 533. Barry's source is Oscar Schacter, *Sharing the World's Resources* (New York: Columbia University Press, 1977), p. 124n, p. 159.
43. Barry, 'Humanity and justice in global perspective', p. 533.
44. Beitz outlines (without endorsing) such a model in suggesting that laissez-faire liberals might understand political boundaries as 'delimiting territorial

aggregates composed of chunks of territory (and appurtenant natural resources) initially acquired in legitimate ways by individuals and joined by agreement' (Beitz, 'International liberalism and distributive justice: a survey of recent thought', *World Politics* 51 (1999) 269–96 at pp. 282–3.) He suggests that 'Locke may have held such a view' in his *Two Treatises of Government*. Beitz's assumption here is that a historical entitlement account of international justice would have to be essentially both libertarian and cosmopolitan. He writes, 'Should a historical theory of distributive justice recognize state (or any other political boundaries) as having basic significance? It seems not. If the initial rights belong equally to all human beings and apply to all natural resources, it is hard to see why political boundaries should affect the validity or strength of a person's claims' (p. 281). My claim is that international libertarians can maintain that even if we accept that the *initial* rights belong to individuals, the collective efforts of these individuals to exercise these rights in concert with others can effectively come to invest political boundaries with ethical significance.

45. This, again, is dependent upon an account of how such legitimate acquisition of territory comes about.
46. Exdell, 'Distributive justice: Nozick on property rights', pp. 147–8.
47. Beitz, *Political Theory and International Relations*, p. 137.
48. See also Miller, *Citizenship and National Identity*, pp. 172–4.
49. Walzer, 'Response', p. 292 Walzer then goes on, strikingly, to express the view that these inequalities would matter if they were the result of historic injustice: '... if we tell a different story – of imperial wars; conquests, occupations, and interventions; the political control of trade, and so on – then we are likely at the end not only to be morally troubled but concerned specifically about the *injustice* of the resulting inequalities. We will be concerned because of our own belief, now widely shared that political power in international society should be distributed in accordance with the principle of collective freedom and self-determination ... And if these unjust determinations have deleterious social and economic consequences, then remedial measures are morally required. And those may well extend to far-reaching redistributions of wealth and resources' (Walzer, 'Response', pp. 292–3). This evidently is an explicit commitment to the rectificatory project.
50. David Landes, *The Wealth and Poverty of Nations* (London: Little, Brown & Company, 1988).
51. Rawls, *The Law of Peoples*, p. 117.
52. Rawls, *The Law of Peoples*, p. 108.
53. Rawls, *The Law of Peoples*, p. 108. Caney argues that this is unrepresentative of Landes's position, since 'for all his emphasis on culture, even Landes explicitly disavows any "monocausal explanations" of growth, stating that "culture does not stand alone." ' Caney, 'Review article: international distributive justice', p. 986.
54. Niall Ferguson, *Empire: How Britain Made the Modern World* (London, Allen Lane, 2003), p. 360. See also Beitz, 'Rawls's Law of Peoples', p. 690.

55. Joseph Heath, 'Rawls on global distributive justice: a defence' *Canadian Journal of Philosophy Supplementary Volume*, ed. Daniel Weinstock (Lethbridge: University of Calgary Press, 2007).
56. For further discussion, see Mathias Risse, 'What we owe to the global poor', *The Journal of Ethics* 9 (2005), 81–117. Risse's account of the issue is far more detailed and nuanced than Rawls's, but he does come down, provisionally, and in qualified fashion, in broad support of the overall tenor of Rawls's conclusion, in holding that it is institutions which are the key determinant of a society's prosperity. For more support of Rawls, see David Miller, 'Collective responsibility and international inequality in *The Law of Peoples*', in Rex Martin and David A. Reidy (eds.) *Rawls's Law of Peoples: A Realistic Utopia?* (Blackwell: Oxford, 2006), 191–205 at pp. 194–6. For criticism, see Thomas Pogge's account of 'explanatory nationalism' in *World Poverty and Human Rights*, pp. 143–5.
57. There is a potentially difficult issue here as to what should be done on this account about the fact that certain peoples have historically not received compensation for their below average resource holdings. One possibility would be to maintain that compensation in the present day should take account of this fact, which may well result in substantial liabilities for resource rich countries. Another alternative would be to put forward some version of an institutional account, whereby the duty to transfer resources only becomes active once the institutional capacity to transfer resources comes into existence.
58. See Allen Buchanan, 'Rawls's Law of Peoples: rules for a vanished Westphalian world', *Ethics* 110 (2000) 697–721.
59. See Barry, 'Humanity and justice in global perspective', p. 533.
60. Thompson, *Taking Responsibility for the Past*, p. 57.
61. This should not be taken to mean that 'possession' here can be stretched to 'control with an occupying force'. Cases where there are substantial attempts made to settle a population in a given territory, such as the British in Ulster, are admittedly more difficult. I do not have space to address these complex issues here. For discussion of this and related questions, see Tamar Meisels, *Territorial Rights* (Dordecht: Springer, 2005) and Fabre, *Justice in a Changing World*, pp. 74–94.
62. David Lyons, 'The new Indian claims and original rights to land', in Jeffrey Paul (ed.) *Reading Nozick* (Oxford: Blackwell, 1982), 355–79.
63. The suggestion here is that, insofar as a dispossessed people retain a strong identification with and allegiance for their homeland, their entitlement may remain. The problem, as discussed below, is that others may also acquire an entitlement in their absence.
64. Tamar Meisels, 'Liberal nationalism and territorial rights', *Journal of Applied Philosophy* 20 (2003), 31–43 at p. 31.
65. I should stress here that I am *not* maintaining that improving the land in this way is necessary in order for the possession of sovereignty over territory. My argument here should not be seen as providing a justification for the

dispossession of itinerant Indigenous peoples, for example. The spirit of international libertarianism, in my view, is supportive of different peoples using their territories in whatever way they see fit, and this should be respected. My claim relates to how a people may gain an entitlement to the value they have added which is conceptually distinct from their right to sovereignty over a territory.

66. Waldron, 'Superseding historic injustice', p. 16.
67. Murray N. Rothbard, 'Justice and property rights', in Samuel L. Blumenfeld (ed.), *Property in a Humane Economy* (La Salle, Illinois: Open Court, 1974), 101–22.
68. For Rothbard, this is the case even if the holding in question has been inextricably mixed with resources to which the current possessors are entitled. So, for example, if land has been cultivated and built upon, it must simply be returned to its proper possessors, who bear no responsibility to pay compensation. This, I would suggest, is going too far. The situation actually represents a reversal of the case discussed in the previous chapter concerning the receipt of benefit stemming from historical injustice. Therefore, I would suggest that there might be circumstances when compensation payments from the heirs of the victims of injustice to the heirs of the perpetrators *would* be appropriate following the restitution of property which the heirs of the perpetrators had improved. This rests upon the claim that the heirs of the perpetrators have in effect, become the innocent victims and historic injustice.
69. Thompson, *Taking Responsibility for the Past*, pp. 111–12.
70. Waldron, 'Superseding historic injustice', pp. 14–15.
71. Later in *Taking Responsibility for the Past*, in response to Waldron, Thompson does suggest that we should be generous to the descendants of victims of injustice, in assuming that misfortune would not have befallen them, resulting in the damage or destruction of their property, had the property not been misappropriated. Doing so is generous in the sense that 'those whose forebears were not done an injustice are forced to bear the consequences of outrageous fortune – of fires that destroy treasured possessions, parents who make unwise investments' (p. 123). As I have suggested, this generosity is unnecessary in that the counterfactual account of what would have happened in the absence of the injustice is irrelevant to the inheritance model. But it should perhaps be noted that, in any case, it is not correct to suggest that the descendants of victims have been somehow insulated from risk. It is entirely possible that the possessions in question could have been damaged or destroyed while they were in the wrongful possession of those who misappropriated them, or their heirs. The risk they were subjected to may have been less or more than if they were left *in situ*, depending on the circumstances – in many cases, the circumstances of misappropriation are likely to have subjected them to much greater risk than had injustice not occurred. But nothing turns on the evaluation of risk in this context. Again, the issue of insulation from risk would only be an issue if a claim for the *value* of misappropriated property, rather than the restitution of particular items of property, was being advanced under the harm-based

account, and this is the context within which Waldron raises it ('Superseding historic injustice', pp. 12–13).
72. Waldron, 'Superseding historic injustice', p. 15.
73. Thompson, *Taking Responsibility for the Past*, p. 125.
74. Steiner, 'Justice and entitlement', p. 151.
75. This objection may not be so convincing within societies characterized by primogeniture, whereby property is handed down to (typically) the eldest son, with other offspring, if awarded anything, only being given enough resources to allow them some specified level of well-being. It seems in such cases that there is an argument for maintaining that the entitlement goes to the primary heir of the property – though this may, of course, be challenged within the terms of the domestic principles of distributive justice of the society in question. International libertarians can consistently remain agnostic on this issue.
76. J.W. Harris has argued that this practice is incompatible with libertarianism: 'a consistent historical-entitlement theory must respect only real choices and it cannot vest the state with power to sequestrate ownerless goods' ('Inheritance and the Justice Tribunal', p. 126). His suggestion is that, as according to historical-entitlement theory 'original just titles can be acquired only by appropriative acts', so the resources in question simply become unowned on the death of the owner, in the absence of her having indicated her wishes for its disposal. Therefore, they seem to be open for reappropriation on a first-come, first-served basis. This is not a problem for my argument, since I do not endorse domestic libertarianism. The relevant comparison for international libertarianism concerns the property of an extinct people, and the claim that their property does not automatically become the property of international institutions but is available for reappropriation is, I believe, compatible with the principles of just international interaction.
77. See Thompson, *Taking Responsibility for the Past*, pp. 113–17.
78. Thompson, *Taking Responsibility for the Past*, pp. 128–9.
79. Simmons, 'Historical rights and fair shares', p. 179.

6

Nations, Overlapping Generations, and Historic Injustice

6.1 THE SIGNIFICANCE OF NATIONAL IDENTITY

This chapter considers the specific question of the responsibility that present day generations bear as a result of the actions of their ancestors. In Chapters 4 and 5, I worked within a methodological assumption that treated contemporary states and individuals as innocent third parties in relation to acts of injustice. This is to say that nothing was assumed as to the identity of the states and individuals in question, in relation to the identity of the political communities originally responsible for the historic act of injustice. The arguments advanced in Chapters 4 and 5 did not rely upon the fact that the community with the current day rectificatory duties was, in any sense, the same as that which committed the original unjust act. It is possible to imagine that a quite separate group has benefited from another group's historic injustice, or is in possession of misappropriated property without actually having misappropriated the property in question. In practice, it may well be the descendants of the perpetrators of injustice who have most often benefited from the actions of their ancestors, or who currently have possession of stolen or illegitimately retained property. But the arguments of Chapters 4 and 5 do not depend upon the presence of this relationship. In this chapter, I wish to move away from this methodological assumption, and put forward a new way of thinking about our relationship with past wrongdoing in order to consider specifically the significance of the fact that present day individuals are members of nations that have acted unjustly in the past. The focus, then, is on the national identity of present day generations. I shall suggest that it may well be that we are not only *connected* to past wrongdoing in such a way that gives rise to restitutive and/or compensatory obligations, but that we are potentially *implicated* in wrongdoing, in that we are ourselves collectively responsible for acting unjustly in relation to current generations. The implications of such a conclusion are important, for the moral obligations of those who are perpetrators of injustice differ significantly from the obligations of compensation and restitution outlined in Chapters 4 and 5 in two respects. First, they are potentially more extensive in terms of what they demand of us in material terms. The obligations described in Chapter 4, derived from the involuntary receipt of benefits stemming from injustice, are limited in that present day generations are only obliged to pay compensation up to the point where they are no longer benefiting from the act of injustice in question. The restitutive obligations in relation to the retention of misappropriated property described in Chapter 5 are similar in that they simply require the return of the property in question (although this may, in practice, leave the current possessors worse off than they would have been had the act of misappropriation never taken place). The compensatory obligations incurred by perpetrators of injustice, however, are potentially more extensive still, in that we generally believe that perpetrators should pay full compensation for injustice for which they are responsible. Secondly, the issue of apologies enters the picture. We generally believe that perpetrators of injustice have a moral obligation to apologize to the victims of their action. If there is a sense in which current generations are implicated in wrongdoing to other contemporary individuals, then the nature of the rectificatory project changes significantly.

There is an obvious sense in which it might be said that present day individuals are connected to historic acts of injustice, on account of the fact that they are members of the nations that were originally associated with the acts in question. Nations are historically continuous bodies. This idea is common to any plausible definition of nationhood: thus, for example, David Miller claims that a definitional feature of nationality, 'is that it is an identity that embodies historical continuity',[1] while Yael Tamir argues that a nation 'may be defined as a community whose members share...beliefs in a common ancestry and a continuous genealogy.'[2] As such, the existence of nations can and does stretch over many different generations. But what follows from the fact that we can share a national identity with persons who were the perpetrators or victims of past injustice? Is this a morally irrelevant fact, akin to the observation that we can share an eye colour with people who were the perpetrators or victims of past injustice, or is there some sense in which historic acts can affect modern day responsibilities and entitlements? The question has proved problematic within the context of liberal political philosophy because of the discipline's commitment to axiological individualism, which suggests that individuals can only be held responsible for their own actions or inactions, and not those of their predecessors. As James Fishkin writes, 'It hardly seems appropriate to hold people responsible for acts committed by their ancestors.'[3] As such, the idea that modern day individuals bear duties of compensation and/or of apology as a result of historic actions is highly controversial, and has led several theorists to devise ingenious solutions, which link present day individuals with the actions of their predecessors by, for example, the respect and affection descendants show to their ancestors,[4] or active association with the actions of these ancestors,[5] or by recasting historical injustice as a failure to create appropriate trans-generational commitments to other societies.[6] The same issues of identity lie at the heart of claims that modern day individuals can be entitled to compensation as a result of actions perpetrated against their ancestors. Janna Thompson refers in this context to 'the Exclusion Principle' that 'individuals or collectives are entitled to reparation only if they were the ones to whom the injustice was done'.[7] Can it really be right to say that present day generations are themselves victims of injustice?

In what follows, I put forward a new way of thinking about our relationship with past wrongdoing. I do this by drawing upon an idea taken from economic theory. The idea in question is that when we think of the existence of communities over time, a model of *overlapping* generations is more realistic than a model of *successive* generations.[8] I shall suggest that the bulk of theoretical consideration of our relation to ancient wrongs has taken place within the context of the latter assumption, which can be broadly described as the idea that one generation replaces another. This in turn leads us to assume that we have little or no morally relevant connection to historic injustice: the acts in question were performed by previous generations, not by our own current generation. I shall suggest that this way of thinking about past wrongdoing does not take sufficient account of the important idea that the ongoing failure to fulfil restitutive and compensatory obligations itself constitutes an ongoing act of injustice. It is this idea that leads to the suggestion that current day individuals may be guilty of wrongdoing as a result of their connection with historic injustice. I shall therefore first consider three relatively uncontroversial propositions, and draw attention to how they fit together. These relate to:

1. The nature of rectificatory duties
2. Nations and collective responsibility
3. Nations and overlapping generations

6.2 THE NATURE OF RECTIFICATORY DUTIES

The commission of injustice gives rise to duties of rectification, that typically, although not necessarily exclusively, fall upon the wrongdoer. The wrongdoer bears a moral obligation to seek to undo the effects of her actions. This involves seeking to repair the harm her action has caused to the victim, which may require either seeking to reverse the act, as in the case of the restitution of stolen property, for example, and/or paying compensation, in an effort to provide counterbalancing losses to make up for the harm. She also faces a moral obligation to apologize for her actions. If these duties are not fulfilled, the injustice of her actions continues and is not remitted. Waldron considers the example of the theft of my car. The theft itself is, of course, unjust. But, he notes, 'the matter does not end there':

> For now there is a continuing injustice: I lack possession of an automobile to which I am entitled, and the thief possesses an automobile to which she is not entitled. Taking the car away from the thief and returning it to me, the rightful owner, is not a way of compensating me for an injustice that took place in the past; it is a way of remitting an injustice that is ongoing into the present. Phrases like 'Let bygones be bygones' are inappropriate here. The loss of my car is not a bygone: it is a continuing state of affairs.[9]

This is right as far as it goes, but it can be taken further. What Waldron does not specify is the ongoing agency of the misappropriator. It is not only that I lack an automobile to which I am entitled, and that the thief possesses an automobile to which she is not entitled. It is also the case that the thief knows this, knows that it is in her power to rectify (or at least seek to repair) the situation, but does nothing. Consider the following example: imagine that, following the theft, the thief had driven home to her house, and gone to sleep. In the course of the night, she is struck by amnesia. The next morning, she has no memory of the act of theft, but finding the car outside her house and the car keys in her possession, she assumes that it belongs to her. This is the same as the situation Waldron describes – a continuing injustice as a result of the unrectified distribution of resources following an unjust act of appropriation. The situation where amnesia does *not* occur is also a continuing injustice, but in a more profound sense. It is not simply the case that we have what we might call (following Nickel's terminology) a 'distortion' within the scheme of distribution;[10] in addition, the agent responsible for causing the distortion chooses to perpetuate it. In doing so, she acts wrongly. As the result of her actions in misappropriating the car, she has acquired restitutive and compensatory obligations to me. If she fails to fulfil these obligations, she commits a further act of injustice against me.

Thus, the point that needs to be underlined in this section is the observation that the failure to fulfil compensatory or restitutive obligations constitutes an act of injustice.[11] This is in many ways a self-evident point: if we have moral obligations that we do not meet (in the absence of a morally compelling reason for why we cannot or should not meet them) then we act wrongly. This is the case regardless of whether the agent who bears the duties has acquired them through her own actions. Consider the following example in relation to the restitution of misappropriated property. Suppose that 200 years ago the rulers of Nation A misappropriated X, an item of property that belonged collectively to the people of Nation B. The rulers of Nation A hid it in a secret location within A's territory. As time passed, the knowledge of the hiding place of X was lost. Now suppose that, earlier this year, X was discovered by a member of Nation A, and, in accordance with A's laws, was handed over to A's government. If we accept that X properly belongs to the current members of Nation B,[12] then it seems that X must be returned to them. But what if the government of Nation A refuses to do this? It is clear that in this instance a fresh act of injustice is committed. We now have two incidents of injustice to consider. The first was committed 200 years ago, and those responsible for it are no longer with us. To suggest that any present day individuals were morally responsible for the commission of this act seems wrong. But the second act of injustice is different. It has just been performed by current day individuals. As such, the government of Nation A now owes an apology to Nation B, and may owe further compensation. Now that they are guilty of an act of injustice, the government of Nation A is responsible for harm that Nation B suffers as a result of its actions. For example, suppose that X is a wonderful work of art. If X was in Nation B's possession it would be able to exhibit it in its national museum, with beneficial consequences in terms of international tourism, not to mention potential benefits that might result from an increase in national tourism, or from the inspiration that could be drawn by members of Nation B from viewing X. The government of Nation A is now responsible for these losses, in a way that it was not prior to the rediscovery of X.

So, the first part of the argument holds that although restitutive and compensatory obligations can be acquired in the absence of moral responsibility for an act of injustice, these obligations are nonetheless moral obligations that compel their holders to act. If such action is not forthcoming, then the bearers of the obligations are themselves the perpetrators of a fresh injustice against the victims of the original act of injustice.

6.3 NATIONS AND COLLECTIVE RESPONSIBILITY

The second step of the argument rests upon a claim that is commonplace within this debate; namely, that it can be possible to hold nations collectively responsible for the actions of their political leaders. The claim requires some explanation. First, it is limited in that it only claims that holding nations collectively responsible is theoretically possible. This is because of the wide variety of relations that might obtain between a people of a given nation and their political leaders. For example, we might, following Miller, posit a continuum of national self-determination, with imperial rule by another power at one extreme and a strong form of democracy at the other.[13] If we locate a given nation at a point on the continuum, it remains an open question whether we should hold the people of the nation collectively responsible for the actions of their leaders. Such judgements depend on the degree of our faith in the efficacy of democratic institutions, on our beliefs as to how the actions of political leaders in non-democratic societies can be said to be determined by, or reflective of, the wishes and beliefs of the people as a whole, and on the extent to which the people are capable of replacing their leaders, should they wish to do so.[14] Nonetheless, it is widely assumed both that it is possible, in some circumstances, to hold nations responsible for the actions of their leaders, and that we should generally hold democratic nations so responsible. Thus, for example, Michael Walzer cites J. Glenn Gray's argument that, 'The greater the possibility of free action in the communal sphere the greater the degree of guilt for evil deeds done in the name of everyone.'[15] While allowing for the possibility of non-democratic national responsibility, Miller nonetheless holds that, '...the more open and democratic a political community is, the more justified we are in holding its members responsible for the decisions they make and the policies they follow.'[16] Ronald Dworkin argues in a similar fashion:

> In a genuine democracy, the people govern...communally. They treat their nation as a collective unit of responsibility, which means that they, as citizens, share derivative responsibility for whatever their government, acting officially, does.[17]

More can be said here about the nature of the 'responsibility' in question. First, we need not maintain that each individual citizen of the polity bears moral responsibility for the actions of their leaders. The individuals in question may have vehemently and vigorously opposed the policy in question. As Walzer argues, 'Even in a perfect democracy, it cannot be said that every citizen is the author of every state policy, though every one of them can rightly be called to account.'[18] The claim is about the obligations of the nation as a whole. As members of the nation, individuals do bear moral obligations to do their part in fulfilling the obligations of the nation itself. Clearly the question of the distribution of costs associated with the fulfillment of these duties is a different matter – there is no presumption that each individual need pay an equal amount regardless of their original stance on, and contribution to, the policy in question (although it will clearly be difficult in practice to find a sensitive allocative mechanism).[19]

Secondly, we can follow David Miller in accepting that even democratic nations do not necessarily bear *moral* responsibility for the actions of their leaders. Miller instead ascribes, in Tony Honoré's words, *outcome* responsibility to such nations:

> When we say that an agent is outcome responsible for the consequences of her action, we are attributing these consequences to her in such a way that, other things being equal, the resulting benefits and burdens should fall to her. If the consequences include harm to others, then outcome responsibility may, depending on the case, entail liability to compensate for that harm.[20]

In broad terms, it seems that we are happy to say that democratic nations are outcome responsible for the actions of their political leaders. The leaders are the representatives of the nation; they are chosen by the nation and act on the nation's behalf. We would perhaps be reluctant to accept the further view that a democratic nation is necessarily morally responsible for the actions of its leaders simply because leaders might act in a way, on a given issue, that does not reflect the will of the nation. The nation has extended a license to its leaders to act on its behalf, and must consequently bear the costs of its agents' actions, but this is not the same as saying it bears moral responsibility for these actions. So we might suggest that the range of cases where the nation is both morally and outcome responsible is a sub-set of the cases where it is outcome responsible. In the real world, the degree of actual control the members of a nation can exercise over its representatives is somewhat limited. But we would also surely want to allow the possibility of cases where leaders *do* act in accordance with the wishes of the nation, so that the nation is morally responsible. Differentiating these cases may well be difficult in practice, although it is also likely that we will find obvious cases of both possibilities. But, in broad terms, we might separate one-off actions from ongoing policies. We might think that it is plausible to ascribe moral responsibility to a nation for a policy that is kept in place over a prolonged period of time, as it is harder to describe such a policy as the result of wayward action by political leaders. This does not, of course, mean that we should think of one-off policies as necessarily unreflective of the nation's wishes; this may or may not be the case.

Furthermore, we might think that even if a given policy is not the result, directly or indirectly, of the will of the nation, it is still the case that the nation is guilty of collective wrongdoing. We might feel that the nation has been culpable in its selection of leaders. If Chris hires a posse of notoriously violent Hells Angels to act as the bouncers at his birthday party, then he acts wrongly, and is blameworthy. If the Hells Angels subsequently vanish without trace, having roughed up several of his guests, we might believe that his obligations go further than fulfilling the requirements of outcome responsibility. His actions were immorally negligent, and as such he possesses duties not only of compensation but of apology for his own actions. Whether we want to say that he is actually morally responsible for any injuries suffered by his guests can be left as an open question (undeniably, the Hells Angels in question are themselves morally responsible).[21] As Steven Sverdlik argues, 'We regard people who negligently cause harm as less blameworthy than those who, say, intentionally cause it, but we do regard them as somewhat blameworthy.'[22] So a judgement that I have not directly authorized my agent to commit X does not mean that I am off the hook altogether in terms of moral responsibility for wrongdoing in connection with X. The situation is different from that where I hire a reputable security firm whose employees subsequently, and unpredictably, run amok. Whether I am outcome responsible in such a way as to bear remedial obligations in such a case is, perhaps, an open question, but there is no suggestion of wrongdoing on my part.

Does it matter whether we hold the nation simply outcome responsible or also morally responsible for the injustice? The compensatory duties will be the same in either case, but we might think that the question of whether apology should be made will differ. Miller, in claiming that the question of the assignation of outcome responsibility is centrally at issue in discussions of national responsibility, suggests not:

> When people apologize, they often do so as a way of acknowledging their moral responsibility for what has happened – in other words they are admitting that they are to blame. But this need not always be so. If someone pushes against me on the Underground and I topple back and tread heavily on someone else's feet, I will certainly apologize for what has happened, as the agent who has directly imposed the harm, but it would surely be wrong to interpret this as admitting moral responsibility. Perhaps, then, we should treat national apologies as a way of acknowledging outcome responsibility for the damage that has been inflicted on the victims, which sometimes, but not always, will involve admitting moral responsibility too.[23]

What this account obscures is the fact that the form of the apology will be different depending on whether an admission of moral responsibility is involved. Within contemporary discussions of national apologies, the question of the form of the apology is very much a live issue. Again, the issue of identity lies at its heart. The question is precisely that of the relation between the act and the agent apologizing for the act. It is quite possible to say that one is *sorry* for a given act without acknowledging any relation whatsoever. As Michael Cunningham notes:

> In common parlance 'sorry' can be used in at least three different ways: to express one's regret at a situation in which one has no responsibility ('I'm sorry your father is ill'); to express regret for a situation in which one was responsible

but intent was absent ('I'm sorry I knocked over your pint'); and to express contrition for an action for which one was responsible with intent ('I'm sorry I knocked over your pint deliberately in a fit of temper').[24]

We could introduce a fourth case here: that of negligence, where one is culpable but lacks specific intent, and distinguish it from versions of the second case where one is responsible for an outcome, but not blameworthy. It is clear that the language of apology, reparation, and responsibility is only appropriate in the second, third, and fourth cases. But which is the most appropriate within the consideration of historic injustice? Cunningham raises the possibility that real world apologies may in fact correspond most closely to his first category, noting that:

> If Blair expresses regret for past wrongs done to Ireland, or Clinton over the slave trade... this could mean no more than that they are dismayed or appalled that such things happened, but bear no responsibility for them – in which case one can presumably go around being sorry promiscuously about all sorts of things.[25]

Clearly, if we are linking apology to national responsibility for injustice, something else beyond an expression of regret of this kind must be intended. According to Miller's typology, one would have outcome responsibility in Cunningham's second and third cases and in our new fourth case, but moral responsibility in only the third and fourth cases. An apology would indeed still be appropriate in the second case as an acknowledgement of outcome responsibility.[26] But such an apology falls well short of what Paul Davis has called a 'Consummate Apology'. Davis argues that a Consummate Apology is three-pronged, consisting of doxastic, affective, and dispositional elements. Taken together, these entail the following:

1. One believes that one has transgressed
2. One has a more specific belief about the morally relevant features of the situation that made one's performance transgressive
3. One is affected by feelings of self-reproach
4. One is disposed to avoid this transgression in future[27]

So even if we accept that an apology is appropriate both in cases where we bear moral responsibility for a wrongful harm and where outcome responsibility alone is involved, it is still the case that our judgement as to whether moral responsibility is at stake will affect the nature of the apology in question. A Consummate Apology requires more than simply an acknowledgement of responsibility; it also involves a process of critical self-reflection, the evident presence of self-reproach, which may best be characterised in terms of guilt and shame, and evidence of a determination to alter future behaviour.[28] And even within cases where we accept that the nation is collectively responsible for wrongdoing, an analysis of the wrongdoing is necessary in order to determine whether the problem lay in the nation's negligent selection of leadership, or in the collective action or inaction of the nation itself. None of this need be necessary in cases where an agent bears outcome responsibility but is not at fault.

We can now bring the argument of the two preceding sections together. The decision not to fulfil one's compensatory or restitutive duties constitutes an act of injustice. Insofar as it is nations which are failing to fulfil their duties, we believe that it is possible to hold the nation as a whole collectively responsible for this act of injustice, and in the case of democratic nations, we generally believe that we should do so. Finally, when a failure to fulfil such duties constitutes an ongoing policy, sustained over time, rather than a wayward, one-off governmental act, it is likely that the relevant nation is collectively responsible not only in terms of outcome responsibility but also in the stronger sense of moral responsibility. This is significant in terms of the apology owed to the victims of the nation's action, and it should also have a material impact on the particular conception of national identity shared by individual members of the nation.

6.4 NATIONS AND OVERLAPPING GENERATIONS

It is at this point that the idea of overlapping generations should be introduced. The conventional view of historic injustice sees its commission as the moral responsibility of previous generations. The question normally asked is whether we, who are innocent of injustice, nonetheless have obligations to the victims of injustice. But this is not necessarily the most helpful way to consider the matter. Consider again the previous example of the moral obligations of Nation A, which is refusing to return X to Nation B. Suppose that the discovery of X, and the refusal to return it, happened at time T. It is now T1: one year after T. What moral obligations does Nation A have to Nation B? Evidently, its restitutive obligation concerning X remains: it should return it to B. But now compensatory duties have entered the picture. Nation A was responsible for an act of injustice against Nation B at T. So it should not only return X but apologize for the fact that it was not returned at T, and compensate B for any harm B has suffered as a result.

This claim evidently rests upon the assumption that the Nation A we are talking about is the same Nation A which we were discussing at T1. But this might not be strictly accurate. The set of individuals comprising Nation A at T1 is not exactly the same as at T. Some individuals who were alive at T have died in the intervening year. Other new individuals have joined the nation. For ease of argument, let us assume that these are 18 year olds, whom we deem to be socially responsible adults within A with, for example, the right to vote. Is it open to Nation A to maintain that it does not bear moral responsibility for its actions at T, as it is not the same entity? Such an argument might be plausible if the composition of Nation A was radically different. Imagine that a peculiar plague (which we might call duodevigintitis) had befallen Nation A six months ago, killing every individual over the age of 18. Nation A is now constituted solely by those adults who turned 18 in the intervening six months. In such a case we might suppose that it is unfair to hold the actions of the preceding generation against them. But, manifestly, this is not how generations work in the real world. Generations do not in fact succeed one another, they overlap. The composition of a nation is constantly changing, with individuals being born (or reaching their majority) and dying every hour. So A is not composed of literally the same individuals at T1 as at T, but it does have (we might assume) 95 per cent of the same people. In this way, the nation is what Peter French has called a 'conglomerate collectivity':

> A conglomerate collectivity is an organization of individuals such that its identity is not exhausted by the conjunction of the identities of the parties in the organization. The existence of a conglomerate is compatible with a varying membership. A change in the specific persons associated in a conglomerate does not entail a corresponding change in the identity of the conglomerate.[29]

As a conglomerate collectivity, the obligations Nation A possesses, collectively as a result of its actions at T remain. So at T1 Nation A has moral obligations to Nation B as a result of Nation A's previous actions at T. For 95 per cent of the population this seems straightforward: they acquired the obligations as a result of their actions at T, and these obligations remain. But what of the new 5 per cent? It cannot be said that they are morally responsible for the wrongdoing at T, any more than the remaining 95 per cent were responsible for the original misappropriation of X. But they are now members of a collective which does bear obligations to B, as a result of the obligations of an overwhelming majority of their fellow members. If, at T1, A once again refuses to return X, they are implicated in the wrongdoing as members of the collective, just as the other 95 per cent were at T. But A has compensatory duties as well as restitutive obligations at T1, as a result of the decision not to return X at T. So, in a sense, *two* acts of injustice are perpetrated at T1. First, X is not returned, and secondly, compensation is not paid for the immoral retention of X. This can clearly be seen if we imagine that a decision is taken at T1 to return X but not to compensate B for its retention over the past twelve months. This would still constitute a new, albeit single, act of injustice. And just as the original 95 per cent were implicated in this decision at T, so all 100 per cent of the population are implicated at T1. If we can hold nations responsible for democratic outcomes, then Nation A is collectively responsible for wrongdoing at T1.

Fairly obviously, this process can be run over and over again. Let us take a simplified version of the example. Imagine that, at T, a referendum is held in A. One hundred per cent of the population votes against the return of X. As a result, the assignation of moral responsibility is straightforward. The nation as a whole is collectively responsible for the decision. Each individual is also, individually, morally responsible for her own actions. Both the nation, and each individual within the nation, has acted wrongly. The members of Nation A are nonetheless conscious of the demands being made by the members of Nation B, and so decide to hold a referendum on the subject of X every year. By T1, things have changed somewhat. A majority of Nation A resolves to return X to B, and this duly happens. But the issue of the yearlong wrongful retention of X is not so happily resolved. In fact, at T1 100 per cent of the population vote against paying Nation B compensation for the retention of X. In so doing, they all act wrongly, even the 5 per cent of the population who were not responsible for the decision at T. The question the new 5 per cent have faced is not that of whether they are morally responsible for the actions at T; it is whether the nation as a collective is responsible. Had the composition of the nation changed entirely between T and T1, the answer to this question would be negative. But given that the membership of the vast majority of the nation is the same at both T and T1, the collective responsibility remains. The result is that a new incidence of injustice is committed. Again, Nation A is collectively responsible for the outcome, and every member of Nation A is also individually to blame for acting wrongly. If the pattern is repeated every successive year, we can say that a new act of injustice is committed every year. So at T50, fifty-one separate acts of injustice have been committed by Nation A against Nation B. Even if the population of A is completely different at T50 than at T or at T1, in that not a single member of A at T1 is still alive, every member of Nation A has acted wrongly in relation to Nation B. As such, they are perpetrators of injustice in relation to B. They owe Nation B an apology and may owe them compensation for harm suffered.

The conclusion on compensation is conditional, while that on apologizing is not, because B is only entitled to compensation insofar as it has suffered as an automatic result of the acts of injustice which A has committed. Of course, it may be that after fifty years there is no longer a perceptible harm which has resulted from A's actions. If the people of B gradually lose awareness of and interest in the situation, it will cease to be significant from a moral viewpoint. But this need not necessarily be so. As noted previously, in the case of major incidents of international wrongdoing, which, for example, upset the balance of international trade, or severely damage a nation's political or economic infrastructure, the automatic effects of injustice may be extremely long-lasting. It is also possible that A's actions will continue to rankle with the people of B, who resent A's continual unwillingness to fulfil its obligations.[30] A key point here is that we do not assess the harm to B by simply looking at the effects on B of the original act of injustice, that is, the harm suffered between T and T1. When we look at the present population of B, we must assess the extent to which members of B have been harmed by each incidence of injustice which has occurred within their own lifetime. So the question is not simply whether the present members of Nation B have been harmed by the original non-return of X. The question is whether they have been harmed by Nation A's refusal not to compensate Nation B for the non-return of X, or by Nation A's refusal to compensate Nation B for their earlier refusal to compensate Nation B for the non-return of X, and so on. In some cases, the harm caused may dwindle with the passing of time and become negligible or non-existent. But this need not happen. Note that in contrast with the argument in Chapter 4, it is not necessary that Nation A be benefiting from any of the injustices in order for A's compensatory duties to persist.

The situation with apology is more straightforward. For as long as an apology is not forthcoming, an apology is owed. The precise nature of the apology will inevitably change over time. As the generations overlap, it will not be the case that Nation A will be apologizing for action Y *per se*. Rather, they will be apologizing for not apologizing for Y, or apologizing for not apologizing for not apologizing for Y, and so on. As with compensation, it is possible for the question of the apology to become unimportant. But, unlike compensation, it is not possible for it actually to disappear. The nature of the obligation to apologize for wrongdoing means that the obligation exists even in the absence of harm to the victim.

It should be clear that the above example is simplified in two important aspects. First, 100 per cent of the population are opposed to a just resolution of the situation. Second, these individuals take a conscious and deliberate decision to act unjustly. But neither simplification, if relaxed, affects the substantive argument. In the first instance, let us suppose that the decision not to compensate Nation B is more controversial than the above example suggests. Perhaps, in the referendum, 40 per cent of the population support a just resolution while 60 per cent oppose it. The outcome is nonetheless unjust, and, as members of Nation A, the 40 per cent who voted justly are nonetheless implicated in the decision. To be sure, their level of implication is not the same as the other 60 per cent. They are not themselves morally at fault. But it is still the case that their nation has acted unjustly. As such, as moral agents, they have a moral duty to support moves in favour of the reversal of the decision. The nation has collectively acted wrongly, despite their best efforts, and so they should vote in favour of a just resolution at the next referendum.

The second simplification concerns the fiction of yearly referenda on a nation's restitutive obligations. The issue of the annual nature of these referenda is, obviously, merely a way of conceptualizing the ongoing nature of a nation's refusal to meet its restitutive obligations. Nations do not face the question of whether to meet their obligations every year; they face them constantly, in that an ongoing refusal to so do represents a continuous act of injustice. It is true that these obligations are not normally explicitly put to a single public vote, far less to a regular series of such votes. But if we are willing to hold a people responsible for the actions and inactions of their governments then there is no reason why we should not be prepared to state that they act unjustly insofar as they fail to fulfil their ongoing collective responsibilities to others.[31]

Finally in this section, a focus on the concept of overlapping generations also allows us a ready response to those who follow Derek Parfit in arguing that present day individuals cannot be deemed to have been harmed by historic events which caused the said individuals to come into existence. As noted previously, such a claim is extremely common in the literature. Thus, Jeremy Waldron, in discussing the counterfactual approach to the rectification of injustice, notes:

> ...the events of justice and injustice may make a considerable difference in who exists at a later time. Children may be born and leave descendants, who would not have existed if the injustice had not occurred. Short of putting them to death for their repugnancy to our counterfactuals, the present approach offers no guidance at all as to how their claims are to be dealt with.[32]

Samuel C. Wheeler III argues in similar fashion:

> I take it as a premise that an individual is entitled to reparations for an unjust event only if the individual would still exist if the unjust event had not happened.[33]

If we consider these individuals as members of a nation within the context of the continuing non-rectification of injustice, the problem disappears.[34] Consider the following example. At time T, Nation C wrongs Nation D by committing action Z. At T 0.1, 36.5 days after T, M is conceived. Z had a major effect on M's parents – it is unlikely that they would have even met had Z not occurred, and wildly unlikely that the precise individual M would have been conceived. So we may, broadly speaking, say that not only has M benefited from Z, but that M owes her existence to Z. This is often, within the literature on the subject, taken as sufficient to nullify, or at least to call into question, M's claim to compensation for Z, on the basis that M has not been harmed by Z. Once we understand that it is not simply Z for whom compensation is being paid, however, this objection ceases to have force. Again using a year as our basic unit, we can imagine that at T1, T2, and so forth Nation D is harmed by Nation C's ongoing unwillingness to pay compensation. Once more, it should be stressed that this is not just an unwillingness to pay compensation for Z. It is also an unwillingness to pay compensation for not paying compensation at T1, T2, and so on. As a member of Nation D, M is harmed by each of these subsequent acts of injustice.[35] Let us take, for example, year T20. M is now an adult member of Nation D. Nation D is still owed compensation, and an apology, for Z (leaving to one side the subsequent injustices at T1, T2, etc.). A majority of the members of Nation D were alive, and full members of Nation D, at T. As a member of Nation D, M is also owed compensation and an apology. When this is not forthcoming at T20, she is harmed and wronged. Thus, it is not justifiable for the members of Nation C to claim, at, let us say, T50 that the majority of members of Nation D were not alive at the time of Z, and in fact owe their existence to Z. This may well be true. But the basis on which members of D are claiming compensation at T50 is not the harm they have suffered at T. Instead, they are claiming compensation for harm caused to them by Nation C's ongoing refusal to compensate their nation in the intervening years after T and up to T50. Because each refusal by C to compensate D constitutes a separate act of injustice, the question of M's relation to Z is beside the point. M does *not* owe her existence to the acts of injustice at T1, T2, T3, or T4. Each of these constitutes a separate act of injustice and, as such, leaves C open to morally valid compensation claims. Historic injustice casts a long shadow.

6.5 HISTORIC JUSTIFIED RIGHTS INFRINGEMENTS AND PRESENT DAY OBLIGATIONS

In this final section, I wish to return to the discussion of justified rights infringements commenced and postponed at the end of Chapter 3. The suggestion was that there could be a class of historical actions which infringed the rights of historical persons and/or groups but which did not constitute acts of injustice *per se*. Such a judgement accepts that the actions in question infringed the rights of others, but justifies the actions in terms of the rights of self-preservation of those committing the actions. It was further held that, unlike cases where actions against aggressors are justified by reference to self-defence, justified rights violations do not close the door on rectificatory justice, in that those responsible for the actions face duties to pay appropriate compensation. If this is not done, they act wrongly and unjustly. This is the sense in which the action is justified but the outcome is unjust: this is only the case insofar as the outcome is not subsequently rectified. If such rectification does take place, then there is no further case for anyone to answer. So the first point to note is that the commission of a justified rights infringement creates a compensatory duty. As such, the situation is the same as in the examples cited above whereby a party not morally responsible for an act of injustice acquires a compensatory duty. The duty in question is a moral obligation. If the duty is not fulfilled then an act of injustice is committed. So, if we find a historical case where we deem the original action to be legitimate *qua* justified rights infringement, this is not the end of the matter. We must further ask whether the compensatory duty which the action created was subsequently fulfilled. To return to the earlier example, we may maintain that the imperiled backpacker acts justifiably in infringing the property rights of the cabin owner, but we should determine whether the backpacker did pay compensation. If not, an act of injustice was committed, with all that this entails, in terms of further compensatory duties and apologies. At this point, we can return to the start of the argument of the current chapter and consider the question of collective responsibility for *this* act of injustice.So the primary claim of this section is that the question of compensation for historic actions is not dismissed by the observation that the action in question was justified since it was performed from necessity. If unrectified, then apology and compensation are due, not simply for the original act itself (for which, it might be said, compensation is due but apology, in terms of acknowledgement of wrongdoing, is not) but for the subsequent failure to fulfil the duties which arose as a result of the action. The suggestion is that the extent to which the rights-infringing actions of our ancestors can be justified turns not simply on the actions in question, but on their subsequent response to those actions. If this response was morally inadequate, an act of injustice was committed.

A further possibility suggests itself, however. What if it is suggested that it was not possible for the rights infringer to pay compensation? For many, this may seem fanciful in practice, but the point needs to be addressed in order to complete the argument. One reason such a situation could theoretically arise would be if the entire point of the justified rights infringement was the acquisition of resources. Consider the following example. Groups A and B are locked in a mortal struggle. Group A is manifestly intent on the destruction of Group B. The result is a resource-intensive arms race between the two. Group B knows that if and when Group A gains a decisive advantage over Group B in terms of its armed capability, which in turn is a function of its level of resource holdings, it will launch a deadly attack. As such, Group B must do everything it can to try to keep up. I assume here that there is no external authority to whom Group B can appeal for assistance – the situation it faces is do or die. We would likely allow, in such a case, that Group B might justifiably commit acts against other groups which would not normally be permitted. Of course, this is not the same as maintaining that *any* acts against other groups are justified – should the members of Group B coincidentally acquire a liking for hunting the members of Group C for sport, this would obviously not be permitted. Nor is it the case that we need allow that any actions designed to further Group B's security would automatically be permitted. As with just war theory in general, we would insist that Group B's actions should be proportionate, in that the harm they inflict should not exceed the harm they seek to avoid. And we may or may not wish to reject the conclusion that the use of lethal force can be justified in such circumstances.[36] But nonetheless, it might appear justifiable for Group B to seek to appropriate, in a systematic fashion, any useful resources it is able to acquire, regardless of who owns them. In such circumstances, necessity would not be a rare and short-term state; it would be the norm. Actions undertaken under conditions of necessity would not be easily reversed, or compensated for, once normality resumed. If we imagine that our imperiled backpacker is not an unfortunate day-tripper but a vagabond in a post-nuclear-holocaust anarchic state of nature, characterized by extreme competition for resources, then the claim that he should pay compensation to the cabin owner seems less straightforward. I would suggest that, in such circumstances, the act of not paying compensation for a justified rights infringement could itself constitute a justified rights infringement. The situation would be one of two successive, but different, justified rights infringements: first, of the property rights of the cabin owner and, second, of the rights to compensation of the cabin owner.[37] So we could maintain both that the actions of our ancestors were justified in terms of necessity and that they were not guilty of injustice in failing to fulfil their compensatory duties stemming from their justified rights infringements. This can be taken even further, if we maintain that our ancestors were guilty of injustice in terms of the original actions they committed (if, for example, they were unjustifiably disproportionate) but that their failure to pay compensation for their unjust actions was itself legitimate *qua* justified rights infringement. It is clear, however, that this justification for not paying compensation only holds for so long as the circumstances of necessity prevail. An uncompensated justified rights infringement is ongoing in precisely the same way as an unrectified act of injustice, and can be transferred across the generations in precisely the same way. In the absence of necessity, a failure to fulfil one's compensatory duties stemming from justified rights infringements becomes an act of injustice.

Therefore, to excuse the actions of our ancestors as justified rights infringements is to create a sort of moral time bomb. The assignation of injustice is only avoided insofar as one is justified in one's actions by some kind of necessity. The compensatory duties which one avoids in the short-term, however, do not disappear. They re-emerge, in binding form, when circumstances change and their fulfilment becomes a real possibility. This raises an intriguing idea about the way we view historic injustice. I suggested at the start of this chapter that the problem of historic injustice is typically portrayed as that of how we, who are not guilty of wrongdoing, can be asked to pay or to apologize for the wrongdoing of others. But this could be quite mistaken. Instead, if we believe that our ancestors' rights-infringing actions were justified by the particular circumstances of the time, it may in fact be recent and/or current generations, who live in relevantly different times, who bear, and who, in many cases, have failed to fulfil their compensatory obligations. As such, we exculpate our ancestors at the risk of inculpating ourselves. Regardless of whether we see our predecessors as innocent or guilty, an ongoing collective refusal to fulfil rectificatory duties can roll across generations, from past to present. It may be that, far from being innocent third parties in relation to particular historic acts of apparent injustice, it is we who are guilty of wrongdoing, and so bear obligations of compensation and apology to the groups affected.

NOTES

1. Miller, *On Nationality,* p. 23.
2. Yael Tamir, 'The enigma of nationalism', *World Politics* 47 (1995), 418–40 at p. 425.
3. Fishkin, 'Justice between generations', pp. 85–96.
4. Wheeler, 'Reparations reconstructed'.
5. Abdel-Nour, 'National responsibility'.
6. Thompson, *'Taking Responsibility for the Past'.*
7. Thompson, 'Historical injustice and reparation: justifying claims of descendants', p. 116.
8. Reference to overlapping generations is common in discussions of intergenerational justice which focus on duties to future generations, but is noticeably lacking in most discussion of what we owe as a result of past wrongdoing.
9. Waldron, 'Superseding historic injustice', p. 14.
10. Nickel, 'Justice in compensation', p. 382.

11. George Sher also makes this point in 'Transgenerational compensation', 190–200. My account was formulated separately, and appears in Daniel Butt, 'Nations, overlapping generations and historic injustice', *American Philosophical Quarterly* 43 (2006), 357–67. There are notable similarities in the way that both arguments unfold, in that Sher also considers a version of the overlapping generations argument, in an attempt to address the non-identity problem. His account, however, is based upon a single family line, as opposed to my rather different focus on collectives.
12. Evidently, as Chapter 5 makes clear, such a claim would need to be justified by reference to an appropriate argument concerning the justifiability of inheritance.
13. Miller, 'Holding nations responsible', *Ethics* 114 (2004), 240–68 at p. 259. Fabre suggests that if we focus on democratic states, then cases covered include claims by African Americans against the U.S. state for the wrongs done them by slavery and by subsequent failures to compensate them, similar claims made by Maoris against the New Zealand state and claims by populations of countries colonized in the nineteenth century by France and Britain (*Justice in a Changing World*, p. 147).
14. This issue is discussed at length by Miller in 'Holding nations responsible', pp. 260–2.
15. Cited in Walzer, *Just and Unjust Wars*, p. 298. As Walzer notes, the term 'guilt' is controversial here, but if we replace it with 'responsibility' it seems less problematic.
16. Miller, 'Holding nations responsible', p. 262.
17. Ronald Dworkin, 'Equality, democracy and constitution: we the people in court', *Alberta Law Review* 28 (1990), 324–46 at p. 337.
18. Walzer, 'Just and unjust wars', p. 299.
19. See Erin Kelly, 'The burdens of collective liability', in Deen K. Chatterjee and Dan E. Scheid (eds.), *Ethics and Foreign Intervention* (Cambridge: Cambridge University Press, 2003), pp. 118–39.
20. Miller, 'Holding nations responsible', pp. 244–5.
21. Miller describes moral responsibility as being linked conceptually to liability for blame, so that, 'to say of A that he is morally responsible for state S is to say that he has contributed to the bringing about of S in such a way as to incur blame' (Miller, 'Distributing responsibilities', p. 459.) Such a definition explicitly includes in its scope negligent action that leads to harm. The contrary view is put forward by J.L. Mackie, who adopts 'the straight rule of responsibility: an agent is responsible for all and only his intentional actions.' This means that we should not hold a person responsible for unforeseen consequences of 'inadvertent negligence'. Quoted in Peter Cane, 'Responsibility and fault: a relational and functional approach to responsibility', in Cane and Gardner (eds.), *Relating to Responsibility* (Oxford: Hart Publishing, 2001), 81–110 at p. 95.

22. Steven Sverdlik, 'Pure negligence', *American Philosophical Quarterly* 30 (1993), 137–49 at p. 137.
23. Miller, 'Holding nations responsible', p. 246. It is not clear to me that if someone pushes against me on the Underground in this way then I do bear outcome responsibility for what happens. If my toppling is simply the result of another agent's pushing, then we might well suppose that it is the other agent, and not I, who bears responsibility for the outcome. I am not an agent in a morally relevant sense here, but a falling object. My situation is the same as the third party who has been thrown down a well at me in Robert Nozick's famous example of an 'Innocent Threat': 'someone who innocently is a causal agent in a process such that he would be an aggressor had he chosen to become such an agent.' Nozick, *Anarchy, State, and Utopia*, p. 34. As such, my apology may not in fact be intended to be an acceptance of outcome responsibility, but rather be intended to assure the unfortunate owner of the feet that my actions were not deliberate. As such, my apology might constitute an express *denial* of responsibility.
24. Michael Cunningham, 'Saying sorry: the politics of apology', *The Political Quarterly* 70 (1999), 285–93 at p. 287.
25. Michael Cunningham, 'Saying sorry: the politics of apology', p. 287.
26. Honoré argues explicitly for the assumption of responsibility, and for a subsequent obligation to apologize, for the unintended results of state action: 'Our identity and integrity depend upon taking responsibility for the way in which we act or have acted in the past even in its unintended aspects. The same is true by analogy of states. To accept responsibility for the unintended consequences of state action or default (e.g. the deaths in the Irish famine of 1845, the Armenian deportations of 1915 onwards, the concentration camps of the Boer War), can be for a nation the condition of self-respect and of reconciliation with the unintended victims of government action', Tony Honoré, 'Being responsible and being a victim of circumstance', in *Responsibility and Fault* (Oxford: Hart Publishing, 1999), 121–42 at p. 133. His argument here mirrors his general argument, elsewhere more commonly expressed in terms of individuals, that outcome responsibility is 'crucial to our identity as persons' ('Responsibility and luck', p. 29.)
27. Paul Davis, 'On apologies', *Journal of Applied Philosophy* 19 (2002), 169–73 at pp. 170–1.
28. For discussion of the impact of shame at one's nation's actions, see Abdel-Nour, 'National responsibility', pp. 711–12. Abdel-Nour suggests that an agent's national shame can induce her 'to transform the myths of her nation'. He writes: 'The cultural left in America, whose focus on national shame Richard Rorty finds so distasteful, has made this its focus, as have the "New Historians" in Israel. The promise of their work of debunking national myths is that it shakes the self-righteous indignation and smug self-satisfaction that these myths have tended to foster amongst members of the nation' (p. 712).

29. Peter French, *Collective and Corporate Responsibility* (New York: Columbia University Press, 1984), p. 13.
30. Of course, this is especially likely to be the case given the unlikely scenario of specific annual decisions not to fulfil these commitments. But it may still generally be the case that the fact of an ongoing, deliberately unrectified injustice will continue to rankle. From the victim's perspective, it may be the case that an unrectified injustice does not grow less significant but more significant with time. The ongoing refusal to address the issue in such a case simply makes the situation worse.
31. May distinguishes between democratic decisions which are the result of collective *omission* and of collective *inaction* as follows: 'If people are able to decide how to act as a group, and they decide not to act, then their failure to act constitutes a collective omission. If people are able to decide how to act as a group, but they do not reach any decisions, and as a result nothing is done, then this is a clear case of collective inaction.' In either case, it seems legitimate to ascribe responsibility to the group. Larry May, *Sharing Responsibility* (Chicago: University of Chicago Press, 1992), p. 108.
32. Waldron, 'Superseding historic injustice', p. 12.
33. Samuel C. Wheeler III, 'Reparations reconstructed', *American Philosophical Quarterly* 34 (1997), 301–18 at p. 302.
34. This point is also suggested in Sher, 'Transgenerational compensation'.
35. There is an obvious, and deliberate, asymmetry here between the ages at which I deem individuals to be responsible for the actions of their nation and that at which I deem them to be harmed by harms to their nation. This simply reflects the degree of agency necessary for responsibility in the former case.
36. It is possible to maintain a general prohibition against lethal force in such circumstances, without considering, for example, extreme examples where huge numbers of a given nation will die unless we kill a small number of another nation. In such situations of (to use Nozick's expression) Catastrophic Moral Horror, it is possible simply to maintain that numbers do matter (*Anarchy, State, and Utopia*, p. 30).
37. Obviously, such a claim would rest upon an account of property rights sufficiently robust to survive the transition to a post-nuclear-holocaust anarchic state of nature.

Conclusion

'I will live in the Past, the Present, and the Future! The Spirits of all Three shall strive within me.'

Ebeneezer Scrooge, *A Christmas Carol*

The preceding chapters have aimed to shed light, from an international libertarian perspective, on the duties that members of modern day states owe to non-nationals as a result of events which occurred many years ago. They have outlined three morally relevant forms of connection with the past. Modern day individuals are connected to historic injustice insofar as they benefit, and others suffer, from its effects. They are connected insofar as they have possession of misappropriated property which properly belongs to others. And they are connected insofar as they are members of political communities which have failed to fulfil their rectificatory duties to non-nationals. The three forms of connection are complementary, but distinct. No one argument rests upon another. Even if one rejects one, or even two, of these forms of connection, one can still maintain that modern day persons possess significant rectificatory duties as a result of historic injustice.

I have aimed in this book to give an exposition of the principles underlying these duties. The question of what precisely particular modern day states owe to non-nationals obviously depends on the results of an empirical investigation into the particular history of the political communities in question. But it seems to me likely that many Western states owe extensive duties of rectification to a wide range of countries in the developing world. This conclusion has been explicitly endorsed by some international libertarians. For example, in seeking to defend John Rawls's international libertarian theory, as laid out in *The Law of Peoples*, Samuel Freeman complains that many criticisms of Rawls ignore the fact that the Law of Peoples is drawn up for the ideal case of well-ordered societies and peoples. So he writes:

> As Rawls maintains in the case of social justice, the transition principles that apply to the non-ideal case to bring about a well-ordered society often must go beyond the principles of justice, and by implication beyond the Law of Peoples, to establish remedial conditions that would not be appropriate in a well-ordered

society. So, just as Rawls might have supported as a provisional measure preferential treatment of minorities, though it infringes fair equality of opportunity, in order to remedy generations of pernicious discrimination, so, too, he could have supported as a temporary measure a global distribution principle, to rectify the history of exploitation, expropriation, and gross violation of human rights endured by burdened peoples around the world. But the important point is that such a global principle would be remedial, not permanent.[1]

This is a striking passage. Freeman's words here are strongly reminiscent of those of Robert Nozick, at the end of his discussion of distributive justice in *Anarchy, State, and Utopia*. As noted previously, Nozick considers a one-off application of the difference principle as a rough rule of thumb to 'approximate the general results of applying the principle of rectification of injustice', arguing that 'Although to introduce socialism as the punishment for our sins would be to go too far, past injustices might be so great as to make necessary a more extensive state in order to rectify them.'[2] This again underlines the extent to which the distributive conclusions of international libertarians at a global level reflect those derived by libertarians at a domestic level. But equally significant is the scope of Freeman's suggestion. In proposing a global principle, Freeman implies that the history of international injustice is so all-pervasive as to call the legitimacy of contemporary resource holdings into question all across the world. Chapter 1 argued that cosmopolitan theorists had good reasons to think carefully about framing at least some of their arguments in terms of the rectificatory project if they sought to have an effect on policy making in the real world. If one concludes that the demands of the rectificatory project are, in the short run, at least, so extensive as largely to coincide with the demands of cosmopolitan distributive justice, then this argument seems compelling.

At the start of 'The problem of global justice', Thomas Nagel writes, 'We do not live in a just world. This may be the least controversial claim one could make in political theory.'[3] It is of vital importance that international libertarians take this claim seriously. It is obviously true for redistributive cosmopolitans, who see a gigantic gulf between the demands of their ideal theories of distributive justice and the starkly inegalitarian realities of world politics. In this book, I have tried to show that it is obviously true for international libertarians also. My account maintains, therefore, that the citizens of Western states are members of collectives which are failing to fulfil their moral duties. Those of us who live in such states are collectively responsible for ongoing acts of injustice. For this failing alone, compensation and apology are owed. I have argued that ideas of rectificatory justice have particular, compelling force; that arguments relating to the righting of wrongs can motivate action in a way which is not the case for claims made from within ideal theory accounts of distributive justice. This is not to say that persuading people that they possess such rectificatory duties is straightforward. In the real world, it is not unusual for individuals to be uncomfortable with ideas of rectificatory justice, and to reject its demands with considerable indignation. In part, I suspect this stems from the very understandable wish not to be blamed for something which was not one's fault. We are familiar from our everyday experience with the particular harm individuals tend to suffer when they are the object of false accusations – these often appear as full-frontal attacks on one's moral integrity, as slurs on one's character. And sometimes those who seek, or support, rectification word their demands in such a way that it appears that they are blaming contemporary individuals for historic actions. It seems as if they are using notions of national identity and responsibility which do not fit in with modern day understandings of individual agency. The rectificatory project as I have outlined it makes no such claims. No present day individuals are blamed, held morally responsible, or asked to apologize for the actions of their predecessors. But this emphatically does not let these present day individuals off the moral hook. We live in a world where history matters, most particularly in terms of the distribution of resources. We grow up in, are cared for by, are educated by, hold property within, and are members of national communities whose prosperity and well-being are largely determined by what happened many years ago. Our membership of these communities is, for the most part, involuntary. But that does not mean that we can avoid the consequences of our communities' history. The claim that present day individuals are morally responsible for the commission of historic actions is manifestly incorrect. But the claim that present day individuals are guilty of wrongdoing in connection with these actions need not be. In such circumstances, to condemn historic injustice, to disown it, and to distance oneself from it is often insufficient. To do this while refusing to fulfil one's rectificatory duties has the opposite effect of tacitly condoning past injustice, and implicating oneself in its commission. Insofar as the effects of wrongdoing persist, those who bear, but fail to perform, duties to undo these effects stand shoulder to shoulder with the perpetrators of injustice.

What, then, ought an international libertarian who is convinced by the arguments of this book to do? What follows from an acceptance of the idea that one's national community owes extensive rectificatory duties to non-nationals? Should we initiate massive resource transfers immediately, so as to seek to regain a state of moral equilibrium with those who are still feeling the effects of historic wrongdoing? Obviously, this is a difficult policy question which is equally faced by redistributive cosmopolitans who believe, for example, that inequalities in international resource holdings are unjust. There are doubtless cases where resource transfers would indeed be of benefit to those who are entitled to rectification; equally, there are doubtless cases where such a course of action might be counterproductive. What is most important is that consideration of policy in such cases is genuinely motivated by a concern for the best interests of those who are – as a matter of justice – entitled to our assistance. If this means that we who possess rectificatory duties must make sacrifices in terms of our standard of living, then so be it. In circumstances of extensive and pervasive historic international injustice, the rectificatory project calls for an ongoing commitment from those who continue to benefit from past wrongdoing to honour the past victims of injustice by building a world where the descendants of both wrongdoers and victims can live together in peace, and interact with one another in a context of justice.

NOTES

1. Freeman, *Justice and the Social Contract*, p. 312.
2. Nozick, *Anarchy, State, and Utopia*, p. 231.
3. Nagel, 'The problem of global justice', p. 113.

Bibliography

Abdel-Nour, Farid, 'National responsibility', *Political Theory* 31 (2003), 693–719.
Abizadeh, Arash, 'Historical truth, national myths, and liberal democracy: on the coherence of liberal nationalism', *The Journal of Political Philosophy* 12 (2004), 291–313.
Alexander, Larry A., 'Causation and corrective justice: does tort law make sense?', *Law and Philosophy* 6 (1987), 1–23.
Anderson, Elizabeth, 'What is the point of equality?', *Ethics* 109 (1999), 287–337.
Arneson, Richard, 'Equality and equal opportunity for welfare', *Philosophical Studies* 54 (1988), 79–95.
Bales, Kevin, *Understanding Global Slavery: A Reader* (Berkeley: University of California Press, 2005).
Barkan, Elazar, *The Guilt of Nations: Restitution and Negotiating Historic Injustices* (New York: Norton, 2000).
Barker, Kit, 'Unjust enrichment: containing the beast', *Oxford Legal Studies* 15 (1995), 457–75.
Barry, Brian, 'Humanity and justice in global perspective', in R. Goodin and P. Pettit (eds.), *Contemporary Political Philosophy: An Anthology* (Oxford: Blackwell, 1993), 525–40.
—— 'International society from a cosmopolitan perspective', in David Mapel and Terry Nardin (eds.), *International Society: Diverse Ethical Perspectives* (Princeton: Princeton University Press, 1998), 144–63.
Beitz, Charles, *Political Theory and International Relations* (Princeton: Princeton University Press, 1979).
—— 'Cosmopolitan ideals and national sentiment', *Journal of Philosophy* 80 (1983), 591–600.
—— 'Social and cosmopolitan liberalism', *International Affairs* 75 (1999), 515–29.
—— 'Rawls's Law of Peoples', *Ethics* 110 (2000), 669–96.
Berges, Sandrine, 'Interview with Professor Thomas Pogge', *Éthique et économique/ Ethics and Economics*, 5 (2007).
Birks, Peter, *An Introduction to the Law of Restitution* (Oxford: Clarendon Press, 1989).
—— *The Foundations of Unjust Enrichment* (Wellington: Victoria University Press, 2002).
Blake, Michael, 'Distributive justice, state coercion, and autonomy', *Philosophy and Public Affairs* 30 (2002) 257–96.
Boxhill, Bernard, 'The morality of reparation', in Gross (ed.) *Reverse Discrimination* (Buffalo: Prometheus, 1977), 270–8.
Brooks, Roy L., *When Sorry Isn't Enough: The Controversy over Apologies for Human Injustice* (New York: New York University Press, 1999).

Brown, Christopher, *Sovereignty, Rights and Justice: International Political Theory Today* (Cambridge: Polity, 2002).
Buchanan, Allen, 'Judging the past: the case of the human radiation experiments', in Ronald Munson (ed.), *Intervention and Reflection: Basic Issues in Medical Ethics* (Belmont, California: Wadsworth, 2000), 525–30.
—— 'Rawls's Law of Peoples: rules for a vanished Westphalian world', *Ethics* 110 (2000) 697–721.
—— *Justice, Legitimacy and Self-Determination: Moral Foundations for International Law* (Oxford: Oxford University Press, 2004).
Burrows, Andrew, *The Law of Restitution* (London: Butterworths, 1993).
Butt, Daniel, 'Principles of Compensation and Restitution in International Justice' (Oxford D.Phil. thesis, 2005).
—— 'Nations, overlapping generations and historic injustice', *American Philosophical Quarterly* 43 (2006), 357–67.
Cane, Peter, *Atiyah's Accidents, Compensation and the Law* (London: Butterworths, 1993).
—— 'Responsibility and fault: a relational and functional approach to responsibility', in Cane and Gardner (eds.), *Relating to Responsibility* (Oxford: Hart Publishing, 2001), 81–110.
Caney, Simon, 'Review article: international distributive justice', *Political Studies* 49 (2001), 974–97.
—— 'Survey article: cosmopolitanism and the Law of Peoples', *The Journal of Political Philosophy* 10 (2002), 95–123.
—— 'A reply to Miller', *Political Studies* 50 (2002), 1013–18.
—— *Justice Beyond Borders: A Global Political Theory* (Oxford: Oxford University Press, 2005).
—— 'Global poverty and human rights: the case for positive duties', in Thomas Pogge (ed.), *Freedom from Poverty as a Basic Right* (Oxford: Oxford University Press, 2007), 275–302.
Card, Claudia Falconer, 'Rectification and remainders', in Edward Craig (ed.), *Routledge Encyclopaedia of Philosophy*, (London: Routledge, 1998), available at http://www.rep.routledge.com/article/L082/.
—— *The Atrocity Paradigm: A Theory of Evil* (Oxford: Oxford University Press, 2002).
Chapman, John W. (ed.), *Nomos XXXIII: Compensatory Justice* (New York: New York University Press, 1991).
Chen, Shaohua and Ravallion, Martin, 'How have the world's poorest fared since the early1980s?', *The World Bank Research Observer* 19 (2004), 141–69
Cohen, G.A., 'On the currency of egalitarian justice', *Ethics* (1989), 906–44.
—— *Self-Ownership, Freedom, and Equality* (Cambridge: Cambridge University Press, 1995).
—— *If You're an Egalitarian, How Come You're So Rich?* (Cambridge, MA: Harvard University Press, 2000).
—— 'Facts and principles', *Philosophy & Public Affairs* 31 (2003), 211–45.

Cohen, Joshua and Sabel, Charles, '*Extra rempublicam nulla justitia?*', *Philosophy and Public Affairs* 34 (2006), 147–75
Cohen, Marshall, 'Moral skepticism and international relations', *Philosophy and Public Affairs* 13 (1984), 299–346.
Coleman, Jules L., 'Justice and the argument for no-fault', *Social Theory and Practice* 3 (1974), 161–80.
—— 'The morality of strict tort liability', *William and Mary Law Review* 18 (1976) 259–86.
—— *Markets, Morals and the Law* (Cambridge: Cambridge University Press, 1988).
—— *Risks and Wrongs* (Cambridge: Cambridge University Press, 1992).
—— 'Corrective justice and property rights', in Rodney C. Roberts (ed.), *Injustice and Rectification* (New York: Peter Lang, 2005), 53–65.
Cunningham, Michael, 'Saying sorry: the politics of apology', *The Political Quarterly* 70 (1999), 285–93.
Daniels, Norman, *Justice and Justification: Reflective Equilibrium in Theory and Practice* (Cambridge: Cambridge University Press, 1996).
Darley, John M. and Pittman, Thane S., 'The psychology of compensatory and retributive justice' *Personality and Social Psychology Review* 7 (2003), 324–36.
Davis, Paul, 'On apologies', *Journal of Applied Philosophy* 19 (2002), 169–73.
de-Shalit, Avner, 'Transnational and international exploitation', *Political Studies* 46 (1998), 693–708.
Dower, Nigel, 'World poverty', in P. Singer (ed.), *A Companion to Ethics* (Oxford: Blackwell, 1991), 273–83.
Dworkin, Ronald, 'Equality, democracy and constitution: we the people in court', *Alberta Law Review* 28 (1990), 324–46.
Erreygers, Guido and Vandevelde, Toon (eds.), *Is Inheritance Legitimate?* (Heidelberg: Springer-Verlag Berlin, 1997).
Exdell, John, 'Distributive justice: Nozick on property rights', *Ethics* 87 (1977), 142–9.
Ezorsky, Gertrude, *Racism and Justice: The Case for Affirmative Action* (Ithaca: Cornell University Press, 1991).
Fabre, Cécile, *Justice In a Changing World* (Cambridge: Polity, 2007).
Fagan, Eduard, 'The constitutional entrenchment of memory', in Sarah Nuttall and Carli Coetzee (eds.), *Negotiating the Past: The Making of Memory in South Africa* (Cape Town: Oxford University Press, 1998), 249–62.
Farrelly, Colin, 'Justice in ideal theory: a refutation' *Political Studies* 55 (2007), 844–64.
Feinberg, Joel, 'Voluntary euthanasia and the inalienable right to life', *Philosophy and Public Affairs* 7 (1978), 93–123.
—— 'Wrongful life and the counterfactual element in harming', in *Freedom and Fulfillment: Philosophical Essays* (Princeton: Chichester, 1992), 3–36.
Ferguson, Niall, *Empire: How Britain Made the Modern World* (London, Allen Lane, 2003).
Fishkin, James, 'Justice between generations', in John W. Chapman, (ed.), *Nomos XXXIII: Compensatory Justice* (New York: New York University Press, 1991), 85–96.

Freeman, Samuel, *Justice and the Social Contract: Essays on Rawlsian Political Philosophy* (New York: Oxford University Press, 2007).
—— *Rawls* (Abingdon: Routledge, 2007).
French, Peter, *Collective and Corporate Responsibility* (New York: Columbia University Press, 1984).
Frost, Melvyn, *Ethics in International Relations: A Constitutive Theory* (Cambridge: Cambridge University Press, 1996).
Fuller, Lon L. and Purdue Jr., William R., 'The reliance interest in contract damages', *Yale Law Journal* 46 (1936), 52–96.
Fullinwider, Robert, *The Reverse Discrimination Controversy* (Totowa, New Jersey: Rowman & Littlefield, 1980).
—— 'Preferential hiring and compensation' in Steven M. Cahn, *The Affirmative Action Debate* (New York: Routledge, 2002), 68–78.
Gaus, Gerald, 'Does compensation restore equality?', in John W. Chapman (ed.), *Nomos XXXIII: Compensatory Justice* (New York: New York University Press, 1991), 45–81.
Gellner, Ernest, *Thoughts and Change* (London: Weidenfeld & Nicolson, 1964).
Gewirth, Alan, *Reason and Morality* (Chicago: University of Chicago Press, 1978).
—— 'The epistemology of human rights', *Social Philosophy and Policy* 1 (1984), 1–24.
—— 'War crimes and human rights', in Aleksander Jokić (ed.), *War Crimes and Collective Wrongdoing* (Oxford: Blackwell, 2001), 48–56.
Gibbard, Allan, 'Constructing justice', *Philosophy and Public Affairs* 20 (1991), 264–79.
Goodin, Robert E., 'Exploiting a situation and exploiting a person', in Andrew Reeve (ed.), *Modern Theories of Exploitation* (London: Sage, 1987), 166–200.
—— 'Compensation and redistribution' in John W. Chapman (ed.), *Nomos XXXIII: Compensatory Justice* (New York: New York University Press, 1991), 143–77.
—— 'Political ideals and political practice', *British Journal of Political Science* 25 (1995), 37–56.
Gosseries, Axel, 'Historical emissions and free-riding', *Ethical Perspectives* 11 (2004), 38–62.
Gray, John, *Mill On Liberty: A Defence* (London: Routledge, 1996).
Griffiths, Martin, *Realism, Idealism and International Politics: A Reinterpretation* (London: Routledge, 1992).
Harris, J. W., *Property and Justice* (Oxford: Oxford University Press, 1996).
—— 'Inheritance and the justice tribunal', in Stephen R. Munzer (ed.), *New Essays in the Legal and Political Theory of Property* (Cambridge: Cambridge University Press, 2001), 106–37.
Haslett, D.W., 'Is inheritance justified?', *Philosophy and Public Affairs* 15 (1986), pp. 122–55.
Heath, Joseph, 'Rawls on global distributive justice: a defence' *Canadian Journal of Philosophy Supplementary Volume*, ed. Daniel Weinstock (Lethbridge: University of Calgary Press, 2007).

Hoffmann, Stanley, 'The political ethics of international relations', in Joel H. Rosenthal (ed.), *Ethics and International Affairs: A Reader* (Washington D.C.: Georgetown University Press, 1999), 28–49.

Honoré, Tony, 'Responsibility and luck', *Law Quarterly Review* 104 (1988), 530–53.

—— 'Being responsible and being a victim of circumstance', in *Responsibility and Fault* (Oxford: Hart Publishing, 1999), 121–42.

Horvath, Ronald J., 'A definition of colonialism', *Current Anthropology* 13 (1972), 45–57.

Howard, Michael, *The Causes of Wars* (London: Maurice Temple Smith, 1987).

Jaja, Cheedy, 'Hobbes's theory of colonialism and the African colonial experience: structural and programmatic affinities', *American Philosophical Association Newsletters* 97 (1998), available at http://www.apa.udel.edu/apa/archive/newsletters/v97n2/black/hobbes.asp/.

Jokić, Aleksander (ed.), *War Crimes and Collective Wrongdoing* (Oxford: Blackwell, 2001).

Jones, Charles, *Global Justice: Defending Cosmopolitanism* (Oxford: Oxford University Press, 1999).

Jones, Hardy E., 'On the justifiability of reverse discrimination', in Barry Gross (ed.), *Reverse Discrimination* (Buffalo: Prometheus, 1977), 348–57.

Kegley Jr., Charles W., and Raymond, Gregory A., 'Preventive war and permissive moral order', *International Studies Perspectives* 4 (2003), 385–94.

Kelly, Erin, 'The burdens of collective liability', in Deen K. Chatterjee and Dan E. Scheid (eds.), *Ethics and Foreign Intervention* (Cambridge: Cambridge University Press, 2003), pp. 118–39.

Kennan, George F., 'Morality and foreign policy', *Foreign Affairs* 64 (1985/86), 205–18.

Kershnar, Stephen, 'Are the descendants of slaves owed compensation for slavery?', *Journal of Applied Philosophy* 16 (1999), 95–101.

Klosko, George, *The Principle of Fairness and Political Obligation* (Lanham: Rowman & Littlefield, 1992).

Kramer, Matthew, 'Of Aristotle and ice cream cones: reflections on Jules Coleman's theory of corrective justice' in B. Bix (ed.), *Analyzing Law: New Essays in Legal Theory* (Oxford: Oxford University Press, 1998), 163–80.

Landes, David, *The Wealth and Poverty of Nations* (London: Little, Brown & Company), 1998.

Lawrence III, Charles R., and Matsuda, Mari J., *We Won't Go Back: Making the Case for Affirmative Action* (Boston: Houghton Mifflin Company, 1997).

Levmore, Saul, 'Variety and uniformity in the treatment of the good-faith purchaser', *Journal of Legal Studies* 16 (1987), 43–65.

Levy, Michael B., 'Liberal equality and inherited wealth', *Political Theory* 11 (1983), 545–64.

Linklater, Andrew, *The Transformation of Political Community: Ethical Foundations of the Post-Westphalian Era* (Cambridge: Polity, 1998).

Locke, John, *Two Treatises of Government*, Peter Laslett (ed.) (Cambridge: Cambridge University Press, 1988).

Lomasky, Loren E., *Persons, Rights, and the Moral Community* (New York: Oxford University Press, 1987).
—— 'Compensation and the bounds of rights', in John W. Chapman (ed.), *Nomos XXXIII: Compensatory Justice* (New York: New York University Press, 1991), 13–44.
Lyons, David, 'The new Indian claims and original rights to land', in Jeffrey Paul (ed.) *Reading Nozick* (Oxford: Blackwell, 1982), 355–79.
McDermott, Daniel, 'Fair-play obligations' *Political Studies* 52 (2004), 216–32.
McMahan, Jeff, 'War as self-defense', *Ethics and International Affairs*, 18 (2004), 13–18.
McWhorter, John, *Losing the Race: Self-Sabotage in Black America* (New York: Perennial, 2001).
—— 'Against reparations', *The New Republic* 23 July 2001.
Mapel, David R., 'Realism and the ethics of war and peace', in Terry Nardin (ed.), *The Ethics of War and Peace: Religious and Secular Perspectives* (Princeton: Princeton University Press, 1996), 54–77.
Matravers, Matt, *Responsibility and Justice* (Cambridge: Polity, 2007).
May, Larry, *Sharing Responsibility* (Chicago: University of Chicago Press, 1992).
Meisels, Tamar, 'Liberal nationalism and territorial rights', *Journal of Applied Philosophy* 20 (2003), 31–43.
—— *Territorial Rights* (Dordecht: Springer, 2005).
Mill, John Stuart, *'On Liberty'and Other Writings,* Stefan Collini (ed.) (Cambridge: Cambridge University Press, 1989).
Miller, David, 'Exploitation in the market', in Andrew Reeve (ed.), *Modern Theories of Exploitation* (London: Sage, 1987), 149–65.
—— *On Nationality* (Oxford: Clarendon Press, 1995).
—— 'Introduction' to D. Miller and M. Walzer (eds.), *Pluralism, Justice and Equality* (Oxford: Oxford University Press, 1995), 1–16.
—— 'Justice and global inequality', in A. Hurrell and N. Woods (eds.), *Inequality, Globalization, and World Politics* (Oxford: Oxford University Press, 1999), 187–210.
—— *Principles of Social Justice* (Cambridge, MA: Harvard University Press, 1999).
—— *Citizenship and National Identity* (Cambridge, MA: Polity, 2000).
—— 'Distributing responsibilities', *Journal of Political Philosophy* 9 (2001), 453–71.
—— 'Caney's "International distributive justice": a response', *Political Studies* 50 (2002), 974–7.
—— 'Holding nations responsible', *Ethics* 114 (2004), 240–68.
—— 'Collective responsibility and international inequality in *The Law of Peoples*', in Rex Martin and David A. Reidy (eds.) *Rawls's Law of Peoples: A Realistic Utopia?* (Blackwell: Oxford, 2006), 191–205.
—— *National Responsibility and Global Justice* (Oxford: Oxford University Press, 2007).
Moellendorf, Darrel, *Cosmopolitan Justice* (Boulder, CO: Westview, 2002).
Munzer, Stephen, *A Theory of Property* (Cambridge: Cambridge University Press, 1990).
Murphy, Liam, *Moral Demands in Nonideal Theory* (Oxford: Oxford University Press, 2000).

Murphy, Liam and Nagel, Thomas, *The Myth of Ownership: Taxes and Justice* (Oxford: Oxford University Press, 2002).

Nagel, Thomas, *Equality and Partiality* (New York: Oxford University Press, 1991).

—— 'The problem of global justice', *Philosophy and Public Affairs* 33 (2005) 113–47.

Nardin, Terry, *Law, Morality and the Relations of States* (Princeton: Princeton University Press, 1983).

—— 'Philosophy of war and peace', in Edward Craig (ed.), *Routledge Encyclopedia of Philosophy* (London: Routledge, 1998), available at http://www.rep.routledge.com/article/S066/.

Nickel, James W., 'Justice in compensation', *William and Mary Law Review* 18 (1976), 379–88.

—— 'Preferential policies in hiring and admissions: a jurisprudential approach', in Barry Gross (ed.), *Reverse Discrimination* (Buffalo: Prometheus, 1977), 324–47.

—— 'Human rights' in Edward N. Zalta (ed.), *The Stanford Encyclopedia of Philosophy (Summer 2003 Edition)* available at http://plato.stanford.edu/archives/sum2003/entries/rights-human/.

Nozick, Robert, *Anarchy, State, and Utopia* (New York: Basic Books, 1974).

O'Neill, Onora, *Faces of Hunger* (London: Allen & Unwin, 1986).

—— 'Rights to compensation,' *Social Philosophy and Policy* 5 (1987), 72–87.

—— *Bounds of Justice* (Cambridge: Cambridge University Press, 2000).

Osgood, Robert and Tucker, Robert, *Force, Order and Justice* (Baltimore: The Johns Hopkins Press, 1967).

Otsuka, Michael, 'Killing the innocent in self-defense', *Philosophy and Public Affairs* 23 (1994), 74–94.

Palmer, Tom, 'A Cosmopolitan Theory of Justice' (Oxford D.Phil. thesis, 2000).

Parfit, Derek, *Reasons and Persons* (Oxford: Clarendon Press, 1984).

Patten, Alan, 'Should we stop thinking about poverty in terms of helping the poor?', *Ethics & International Affairs* 19 (2005).

Paul, Ellen Frankel, 'Set-asides, reparations, and compensatory justice', in John W. Chapman (ed.), *Nomos XXXIII: Compensatory Justice* (New York: New York University Press, 1991), 97–139.

Perry, Stephen R., 'On the relationship between corrective and distributive justice' in J. Horder, (ed.), *Oxford Essays in Jurisprudence* (Oxford: Clarendon Press, 2000 – Fourth Series), 237–63.

Pogge, Thomas W., *Realizing Rawls* (Ithaca: Cornell University Press, 1989).

—— *World Poverty and Human Rights* (Cambridge: Polity, 2002).

—— ' "Assisting" the global poor', in Deen K. Chatterjee (ed.), *The Ethics of Assistance: Morality and the Distant Needy* (Cambridge: Cambridge University Press, 2004), 260–88.

—— 'Symposium: World Poverty and Human Rights', *Ethics and International Affairs* 19 (2005), 1–7.

—— (ed.), *Freedom from Poverty as a Basic Right* (Oxford: Oxford University Press, 2007), 275–302.

Pogge, Thomas and Reddy, Sanjay G., 'Unknown: the extent, distribution and trend of global income poverty' (2006) – available at http://ssrn.com/abstract = 936772

Rawls, John, *A Theory of Justice* (Oxford: Oxford University Press, 1972).

—— 'The independence of moral theory', *Proceedings and Addresses of the American Philosophical Association*, 48 (1974/5), 5–22.

—— *Political Liberalism* (New York: Columbia University Press, 1993).

—— *The Law of Peoples* (Cambridge, MA: Harvard University Press, 1999).

Raymond, Gregory A., 'Necessity in foreign policy', *Political Science Quarterly* 13 (1998/99), 673–88.

Raz, Joseph, *The Morality of Freedom* (Oxford: Clarendon Press, 1986).

Richards, David A.J., 'International distributive justice' in J.R. Pennock and J.W. Chapman (eds), *Nomos XXIV: Ethics, Economics, and the Law* (New York: New York University Press, 1982), 275–99.

Ripstein, Arthur, *Equality, Responsibility and the Law* (Cambridge: Cambridge University Press, 1999).

Risse, Mathias, 'How does the global order harm the poor?', *Philosophy & Public Affairs* 33 (2005).

—— 'What we owe to the global poor', *The Journal of Ethics* 9 (2005), 81–117.

Roberts, M. A., 'The non-identity fallacy: harm, probability and another look at Parfit's depletion example', *Utilitas* 19 (2007), 267–311.

Robinson, Randall, *The Debt: What America Owes to Blacks* (New York: Plume, 2001).

Rodin, David, *War and Self-Defense* (Oxford: Oxford University Press, 2002).

Rothbard, Murray N., 'Justice and property rights', in Samuel L. Blumenfeld (ed.), *Property in a Humane Economy* (La Salle, Illinois: Open Court, 1974), 101–22.

Russell, Paul, 'Nozick, need and charity', *Journal of Applied Philosophy* 4 (1987), 205–16.

Salter, Mark B., *Rights of Passage* (Dordrecht: Lynne Rienner, 2003).

Sangiovanni, Andrea, 'Global justice, reciprocity and the state', *Philosophy and Public Affairs* 35 (2007), 3–39.

Schacter, Oscar, *Sharing the World's Resources* (New York: Columbia University Press, 1977).

Schmidtz, David, *Elements of Justice* (Cambridge: Cambridge University Press, 2006).

Shapiro, Ian and Brilmayer, Leo (eds.), *Nomos XLI: Global Justice* (New York: New York University Press, 1999).

Shei, Ser-Min, 'World poverty and moral responsibility' in Andreas Follesdal and Thomas Pogge (eds.), *Real World Justice: Grounds, Principles, Human Rights, and Social Institutions* (Dordrecht: Springer, 2005), 139–56.

Sher, George, 'Ancient wrongs and modern rights', *Philosophy and Public Affairs* 10 (1980), 3–17.

—— *Approximate Justice: Studies in Non-Ideal Theory* (Lanham: Rowman & Littlefield, 1997).

—— 'Transgenerational compensation' *Philosophy and Public Affairs* 33 (2005), 181–200.
Shiffrin, Seana Valentine, 'Lockean arguments for private intellectual property', in Munzer (ed.), *New Essays in the Legal and Political Theory of Property* (Cambridge: Cambridge University Press, 2001), 138–67.
Shue, Henry, *Basic Rights: Subsistence, Affluence and U.S. Foreign Policy* (Princeton: Princeton University Press, 1996).
Simmons, A. John, 'Historical rights and fair shares', *Law and Philosophy* 14 (1995), 149–84.
Singer, Peter, 'Famine, affluence and morality', *Philosophy and Public Affairs* 1 (1972), 229–43.
Solignac Lecomte, Henri-Bernard, McDonnell, Ida, and Wegimont, Liam (eds.), *Public Opinion and the Fight Against Poverty* (Paris: OECD, 2003).
Steiner, Hillel, 'Justice and entitlement', *Ethics* 87 (1977), 150–2.
—— 'Nozick on appropriation', *Mind* 87 (1978), 109–10.
—— 'Liberty and equality', *Political Studies* 29 (1981), 555–69.
—— 'Exploitation: a liberal theory amended, defended and extended', in Andrew Reeve (ed.), *Modern Theories of Exploitation* (London: Sage, 1987), 132–48.
—— *An Essay on Rights* (Oxford: Blackwell, 1994).
—— 'Territorial justice', in Simon Caney, David George, and Peter Jones (eds.), *National Rights, International Obligations* (Boulder, CO: Westview, 1996), 139–48.
—— 'Hard borders, compensation and classical liberalism' in David Miller and Soheil H. Hashmi (eds.) *Boundaries and Justice: Diverse Ethical Perspectives* (Princeton: Princeton University Press, 2001), 79–88.
Stemplowska, Zofia, 'What's ideal about ideal theory?' *Social Theory and Practice* 34 (2008), 319–40.
Sunstein, Cass R., 'Incompletely theorized agreements', *Harvard Law Review* 108 (1995), 1733–72.
Sverdlik, Steven, 'Pure negligence', *American Philosophical Quarterly* 30 (1993), 137–49.
Swift, Adam, 'The value of philosophy in nonideal circumstances' *Social Theory and Practice* 34 (2008), 363–87.
Tamir, Yael, *Liberal Nationalism* (Princeton: Princeton University Press, 1993).
—— 'The enigma of nationalism', *World Politics* 47 (1995), 418–40.
Tan, Kok-Chor, *Justice Without Borders: Cosmopolitanism, Nationalism and Patriotism* (Cambridge: Cambridge University Press, 2004).
Taylor, Charles, 'Atomism', in Taylor, *Philosophy and the Human Sciences: Philosophical Papers 2* (Cambridge: Cambridge University Press, 1985), 187–210.
Thompson, Janna, *Justice and World Order* (London: Routledge, 1992).
—— 'The apology paradox', *The Philosophical Quarterly* 50 (2000), 470–5.
—— 'Historical injustice and reparation: justifying claims of descendants', *Ethics* 112 (2001), 114–35.

Thompson, Janna, *Taking Responsibility for the Past: Reparations and Historical Injustice* (Cambridge: Polity, 2002).
Thomson, Judith Jarvis, *Self-Defense and Rights* (New York: University of Kansas Philosophy Department, 1977).
—— 'Preferential hiring', in *Rights, Restitution and Risk: Essays in Moral Theory* (London: Harvard University Press, 1986), 135–53.
Unger, Peter, *Living High and Letting Die: Our Illusion of Innocence* (New York: Oxford University Press, 1996).
Vallentyne, Peter, 'Brute luck, option luck, and equality of initial opportunities,' *Ethics* 112 (2002), 529–57.
Vernon, Richard, 'Against restitution', *Political Studies* 511 (2003), 542–57.
Waldron, Jeremy, *The Right to Private Property* (Oxford: Oxford University Press, 1988).
—— 'Superseding historic injustice', *Ethics* 103 (1992), 4–28.
Walzer, Michael, *Just and Unjust Wars,* (New York: Basic Books, 1977).
—— *Spheres of Justice* (Oxford: Blackwell, 1985).
—— 'Interpretation and social criticism', in Sterling M. McMurrin (ed.), *The Tanner Lectures on Human Values* (Salt Lake City, Utah: University of Utah Press, 1988), 1–80.
—— 'Nation and universe', in G. B. Peterson (ed.), *The Tanner Lectures on Human Values* (Salt Lake City, Utah: University of Utah Press, 1990), 507–56.
—— *Thick and Thin: Moral Argument at Home and Abroad* (Notre Dame: Notre Dame University Press, 1994).
—— 'Response' in Miller and Walzer (eds.), *Pluralism, Justice and Equality* (Oxford: Oxford University Press, 1995), 281–98.
Wertheimer, Alan, 'Exploitation', in Edward N. Zalta (ed.), *The Stanford Encyclopedia of Philosophy (Winter 2001 Edition)* available at http://plato.stanford.edu/archives/win2001/entries/exploitation/.
Wheeler III, Samuel C., 'Reparations reconstructed', *American Philosophical Quarterly* 34 (1997), 301–18.
White, Stuart, *The Civic Minimum: On the Rights and Obligations of Economic Citizenship* (Oxford: Oxford University Press, 2003).
Williams, Bernard, 'Ethical consistency', *Proceedings of the Aristotelian Society*, supplementary volume 39 (1965), 103–24.
—— 'The idea of equality', in *Problems of the Self: Philosophical Papers, 1956–1972* (Cambridge: Cambridge University Press, 1973), 230–49.
—— *Ethics and the Limits of Philosophy* (London: Fontana, 1985).
—— *Shame and Necessity* (Berkeley: University of California Press, 1993).
Wolfers, Arnold, *Discord and Collaboration* (Baltimore: Johns Hopkins University Press, 1962).
Wolff, Jonathan, *Robert Nozick: Property, Justice and the Minimal State* (Cambridge: Polity, 1991).
—— 'Political obligation, fairness and independence', *Ratio* 8 (1995), 87–99.

—— 'Libertarianism', in Edward Craig (ed.), *Routledge Encyclopedia of Philosophy* (London: Routledge, 1998), available at http://www.rep.routledge.com/article/S036/.

—— 'Rational, fair, and reasonable', in P. J. Kelly, *Impartiality, Neutrality and Justice: Re-reading Brian Barry's Justice as Impartiality* (Edinburgh: Edinburgh University Press, 1998), 35–43.

Woodward, James, 'The non-identity problem', *Ethics* 96 (1986), 804–31 at p. 809.

Index

Abizadeh, Arash 25n
Abdel-Nour, Farid 25n, 193n
Aborigines 53n
  see also indigenous peoples
affirmative action *see* reverse discrimination
Africa 1–2, 87, 103
African Americans, reparations to 2, 21, 134n, 135n, 141, 192n
agency, moral 127–9
aggression, international 5, 9, 16, 32, 66–7, 68, 75–88, 90n
Alexander, Larry 37
Anderson, Elizabeth 98
apology 1–4, 11, 12, 16, 22, 33, 35, 42, 128–9, 133n, 177–91, 193n
Aristotle 121, 152
Arneson, Richard 38, 154
atomism 151–2, 157–8
autonomy 41, 45, 146, 149, 162

Barkan, Elazar 3, 24n
Barker, Kit 53n
Barry, Brian 59, 90n, 116, 153, 171n
basic structure 38, 155
Beitz, Charles 3, 13, 59, 63, 89n, 90n, 115–17, 135n, 136n, 153–5, 169–70n
benefiting from historic actions 6, 17, 99–133, 186
  and duties of assistance 118–22
  and the effects of injustice 122–33
  importance of being a net beneficiary 126–33
  measuring in relation to counterfactuals 102–17
  subjective element in calculation 130–3, 138–9n
Bhopal Disaster 106
Birks, Peter 22, 29n, 137n, 138n
Black Radical Congress 1
Blair, Tony 4, 182
Blake, Michael 59, 64–5
blame 16, 74–5
  see also moral culpability
boundaries, ethical significance of 9–10, 13, 60–5, 169–70n

Bowie, David 62
Boxhill, Bernard, 133n
British Empire 6, 12
Brown, Christopher 90n, 116
Brown, Umberto 1
Buchanan, Allen 15, 75, 92n, 171n
Butt, Daniel 91–2n, 192n

Cane, Peter 97, 192n
Caney, Simon 13, 15, 27n, 29n, 89n, 90n, 116, 170n
Card, Claudia 55n
causal overdetermination 108–9
Chen, Shaohua 28n
Chernobyl Disaster 106
Church of England 3–4
Clinton, Bill 182
Cohen, G.A. 25n, 38, 74, 150–1
Cohen, Joshua 26n
Cohen, Marshall 32
Cold War 3
Coleman, Jules 36, 44–5, 53n, 121–2, 133n
colonialism 1–6, 12, 86–8, 102, 103–4, 107, 109–17, 129, 141, 192n
compensation 20–3, 75, 97–133, 176–8, 183–91
  and counterfactuals 102–15, 122, 123
  and incommensurability 42–3
  and justified rights infringements 86–88, 95n, 188–91
  and moral equilibrium 100–2
  rationale for 36, 42–7, 97–102
  rights and duties of 20–2, 131–2
  and self-defence 83
conglomerate collectivities 183–4
consequentialism 21, 38, 49–50, 103–4, 142–4
cooperation 15, 61–5, 69–70, 82, 111, 116–17, 157–8
corrective justice *see* rectificatory justice
cosmopolitanism 10, 13–19, 58–65
  not necessarily redistributive 10, 60
  non-relational 15, 60–5
  relational 15, 61–5

counterfactuals 47
  and automatic effects of injustice 112–14
  identifying the morally relevant 14, 102–17, 122, 123
  and probability 107–9, 115
  and property acquisition 151
  and relational justice 115–17
  and restitution 163–7, 172–3n
crimes against humanity 1–2
culpability, moral 32–3, 42, 53n, 74–5, 85, 180–3, 192n
cultural property 12, 158, 178
Cunningham, Michael 181–2

Daniels, Norman 27n
Darley, John M. 28n
Davis, Paul 182
de-Shalit, Avner 70, 91n
democracy 33, 179–80, 187, 194n
desert 142–3, 168n
difference principle 38, 49, 59, 63, 116, 196
distributive justice, backward-looking accounts 31–41, 48–52, 141–60
  and compensation 98
  current time-slice principles 37–8, 53–4n
  end-state principles 37–8, 53–4n, 143
  forward-looking accounts 31–2, 39–41, 43–7, 50–2, 141–5
  international 3, 18, 29n, 58–65, 115–17
  relationship with rectificatory justice 8, 29–52
domestic analogy 94n, 148, 157
double practicality 8, 13, 153
Dower, Nigel 18
driveways 125–32
duties, of assistance 8, 9–10, 19, 62, 69–72, 118–22, 143–4
  negative and positive 15–17, 19, 28n, 65
  relation to rights 20–2, 72, 131–2
Dworkin, Ronald 179

egalitarianism 10, 15, 37–9, 45, 60, 64, 99, 117, 142–3
  luck egalitarianism 38–9, 98–9
empires 158, 179
entitlement 17, 111–15, 122, 145–8
  see also historical entitlement, property, restitution
equality, moral 38–9, 51, 55n, 60–1
equality of opportunity 40, 50, 54n
equilibrium, moral 22, 55n, 100–2, 121, 126, 197
expectations 44–7, 160–2

Erreygers, Guido 55n
Exdell, John 150, 154
exploitation 5, 18, 32, 68–71, 91n, 110–14, 117, 135n, 141, 157
Ezorsky, Gertrude 137n

Fabre, Cécile 13, 109, 168n, 171n, 192n
Fagan, Eduard 25n
Farrelly, Colin 25n
Feinberg, Joel 78, 85–7, 108–9, 134n
Filmer, Robert 169n
Fishkin, James 134n, 175
Freeman, Samuel 54n, 59, 168n, 195–6
French, Peter 184
Frost, Mervyn 25n, 59, 90n
Fuller, Lon L. 136n
Fullinwider, Robert 125–7, 132, 137n, 138n

Gaus, Gerald 55n
Gellner, Ernest 25n
generations, overlapping 176, 183–91
  successive 165–7, 176, 184
Gewirth, Alan 79, 83, 93n
Gibbard, Allan 69
globalization see interdependence, global
Goodin, Robert 25n, 29n, 43, 45, 46, 70–1, 91n, 104
Gosseries, Axel 138n
Gray, J. Glenn 179
Gray, John 90n
Griffiths, Mark 93n
Guardian, The 12
guilt 12, 182, 192n
  see also moral culpability

harm 14–16, 38, 46–7, 68–9, 75, 97–9, 101–2, 123, 176–7, 185–6
  measuring in relation to counterfactuals 102–17
Harris, J.W. 149–50, 152, 173n
Haslett, D.W. 54n
Heath, Joseph 155
Hells Angels 180–1
historic actions, judgement of 72–88
  concern with justice, not culpability 74–5
  and different international context 79–88
  and relativism 74, 91–2n
  significance of international law 75–9
historic injustice, net effects of 100–2
historical entitlement 34, 39, 40–1, 48–51, 141–62

history, ethical significance of 8, 10, 31–52, 175–6, 197–8
Hoffman, Stanley 81–2
Honòré, Tony 180, 193n
Horvath, Ronald 5
Howard, Michael 84
human rights 13, 66–7, 71, 83, 85
  relation to legal rights 78–9

ideal theory 6–8, 18, 25n, 37–41
indeterminacy 114–15, 162–7
indigenous peoples 23, 24n, 52n, 76, 86–7
  see also Aborigines, Maoris, Native Americans
inequality, between co-nationals 64–5, 100
  between nations 19, 61, 70–1, 98, 100–1, 154–6
inheritance, justifiability of 14, 40–1, 54–5n, 140–67
inheritance model of rectificatory justice 140–67
  and counterfactuals 140, 151, 163–7, 172–3n
  and indeterminacy 162–7
  and initial acquisition 149–56
  and possession of property 145–8, 160–2
innocence, of present day individuals 23–4, 117, 129–30, 132–3, 140, 174–8, 183–91, 196–7
interdependence, global 15, 62–4, 81–2, 115–17, 129, 157–8
interests, and harm 16, 68, 103, 108–9, 134n
  lifetime transcending 166–7
  vital 78, 80, 87
international law 13, 14, 23, 66–7, 69, 92–3n, 94n, 131, 153, 160
  actions committed prior to development of 2, 75–9, 81–2
international libertarianism 58–88, 98–9, 195–8
  as an account of distributive justice 58–65, 98–9, 143–5, 148–60
  defined 8–9
  real world popularity of 13–14, 153
  relation with cosmopolitanism 13–19, 58–66, 148, 153, 196
  relation with domestic libertarianism 8–10, 25n, 29n, 56–7n, 72, 148, 157, 173n, 196
  relation with realism 10, 65
  significance of history for 31–2, 52, 141, 148–60

  see also principles of just international interaction
intervention, humanitarian 66–7, 71
Iraq 70
Ireland 182
Israel 1, 159

Jaja, Cheedy 95n
Jones, Charles 59–60
Jones, Hardy E. 137n
Jordan 70
judgement *see* historic actions, judgement of
justice 21–2, 34–5, 41–2, 51–2, 69
  see also distributive justice, political justice, rectificatory justice

Kant, Immanuel 15, 61
Kegley Jr., Charles W. 94n
Kelly, Erin 192n
Kershnar, Stephen 107, 133n, 167n
Klosko, George 138n
Kramer, Matthew 53n
Kyototo Protocol on Climate Change 11

land *see* territory
Landes, David 155, 170n
Lawrence III, Charles R. 137n
leaders, actions of 178–83
legitimacy 44–7, 158–60
Levmore, Saul 136–7n
Levy, Michael B. 55n
liberal nationalism 59, 64
libertarianism 8–9, 10, 39, 40–1, 48–51, 56–7n, 60, 72, 99, 148–53, 157, 173n, 196
  see also international libertarianism
life projects 44–7, 50, 56–7n, 147, 160–2
limitations, statutes of 46
Linklater, Andrew 93n
Locke, John 146, 149–53, 156, 169n, 170n
Lomasky, Loren 50, 56n, 57n, 72, 85–6, 91n, 147, 166
Lugard, Frederick 87
Lyons, David 159

McDermott, Daniel 138n
McDonnell, Ida 29n
Mackie, J.L. 192n
McMahan, Jeff 96n
McWhorter, John 21
Maoris 109, 192n
  see also indigenous peoples
Mapel, David 80–1, 83, 85, 90n

Matravers, Matt 54n
Matsuda, Mari J. 137n
May, Larry 194n
Meisels, Tamar 159, 171n
methodological assumption *see* innocence, of present day individuals
Mill, John Stuart 68, 152
Miller, David 13, 23, 26–7n, 30n, 59, 64, 68–70, 89n, 90n, 91n, 117–22, 136n, 138n, 144, 159, 170n, 171n, 175, 179–82, 192n, 193n
minimal state 9
Moellendorf, Darrel 13, 62–4
multinational corporations 30n, 110
Munzer, Stephen 168n
Murphy, Liam 25n, 54–5n

Nagel, Thomas 13, 54–5n, 56n, 59, 64, 196
Nardin, Terry 30n, 59, 76, 90n
nation-states 23–4, 30n
national identity 11–12, 113, 174–6, 178–91
national self-interest 10–12, 65–7, 79–88
nationalism 11–12, 25–6n, 59
nations 11–12, 25n, 174–6, 178–91
  composition of 183–5
  relation to states 23–4, 30n, 63–5
Native Americans 135n, 167
  see also indigenous peoples
natural resources 9, 149–51, 153–6, 159–60
Nazi Germany 2
necessity 10, 65, 80–2, 87, 94–5n, 189–91
negligence 42, 108–9, 180–3, 192n
neo-realism *see* realism
Nickel, James 93n, 104, 121, 177
non-ideal theory 6–8, 13–14, 19, 25n, 41–52
non-identity problem 105–9, 114–15, 128–9, 135n, 187–8, 192n
non-interference *see* non-intervention
non-intervention 9, 66–7
non-nationals, defined 23
Nozick, Robert 8, 29n, 37–9, 40–1, 48–50, 53–4n, 55n, 72, 90n, 91n, 104, 133n, 134n, 138n, 143, 147–53, 168n, 193n, 194n, 196

Obasanjo, Olusegun 1
obligation, political 76–7, 127, 138n
O'Neill, Onora 13, 18, 19, 20, 22, 89n, 124, 131–2, 137–8n
oil 155
original position 61, 63, 116
Osgood, Robert 80–1, 84

Otsuka, Michael 95n
Oxford 6

Palestine 1, 159
Palmer, Tom 89n
Patten, Alan 28n
Parfit, Derek 105–7, 187
Paul, Ellen Frankel 103, 133n, 136n
Perry, Stephen 38, 55n
personal identity 105–7, 114–15, 134n
Pittman, Thane S. 28n
Pogge, Thomas 13, 14–17, 28–9n, 59, 68–9, 101, 133n, 153–5, 171n
political culture 154–6
political justice 33
pollution 68
poverty, global 1, 7, 8, 14–15, 17–19, 28–9n
practicality 6–8
  see also double practicality
prescriptive realism *see* realism
principles of just international interaction 9, 15, 31, 65–72
  core principles 66–7
  further principles 67–72, 118
  historic application of 72–88
property 9, 22–3, 44–52, 56–7n, 140–67
  importance of ongoing possession of 145–8, 160–2
  initial acquisition of 149–56
punishment 8, 32, 38, 42, 83, 93n, 124
purchases, good faith 123–4
Purdue, William R. 136n

racism 1, 32, 82
Ravallion, Martin 28n
Rawls, John 3, 6–7, 9, 10, 13, 14, 27n, 29n, 34–5, 38, 45, 54n, 55n, 59, 61–2, 63, 69, 71, 72, 89n, 90n, 116, 144, 152, 155, 168n, 171n, 195–6
Raymond, Gregory A. 94n
Raz, Joseph 78
realism 10–12, 26n, 58–9, 65, 79–88, 90n, 94n
reciprocity 61, 65, 69–70
reconciliation 12, 21
rectificatory justice, failure to fulfil demands of 14, 132–3, 177–8, 183–91, 197–8
  and justified rights infringements 86–8, 188–91
  international different from domestic 2–3, 31–4, 51–2, 113–14, 134n, 141, 143–5, 147, 166–7

involuntary acquisition of rectificatory
    duties 99, 119–33, 184–91, 197–8
motivational force of 16–17, 196–7
nature of rectificatory duties 42–3, 174–8,
    183–91
relationship with corrective justice 52n
relationship with distributive justice 8,
    29–52, 196
'standard account' of 36, 37–9
rectificatory project 16, 19–22, 131, 170n,
    174–5, 195–8
    counter-productive effects of 1, 20–22,
        55n, 198
    defined 5
    self-interested reasons for adoption
        of 11–12
    strategic reasons for adoption of 14–19,
        196
Reddy, Sanjay G. 28–9n
redistribution of resources 33, 48–52, 142–3
    across national boundaries 6, 8–10, 14–19,
        60–6, 98–9, 143, 197–8
    generational 39–41, 50, 51–2, 65–6, 143
reflective equilibrium 14, 18, 27n,
relativism 74, 91–2n
remainder, moral 55n
reparations, real world demands for 1–5,
    13–14, 16, 20–2, 35, 97, 105–7
    see also compensation, restitution
repentance 42
responsibility 17, 38–9, 53n, 54n, 192n
    causal 118–22, 193n
    collective 178–91
    moral 118–22, 179–91, 192n
    national 143–4, 174–6, 178–91
    outcome 180–3, 193n
    remedial 118–22, 178–91
restitution 22–3, 29n, 140–67, 176–8, 183–91
    defined 22
    law of 36, 53n, 123, 130–1
    rationale for 36, 42–7
    relation to compensation 22–3, 42, 177–8
    see also inheritance model of rectificatory
        justice
reverse discrimination 125–7, 137n
Richards, David 61
rights, justified infringements of 85–8,
    94–5n, 188–91
Ripstein, Arthur 40, 43, 54n
risk bearing, principle of 97–8
Risse, Mathias 28n, 59, 171n
Roberts, M.A. 135n
Robinson, Randall 21

Rodin, David 83, 85, 94n, 95–6n
Rorty, Richard 193n
Rothbard, Murray 161, 172n
Russell, Paul 91n

Sabel, Charles 26n
Salter, Mark B. 93n
Sangiovanni, Andrea 59, 60–1, 65, 69
Schacter, Oscar 169n
Schmidtz, David 38, 56n, 147
Schwarzenberger, Georg 92–3n
Scrooge, Ebeneezer 195
second-best, theory of 7–8, 19
self-defence 65–8, 75, 81, 83–8, 90n, 94n,
    95–6n, 188
    pre-emptive 65, 67, 83–4, 94n
    preventive 84, 87, 94n
self-determination 9, 13, 19, 23, 65, 66–7, 75,
    78, 80, 98, 113, 179
self-ownership 9, 149–50
self-preservation, national 80–8
shame 12, 182, 193n
Sher, George 7, 111–15, 134n, 135n, 192n,
    194n
Shiffrin, Seana Valentine 169n
Simmons, A. John 29n, 108, 113, 114–15,
    167, 167n
Singer, Peter 17, 28n
slave trade 12, 74, 103, 114, 133n, 141, 182,
    192n
    contemporary 4, 24n
    reparations for 1–6, 21, 24n, 33, 107, 134n,
        141
socialism 49–50, 152, 154, 169n
'society of states' 59
Solignac Lecomte, Henri-Bernard 29n
South Africa 12, 25–6n
sovereignty, national 9, 13, 66–7
    over natural resources 9, 153–6
    over territory 158–60
states 23–4
    relation to nations 23–4, 30n, 63–5
Steiner, Hillel 70–1, 89n, 137n, 149, 153,
    165, 168n, 169n
Stemplowska, Zofia 25n
Sunstein, Cass 18
supersession of injustice 46–7, 145–7, 160–2
Sverdlik, Steven 181
Swift, Adam 25n

Tamir, Yael 59, 64, 175
Tan, Kok-Chor 89n
Taylor, Charles 152

territory 5, 9, 76, 140, 148, 153, 158–60, 169–70n
  and first occupancy 158
  and sustained possession 159–60, 171–2n
Thompson, Janna 54n, 68, 76, 86–7, 128–9, 141, 142, 145, 158–9, 162–7, 172–3n, 176
Thomson, Judith Jarvis 85–6, 95n, 125–7, 137n
Times, The 2
tort law 36, 53n
trade 63, 66, 70, 101, 186
treaties 66–7, 76–7
Tucker, Robert 80–1, 84

United Nations 1–2, 30n, 75–6, 81, 153
United Nations World Conference against Racism, Racial Discrimination, Xenophobia and Related Intolerance 1–6, 21
unjust enrichment 36, 53n, 121–3, 130–1

Vallentyne, Peter 54n
Vandevelde, Toon 55n
Vattel, Emerich de 84
Vernon, Richard 22, 52–3n

Wade, Abdoulaye 1
Waldron, Jeremy 22, 29n, 35, 46–8, 52–3n, 56n, 113, 129–30, 135n, 141, 145–8, 149, 159, 160–7, 168n, 172–3n, 177, 187
Waltz, Kenneth 79–80
Walzer, Michael 13, 26n, 59, 63, 68, 75–6, 78, 80, 90n, 92n, 93n, 94–5n, 154, 156, 159, 170n, 179, 192n
war, motives for 83–4
Wegimont, Liam 29n
Wertheimer, Alan 91n
Wheeler, Samuel C. 187
White, Stuart 55n
Williams, Bernard 55n, 89n, 92n
Williams, Rowan 4
Wolfers, Arnold 93n
Wolff, Jonathan 50, 62, 127, 149
Woodward, James 109
World Bank 17
world ownership 150, 153–4
World War II 2, 3, 102

Zephaniah, Benjamin 12